Educating Our Black Children

It is well established that many young black pupils are being excluded from mainstream education. Although social exclusion is a major issue in the government's education policy, recent initiatives and programmes have been criticised for being colour-blind and failing to place targets on areas such as black exclusions. This book goes beyond traditional research and policy analysis by providing actual approaches and programmes. This important collection of essays from distinguished UK and US contributors focuses on positive social inclusion policy and practice. Themes covered include:

- mentoring schemes and how to evaluate mentoring
- masculine identity
- rites of passage programmes and manhood training
- black supplementary schools
- African-centred knowledge systems

Comparing UK and US initiatives, the contributors move the debate forward by providing original and creative approaches to issues in black education, laying the framework for new policies and practices. *Educating Our Black Children* will be an invaluable read for students studying education, social work, psychology and sociology as well as policy makers, academics, practitioners and headteachers/principals.

The contributors to this book include:

David Gillborn, Maud Blair, Diane S. Pollard, Cheryl S. Ajirotutu, Jason W. Osborne, Keith Alford, Patrick McKenry, Stephen Gavazzi, Diane Reay, Heidi Safia Mirza, Mekada Graham, Teresa Gerate-Serafini, Fabricio E. Balcazar, Christopher B. Keys, Julie Weitlauf, Karl Brooks, Denny Grant, Aminifu R. Harvey, Tony Sewell, Vincent Wilkinson, William Gulam, James Earl Davis, Richard Harris and Carl Parsons.

Richard Majors is a former Harvard Medical School Clinical Fellow and is a Senior Fellow at the University of Manchester, in the Department of Social Policy and Social Work. He is the founder and Deputy Editor of the *Journal of African American Men* and has written extensively on education, race, class and gender. His book *Cool Pose: The Dilemmas of Black Manhood in America* (cowritten with J. Billson) was on the Publishers Bestsellers List. He has been selected by the International Biographical Centre as one of the 2000 outstanding people of the twentieth century. Currently Richard Majors is the Deputy Director of the Leigh Education Action Zone. He has been on Working Groups for the Qualifications and Curriculum Authority, Department for Education and Employment and the Commission for Racial Equality. The *New York Times* describes his work as 'being at the forefront of a movement of black social scientists who are seeking ways to understand inner city youths better and to marshal the strengths of the black middle class to help these troubled young people survive'.

Educating Our Black Children

New directions and radical approaches

Edited by Richard Majors

London and New York

First published 2001 by RoutledgeFalmer
11 New Fetter Lane, London EC4P 4EE

Simultaneously published in the USA and Canada
by RoutledgeFalmer
29 West 35th Street, New York, NY 10001

Reprinted 2001

RoutledgeFalmer is an imprint of the Taylor & Francis Group

Typeset in Baskerville by Keystroke, Jacaranda Lodge, Wolverhampton.
Printed and bound in Great Britain by TJI Digital, Padstow, Cornwall

British Library Cataloguing in Publication Data
A catalogue record for this book is available from the British Library

Library of Congress Cataloging in Publication Data
Educating Our Black Children : new directions and
radical approaches/[edited by]
Richard Majors
    p. cm.
  Includes bibliographical references and index.
  1. Children, Black—Education—Great Britain.
  2. Educational change—Great Britain. 3. Afro-American
  children—Education Majors, Richard
LC2806.G7 E392001
371. 829′96041—dc21   00–62793

ISBN 0–7507–0965–0 (hbk)
ISBN 0–7507–0964–2 (pbk)

Dedication

The Fighting Spirit

Familiar Footsteps upon the walk,
The crazy way we used to talk
A baby suckled to its mothers breast . . .
Familiar Footsteps on the walk,
The crazy way we used to talk . . .

Fannie Sue Majors

This book is dedicated to the loving memory of my mother, Fannie Sue Majors. No one has ever exhibited more courage, character, determination and honesty during their life than my mother.

Unfortunately, because of injuries sustained in an horrific car accident she had to call upon these virtues too many times.

But like a phoenix that rises from the ashes, many times our mother met the challenge to come back and fight on, whenever we thought we were going to lose her. This 'fighting spirit', determination and strong will, defined our mother, it is by these virtues that we will always remember you, mother.

Contents

List of figures   xi
List of tables   xii
Preface   xiii
Acknowledgements   xiv
Introduction   1

PART I
**Tackling historical and contemporary education
problems**   **11**

1 **Racism, policy and the (mis)education of black children**   13
   DAVID GILLBORN

2 **The education of Black children: why do some schools
   do better than others?**   28
   MAUDE BLAIR

3 **Academic disidentification: unravelling under achievement
   among Black boys**   45
   JASON W. OSBORNE

PART II
Radical Black approaches to education   **59**

4 **The 'miseducation' of Black children in the British
   educational system – towards an African-centred
   orientation to knowledge**   61
   MEKADA GRAHAM

5 **Lessons from America: the African American Immersion Schools experiment** 79
DIANE S. POLLARD AND CHERYL S. AJIROTUTU

6 **Black supplementary schools: spaces of radical blackness** 90
DIANE REAY AND HEIDI SAFIA MIRZA

PART III
Reflections on social exclusion and inclusion **103**

7 **The exclusion of Black children: implications for a racialised perspective** 105
RICHARD MAJORS, DAVID GILLBORN AND TONY SEWELL

8 **Educational psychologists and Black exclusion: towards a framework for effective intervention** 110
KARL BROOKS AND DENNY GRANT

9 **Black exclusions in a moral vacuum** 128
RICHARD HARRIS AND CARL PARSONS

PART IV
Rites of passage, manhood training and masculinity perspectives **139**

10 **Enhancing achievement in adolescent Black males: the Rites of Passage link** 141
KEITH ALFORD, PATRICK MCKENRY AND STEPHEN GAVAZZI

11 **An after-school manhood development program** 157
AMINIFU R. HARVEY

12 **Black boys at school: negotiating masculinities and race** 169
JAMES EARL DAVIS

13 **Black boys and schooling: an intervention framework for understanding the dilemmas of masculinity, identity and underachievement** 183
TONY SEWELL AND RICHARD MAJORS

PART V
Mentoring and education 203

14 **Mentoring Black males: responding to the crisis in education and social alienation** 205
RICHARD MAJORS, VINCENT WILKINSON AND WILLIAM GULAM

15 **School based mentoring for minority youth: program components and evaluation strategies** 214
TERESA GARATE-SERAFINI, FABRICIO E. BALCAZAR, CHRISTOPHER B. KEYS AND JULIE WEITLAUF

List of contributors 258
Index 264

List of figures

Figures

3.1 Trends in the correlation between grades and self-esteem 50
9.1 Permanent exclusions from schools in England – 1990–98 129
13.1 Model of racial identity development 194
13.2 Extending the model of racial identity development 196
15.1 Evaluation domains 215
15.2 Personal competencies 225

List of tables

 8.1 EPS involvement at different stages of exclusion process   121
15.1 Evaluating a mentoring program   222
15.2 Methods for evaluating mentoring programs   229

Preface

Although it is well established that many young black pupils are being excluded from mainstream education, there has been limited material available that focuses on positive social inclusion policy and practice. This book is a welcome addition, because editor Richard Majors has assembled a distinguished 'cast' of American and British authors that focuses on solution and best practices models, rather than just theory and research. Hopes are sustained whenever there is an emphasis on solving problems rather than on charting and measuring them. Now, at long last, we are witnessing a trans-Atlantic movement of concern and commitment about the need for effective policy and practices initiatives which directly respond to these trends.

One of the great achievements of this collection of essays is that he introduces radical and creative approaches and perspective that could lay the framework for new policies and practices. Typical themes include a critical consideration and the relevance of mentoring, social justice, masculine identity, black supplementary schools and an African-centred knowledge system.

Also, one of the outstanding contributions of this collection of essays is that Dr Majors suggests as many new questions, even as he charts some new answers. Where are the studies of educationally *successful* young black men? How important is gender in understanding boys' classroom behaviour? Why do some Asian pupils perform better than black pupils in school? How significant are social class influences in this regard? Has the John Longborough School, with its particular religious ethos, anything to teach us, or is it merely acting as a rare magnet for both local and metropolitan London black middle-class families?

Once these essays are published it will be crucially important to disseminate their different wisdoms to white and black audiences, professional and non-professional, educationists and the whole spectrum of people workers.

I have no doubt that this book will make a major contribution to the literature and will become a foundation stone for change. Nevertheless, much bridge-building, across the various 'islands of hope', as well as between them and the other social islands in our cities, remains to be done; not just in metropolitan London and its provincial equivalents but also far beyond, where old imperial stereotypes remain. The very existence of this book only serves as a positive encouragement to these challenges and ideas.

Duncan Scott
Senior Lecturer in Social Policy and Social Work, University of Manchester

Acknowledgements

I am deeply indebted to many people. This book could not have been completed without their contributions, advice and encouragement. First and foremost, I wish to acknowledge and recognise my family especially my eldest sister Lynn Owens, younger sisters Holy Small and Lisa Majors, Aunt Yvonne Hughes, my niece Nica Small and family friends Rosetta Jenkins and Louis Wallace.

I am proud and honoured to be a member of this family after witnessing how these individuals loved, supported, took care of and rallied around my Dear Mother, Fannie Sue Majors, during her long illness which ultimately took her life.

Next, I would like to thank Sandy Parker, one of my best friends and my secretary. Few people in my life have given of their time, stood by me, or believed in me in the way that you have, Sandy. For this Sandy, you will always be 'special', I could never ever thank you enough.

As a former Leverhulme Trust Visiting Fellow I would like to thank the Leverhulme Trust for supporting my work in the past. Originally it was this fellowship that enabled me to come to Britain to conduct research on mentoring and Black males. I am also grateful to a number of individuals for their intellectual guidance, personal support or friendship. They are: David Moore, Duncan Scott, Michael Bartram, George Rowan, the late Valerie Karn, Duncan Chapman, Glennis Aspinsall, Philup Arnold, David Davies, Arthur Nikelly, John Guernsey, Vince Young, Vince Wilkinson, Angela O'Donoghue, John Robertson, Paulette Wisdom, Margaret Bullock, Kenneth McIntire, Joel Lilienkamp, Michael Meyerscough, Roy Cochrane and his family, the Richardson family, Steve Clarke and Pat Jones.

For their spiritual guidance and special friendship I wish to express my appreciation to my brother Chan Majors, my sister Theda Lewis, Dr Martin Hastings, my late friends Hollis Head, Dennis Allen, Bertha Denby, Phil Powell, Edward Elders and Pauline Colley and late family member Aunt Marie Paul from Sidcup, Roseman Moyo, the Elders family, Ronald Fitzgerald, Helena Hajkova, Abe and Denise Lee, Sheldon Julius, Joe Tyler, Sheldon Lee, Eddie Faye Gates, John Williams, Jo Jolliffe, Diane Watt, Steve Kwofie, Greg Foster, Johnny Barnes, Thad Branch, Douglas Jenkins and Nehemiah Nixon wherever you may be and my former students David Dommel, Mark Granius and Gina White whose world is their oyster.

I owe enormous gratitude to Anna Clarkson, the Publisher for Routledge Falmer, for her belief in me and her commitment to the project. I would also like to thank Rachel Larman, Kelly Peat, Alan Lowe, and Rosemary Appleyard for their editorial assistance and good-natured dispositions.

Introduction

Understanding the current educational status of Black children

Richard Majors

England is experiencing an education revolution. Few would deny that in the four years since the Labour government came to power they have made major advances in education and social inclusion. For example, in an effort to reduce social exclusion in education they have developed programmes and initiatives in the following areas: excellence in the cities, mentoring, literacy and numeracy, computer technology, Education Action Zones, and breakfast and homework clubs, among other things.

Therefore, the government's agenda should be applauded for its innovative and creative approach to addressing the whole issue of social inclusion. However, if our Black children are to acquire the maximum benefit from these initiatives, further action will be required. Further steps are necessary because many of the policies, programmes and initiatives created by the government are colour-blind and fail to place targets on areas such as Black exclusions (Majors, Gillborn and Sewell, 1998; Thornton, 1999).

BLACK EXCLUSIONS

Black exclusions are an example of the current failure in policy. While the government's social exclusion limit has set the first ever national targets on reducing exclusion (one-third reduction of both fixed term and permanent exclusions by 2002) no targets have been set likewise for a reduction of Black exclusions. In general, while such targets are ambitious and welcomed, conditions for Black pupils could worsen if targets are not set for the reduction of Black exclusions (Thornton, 1999).

Nevertheless, because exclusions, truancy and underachievement have reached crisis point, particularly among minority groups, the Labour government has prioritised social exclusion for action. The engines that drive the government's social inclusion agenda are the Social Exclusion Unit, Estelle Morris's Advisory Group on Ethnic Minority Achievement and the Social Exclusion Practitioner Group. These groups meet periodically to discuss policies and to consider recommendations that impact social inclusion and disaffection.

The Social Exclusion Unit Report (1998) addressed the disaffection of pupils in education. The report stated that approximately 13,000 pupils had been excluded permanently, and over 100,000 had been excluded temporarily over the year. A disproportionate number of these exclusions have been from ethnic minorities, particularly Black males. The government Social Exclusion Unit reported that African-Caribbeans are more than six times more likely to be excluded than their White counterparts. Most of those excluded are male. The number of Black exclusions has become so problematic that, in certain areas of London, Black children are up to 15 times more likely to be excluded from school than their White classmates (Ouseley, 1998). Simply put, if Black exclusions are to be reduced, it is imperative that drastic action be taken to arrest and reverse the current trend. This action should include, but not be limited to, target setting.

The Commission for Racial Equality (CRE) has long argued that specific targets are needed in order to reduce Black exclusions. They believe that one way to disproportionately reduce Black exclusions is to set specific targets within the government's general targets. However, the government has so far resisted setting targets for high-risk groups (Thornton, 1999).

Nevertheless, the Department for Education and Employment (DfEE) has ordered twelve educational authorities with 'extremely high' exclusion rates for Black and other ethnic minority pupils to produce action plans. Experts are sceptical, however, as to whether this action will ultimately have the impact that target setting or a formal investigation would achieve (Ouseley, 1998).

As a result of this scepticism, the CRE is not waiting for the government to solve the problem. In 1998, when Herman Ouseley was the chairperson of the CRE, he threatened to take drastic action, if exclusions were not reduced. He believed that because black exclusions were 15 times higher than whites in some areas were sufficient grounds for his organization to launch a formal investigation. (Ouseley, 1998),

So why are so many Black children excluded? There is evidence that some are excluded for conduct and behavioural problems (although far too many pupils in this category are excluded for trivial and relatively minor offences). However, many are also excluded simply for exhibiting culture-specific behaviours (wearing dreadlocks, braids, having one's hair too short, having tramlines shaved on one's head, demonstrating 'inappropriate' walking styles or eye behaviour. See Majors and Billson, 1992; Sewell, 1997 for discussion).

Many of these exclusions occur because of a lack of cultural awareness, miscommunication, racism and negative stereotyping. Teachers often label or view a Black child who demonstrates certain culture-specific behaviours as 'having an attitude problem' or even as being 'ignorant' rather than characterising the child as one who has pride, confidence and a positive sense of self-esteem and cultural identity (Majors and Billson, 1992). As Irvine (1990) reported, because the culture of Black pupils is (in most instances) so different from that of their teachers, teachers often misunderstand, ignore, or discount Black children's language, non-verbal cues, learning styles and worldview.

When teachers are colour-blind to the culture of others, and therefore ignore or are unwilling to affirm another's culture, it often leads to hostility and conflict between White teachers and Black pupils. Qualitative research, such as that cited by the Office for Standards in Education (OFSTED) in 1996, has frequently highlighted the high level of tension between White teachers and Black pupils, in particular Black boys.

The high levels of exclusion among Black children has inevitably affected their academic performance. The DfEE Youth Cohort Study (1994) revealed that Blacks were academically the least successful when compared to Whites and other ethnic groups. Only 21 per cent of Blacks achieved five or more GCSEs at grades A to C. In contrast, 45 per cent of Indians and Whites achieved five or more GCSEs at grades A to C, and 51 per cent of the other Asians gained five or more GCSEs at grades A to C. Furthermore, the *Raising the Attainment of Minority Ethnic Pupils* report (OFSTED, 1999) noted that 25 local authorities revealed serious underachievement among ethnic minorities. The report noted that Black Caribbean and Travellers' children were well behind other groups by the end of secondary school.

RACISM IN SCHOOLS

Given the proliferation of exclusions among Black pupils and their resulting underachievement, as well the heightened media interest in an inclusive society, a number of well-known organizations and institutions have produced reports to counter disaffection and to raise cultural awareness. These reports include: *Recent Research on the Achievement of Ethnic Minority Pupils* (Gillborn and Gipps, 1996); *Raising the Attainment of Minority Ethnic Pupils: School and LEA's Response* (OFSTED, 1999); *Exclusion from School: The Public Cost* (CRE, 1996); *Making the Difference: Teaching and Learning Strategies in Success-full Multi-Ethnic Schools* (Blair and Bourne, 1998); *Racism and Race Relations in Predominantly White Schools: Preparing Pupils for Life in a Multi-cultural Society* (Hamilton, Rejtman and Roberts, 1999); *The Macpherson Report of the Inquiry into the Racist Murder of Stephen Lawrence* (1999); NASUWT's *Education and Race* report (1999); *Improving Practice: A Whole School Approach to Raising the Achievement of African Caribbean Youth* (Weeks and Wright, 1998).

It is striking how regularly these reports cite racism as one of the most salient features in understanding exclusions and underachievement. In 1998, at the North of England Education Conference, Herman Ouseley went a step beyond invoking racism by remarking that, by failing to tackle racial inequality or cultural diversity, the government was creating an apartheid system in education. Following the criticisms in the Macpherson Report concerning the education system's response to Black underachievement (O'Leary and Betts, 1999), Cliff Gould, OFSTED's head of secondary inspection, similarly stated that many schools were 'institutionally racist'.

Macpherson in fact found that the majority of schools had no idea how their minority pupils were doing, in comparison with White pupils. Only half of the secondary schools in the study, and one in 24 of the primary schools, monitored

Black achievement. Less than a quarter of education authorities had a strategy for raising the academic performance of minorities, and barely a third monitored that performance (O'Leary and Betts, 1999).

Hamilton, Rejtman and Roberts (1999) additionally reported that schools where a majority of the pupils are White are particularly guilty of failing to tackle racism. In many schools in the study, teachers admitted that their pupils left school ill-prepared for life in a multicultural society. The report found that many teachers had little or no idea of how to define a minority, what characterises racism, or how to teach about racism. In addition, openly racist attitudes were often ignored by staff. Seventy-five per cent of the staff in the study reported hearing pupils using racist language, but only two schools documented racist incidents.

Chris Wilkin's study on social and political attitudes even highlighted racism among teacher trainees. According to Wilkin, 5–10 per cent of trainee teachers were 'negative or hostile' towards minorities and others complained of anti-racism and anti-sexism being 'shoved down their throats'. He reported that they used familiar racist rhetoric: Black people are responsible for crime, they take White people's jobs, and they do not want to integrate with Whites (Barnard, 1999).

The Teacher Training Agency (TTA) is the organisation in charge of the curriculum and the setting of guidelines for the training of teachers. The TTA has often been criticised for failing to develop a curriculum and programme that prepares teachers to teach minorities and to deal with racism and cultural diversity effectively. Given such racist attitudes by teachers, Stephen Hillier, head of corporate managers at TTA, said that the TTA was not presently willing to prescribe anti-racist education on the actual curriculum or syllabus (Ghouri, 1998). Reacting to TTA officials, Herman Ouseley called the TTA 'negligent' and 'scandalous' for refusing to put equal opportunity firmly on the teacher-training curriculum, and for neglecting to provide places for qualified Black applicants (Ghouri, 1998).

The CRE (1998) has also spoken out regarding the under-representation of ethnic minorities teachers within the profession. Their investigations have found that less than 2 per cent of teachers were minorities. The fact is, we need to hire more Black teachers if we are to reduce racism. Both Black and White pupils need Black role models in the classroom who can motivate them and challenge the ideas and views that contribute both to racism and to understanding.

Conversely, the Macpherson Report (1999), commissioned to address the racist attack and killing of Stephen Lawrence, a well-liked Black youth, by a gang of White youths, makes several recommendations for education. Regarding racism in the schools, the report suggested that the national curriculum should aim towards 'valuing cultural diversity and preventing racism'. These efforts should not duplicate the superficial multiculturalism of the 1970s that focused on dress, food, religion, holidays, festivals and events. This multicultural model is inappropriate for understanding deeper and more profound aspects of cultures (Majors, Gillborn and Sewell, 1998). Anti-racism should be about challenging and educating individuals about racism, rather than celebrating and reinforcing stereotypes (Blair and Gillborn, 1999).

How multiculturalism should or should not be taught may be a moot issue. The government ministers' response to the Macpherson Report regarding whether anti-racism should be an integral part of the curriculum was that the National Curriculum does presently address the diverse nature of British society. They added that anti-racism education would also be covered by their plan to introduce a citizenship education (Ghouri, 1999).

DIFFERENTIAL TREATMENT

Many racist behaviours and attitudes are manifested in the form of stereotypes, lower expectations and differential treatment toward minorities, particularly Black males (Blair and Bourne, 1998). Wrench and Hassan (1996) reported that young African-Caribbean males felt that teachers often had negative views of them. As Irvine (1990) reported, overt and subtle messages are communicated by teachers to pupils about their reliability and ability to succeed and do well. Sewell (1997) found that not only were Black boys negatively stereotyped by teachers, but also feared by them. He reported that teachers said that they were afraid of Black boys because of their physical size and their views that they were more troublesome than other pupils.

Black pupils are consistently the subject of differential treatment and the victims of double standards. For example, Black pupils have reported that they have observed differential treatment with regard, among other things, to teacher bullying (e.g. harassment, over-monitoring) discipline, length of punishment, the choice of who is to speak in class, and how they are communicated with (Foster, 1995; Sewell, 1997).

A recent study conducted by Watt, Sheriffe and Majors (1999) on mentoring with Black boys found support for Black pupils' views of differential and inappropriate treatment from teachers. The study found that Black boys believed that they were more likely than their White classmates to be disrespected, talked down to, over-monitored, blamed for things they did not do, and to have limited chances to tell their side of the story. Hence, too many social inclusion initiatives focus on pupils' deficits rather than equally addressing teachers' deficits.

Black pupils also experience differential expectations from teachers in the area of academic ability. When Black and White males are compared, teachers tend to predict higher test results for White males than they do for Black males (Irvine, 1990). Teachers' assessments of Blacks are in fact consistently lower than their actual test results (OFSTED, 1999). One Black pupil, Renaldo LaRose, who is taking three A levels, provides evidence regarding the lack of confidence which many teachers display in Black pupils' academic ability. 'After we got our GCSE results', he stated, 'teachers were going up to Black pupils and saying they were surprised they had done so well. They used to put Black pupils down' (Judd 1999).

Research is limited on the psychological impact and long-term consequences on Black children's self-esteem and self-worth as a result of the differential treatment of teachers. However, given their interactions with teachers, many Black pupils become disappointed and overburdened and 'learn helplessness', or just lose interest in school altogether (White and Cones, 1999). In various studies, pupils have repeatedly pointed out the disregard teachers have for social justice and civil rights (Alderson and Arnold, 1999; Watt, Sheriffe and Majors, 1999).

For example, in a study, *Civil Rights in Schools* by Alderson and Arnold (1999), which sampled 2,272 pupils, aged 7–17, it was discovered that pupils were upset by the way teachers dismissed and mistrusted their views. They repeatedly mentioned that they wanted more opportunities to express their own views. In fact, 40 per cent of the sample believed they should have more rights at school, but only 11 per cent of teachers agreed with them. They also disliked the power teachers had to hand out various forms of punishment without explanation.

The fact is, we are obsessed with controlling, monitoring, disciplining, punishment, excluding and labelling rather than focusing on relationships, communication and social justice.

TEACHER STRATEGIES: RELATIONSHIPS AND OPTIMISM

There are two ways to raise attainment and to manage behaviours in the classroom. The first way involves the use of cognitive strategies, exercises and techniques with pupils in the classroom. Positive learning approaches encourage pro-social behaviours in this context. The second way focuses on strategies that promote interpersonal relationships and social justice approaches between teachers and pupils. If a child feels as though they are listened to and valued, they are more likely to attend school and to feel better about themselves, be motivated to learn and therefore less likely to become engaged in conflict with others. For example, Pickering (1997) argued that pupils, particularly boys, were most influenced by human relationships of all types in the classroom. He also found that girls believed that boys' learning was more affected by their relationships with teachers than their own individual relationships. In the study of Kinder, Wakefield and Wilkin (1996), *Talking back, Pupils' Views on Disaffection*, pupils discussed the importance of having good relationships with teachers. Pupils were asked to identify the best way to reduce problems with teachers in the classroom. The second highest response from pupils (next to changing curriculum) was to focus on changing relationships with teachers. The pupils in this study also repeatedly pointed out that teachers did not give them enough respect, and pupils are far more likely to report to school and to co-operate with teachers when they have teachers whom they like and with whom they can communicate. Teachers that utilise humour and a well timed smile, who set high expectations and respect and praise pupils can affect their learning (Pickering, 1997). Every teacher should be willing to learn the interpersonal and social skills which help teachers to cope with even the worst pupils (Abdenoor, 1999).

Recent research has additionally highlighted the importance of hope, optimism and caring in reducing disaffection and raising attainment among pupils in the classroom (Collinson, Killeavy and Stephenson, 1999). As Collinson, Killeavy and Stephenson (1999) write: 'Hope is other-centred, hope sets high expectations and goals for self and others, and hope perseveres even in face of obstacles'.

Steve Preston (conversation, 9 March 2000), currently a headteacher of a high school in the north of Britain, illustrates the power of optimism, hope and caring in the classroom. During Steve's first year of teaching, an experienced senior teacher noticed that he was struggling with a class of disaffected pupils. The senior teacher commented to Steve that, 'You do not like that class do you?' Steve replied, 'No, I don't'. The senior teacher's advice to Steve was to pretend for one month that his troubled class was 'his best class', and the pupils were 'his most favourite pupils', and to think more positive. Steve said it worked. He said that by the end of the year not only did the class become his favourite, but he was actually sad to see them leave. This anecdote highlights the power of positive thinking, optimism, hope and caring when attempting to engage at-risk pupils in the classroom (Seligman, 1998).

Schools have been identified as a primary site for the promotion of optimism, hope and caring relationships. However, Polite's (1994) study of 65 Black high school boys found that many schools were not creating or fostering environments that elicit these attitudes and behaviours. Interviews with Black boys revealed that teachers often did not demonstrate caring. Moreover, Kinney, Eaton, Bain, Williams and Newcombe (1995), and Phelan, Davidson and Cao (1992) reported that pupils expressed a preference for 'caring–friendly' classrooms. Teachers can promote 'caring–friendly' classroom environments by showing pupils an interest in their ideas, experiences, personal lives and 'going the extra miles' (Smith, 1997).

It has often been said that Black males have low self-esteem. However, some studies have found that Black male youths when compared to Whites have higher self-esteem (Dukes and Martinez, 1994; Morgan, 1995). Nevertheless, Spencer (1991) reported a discrepancy between pupils' more general self-esteem and their 'student self'. He noted that in comparison with non-minority pupils, Black youths consistently showed high self-esteem. But the longer a Black male youth stayed in school the more their 'student self' eroded (Smith, 1997).

Given this situation, there is a need to bring Black pupils' general self-esteem more in line with their 'student self'. Therefore there is a need to develop school policies that focus on caring and relationship strategies. Focusing on communication, relationship-building, caring, hope, optimism and social justice approaches can lead to positive differences and academic success (Smith, 1997). Mindful of the importance of hope, optimism, caring relationships and social justice approaches in reducing differential treatment, Leigh Education Action Zone has focussed on developing social justice initiatives. These initiatives will focus on mediation, grievance procedures and teacher empathy programmes, among other schemes. The goal is to provide pupils and families with a genuine and formal procedures or process for getting issues and concerns addressed, heard and acted on. Because many pupil complaints involving differential treatment are often not taken seriously, followed up or mediated, many pupils 'learn helplessness', give up, or stop going to school altogether.

It is the hope of this author that many of these social justice models will be replicated because of their potential to reduce conflict, enhance communication and relationships, raise awareness and empower pupils and teachers alike.

PLAN OF THE BOOK

This book, which involves both British and American scholars, has a number of aims and goals. Firstly, it seeks to document the efforts, currently underway in various schools, agencies, and communities that address issues involving disaffection, racism, differential treatment, low expectancy, negative stereotypes and social justice among Black pupils.

Too many books focus on theory rather than concentrating on solutions or doing both. Thus, the second goal of this book is to describe the latest theories and research findings, but at the same time to offer real solutions to real problems (e.g. providing information on starting up programmes and evaluating them).

Third, this book aims to illustrate and highlight 'best practice' models from the US that could make a difference here in Britain. In the last 40 years since the civil rights movement, African Americans have developed creative and innovative programmes in schools to promote the well-being of African American children. These innovative and creative programmes and approaches, which have met with tremendous success in the Black community and churches, have focused on fatherhood initiatives, mentoring, rites of passage and manhood training programmes, Afrocentric approaches, and establishing African American independent schools. Fundamentally, these programmes and approaches have their roots in the long and proud tradition of Black Self-Help philosophy. This philosophy has been influenced and shaped by such esteemed African Americans as Malcolm X, Martin Luther King and Jesse Jackson, among others.

Overview of chapters

The book covers a broad range of topics concerned with eradicating disaffection, and empowering Black pupils. Therefore, this volume is an attempt to bring those themes together to bear on the issue of schooling for this group, and it is organised into five parts, representing fifteen chapters. Part I (Tackling Historical and Contemporary Education Problems) focuses on policy, best practices in education and new theories that unravel underachievement and disaffection. Part II (Radical Black Approaches to Education) focuses on Black radical schools, paradigms and initiatives that enhance the development and performance of Black pupils. Alternative knowledge systems, such as the African central worldview, challenge existing Eurocentric educational strategies that have undermined many Black pupils. African central worldview attempts to re-engage Black pupils to education and learning by focusing on the pupil's experiences, history, culture and the identity of the Black pupil. Part III (Reflections on Social Exclusion and Inclusion) addresses the complexity of the issue of social exclusion and inclusion around education policy, race and practice. New frameworks and models are proposed for understanding and solving social exclusion and inclusion. Part IV (Rites of Passage, Manhood Training and Masculinity Perspectives) is devoted to understanding how masculine identity influences and shapes the lives of Black pupils in school. This section also introduces and describes how rites of passage, a masculine-oriented scheme challenge and empower Black pupils, particularly at-risk pupils. Part V (Mentoring and Education) is devoted to measuring the effectiveness of mentoring in schools. This section also addresses how mentoring can be utilised as a remediative and intervention tool in education. There is growing evidence that mentoring schemes, particularly those targeting high-risk pupils, can make a difference between wasted and productive lives.

REFERENCES

Abdenoor, A. (1999) 'Inclusion buck stops with you', *TES*, 22 October.

Alderson, P. and Arnold, S. (1999) *Civil Rights in Schools*, London: Economic and Social Research Council.

Barnard, N. (1999) 'One in 10 trainees has racist attitudes', *TES*, 16 April.

Blair, M. and Bourne, J. (1998) *Making the Difference: Teaching and Learning Strategies in Successful Multiethnic Schools*, London: DfEE.

Blair, M. and Gillborn, D. (1999) 'Face up to racism', *TES*, 5 March.

Collinson, V., Killeavy, M. and Stephenson, J. (1999) 'Exemplary teachers: practicing an ethic of care in England, Ireland and the United States, *Journal for a Just and Caring Education*', **5**, 4, p. 349–66.

CRE (1996) *Exclusion from School: The Public Cost*, London: CRE.

CRE (1998) *Ethnic Minority School Teachers*, London: CRE.

DfEE (1994) *Youth Cohort Study*, London: HMSO.

Dukes, R. and Martinez, R. (1994) 'The impact of ethgender on self-esteem among adolescents', *Adolescence*, **29**, 113, pp. 105–115.

Foster, H. (1995) 'Educators and non-educators perceptions of Black males: A survey', *Journal of African American Men*, **1**, 2, pp. 38–42.

Ghouri, N. (1998) 'Race chief attacks training negligence', *TES*, 3 July.

Ghouri, N. (1999) 'Racism log ordered for nation's schools', *TES*, 26 March.

Gillborn, D. and Gipps, C. (1996) *Recent Research on the Achievements of Ethnic Minority Pupils*, London: OFSTED.

Hamilton, C., Rejtman, R. and Roberts, M. (1999) *Racism and Race Relations in Predominantly White Schools: Preparing Pupils for Life in a Multi-cultural Society*, Colchester: Children's Legal Centre.

Irvine, J. (1990) *Black Students and School Failure*, New York: Praeger.

Judd, J. (1999) 'Young, gifted, black – and a living reproach to our racist school system', *The Independent*, 11 March.

Kinder, K., Wakefield, A. and Wilkin, A. (1996) *Talking Back, Pupils' Views on Disaffection*, Slough: NFER.

Kinney, D., Eaton, J., Bain, N., Williams, B. and Newcombe, E. (1995) 'Mentoring Urban Adolescents' Motivation to Learn: A Teacher's Strategies and His Students' Perceptions', Paper presented at the Annual Meeting of the American Sociological Association, Washington DC.

Macpherson, Sir William of Cluny (1999) *The Stephen Lawrence Inquiry*, London: The Stationery Office.

Majors, R. and Billson, J. (1992) *Cool Pose: The Dilemmas of Black Manhood in America*, New York: Lexington Books.

Majors, R., Gillborn, D. and Sewell, T. (1998) 'The Exclusion of Black Children: Implications for a Racialised Perspective', *Multicultural Teaching*, **16**, 3, pp. 35–7.

Morgan, H. (1995) 'Drug use in high school: race and gender issues', *Journal of Educational research*, **88**, 5, pp. 301–8.

OFSTED (1999) *Raising the Attainment of Minority Ethnic Pupils: School and LEA's Response*, London: OFSTED.

O'Leary, J. and Betts, H. (1999) 'Inspectors accuse schools of racism', *The Times*, 11 March.

NASUWT (1999) *Education and Race*, Birmingham: NASUWT.

Ouseley, H. (1998) 'Black exclusions scandal', *TES*, 18 December.

Phelan P., Davidson, A. and Cao, H. (1992) *The Flow of Ethnicity*, New York: Teachers College Press.

Pickering, J. (1997) *Raising Boys' Achievement*, Stafford: Network Educational Press.

Polite, V. (1994) 'The method in the madness: African American males, avoidance schooling and chaos theory', *Journal of Negro Education*, **62**, 4, pp. 588–601.

Seligman, M. (1998) *Optimism*, New York: Pocket Books.

Sewell, T. (1997) *Black Masculinities and Schooling*, Stoke on Trent: Trentham Books.

Smith, V. (1997) 'Caring: Motivation for African American male youth to succeed', *Journal of African American Men*, **3**, 2, pp. 49–63.

Social Exclusion Unit (1998) *Truancy and School Exclusion Report*, London.

Spencer, M. (1991) *Adolescent African American Self-esteem: Suggestions for Mentoring Program Content*. Conference paper series, Washington: Urban Institute.

Thornton, K. (1999) 'Exclusion still highest in minority groups', *TES*, 9 July.

Watt, D., Sheriffe, G. and Majors, R. (1999) *Mentoring Black Male Pupils*, Unpublished manuscript, City College Manchester.

Weeks, D. and Wright, C. (1998) *Improving Practice: A Whole School Approach to Raising the Achievement of African Caribbean Youth*, London: Runnymede Trust.

White, J. and Cones, J. (1999) *Black Man Emerging*, New York: Routledge.

Wrench, J. and Hassan, E. (1996) *Ambition and Marginalisation: A Qualitative Study of Underachieving Young Men of Afro-Caribbean Origin*, London: DfEE.

Part I

Tackling historical and contemporary education problems

1   Racism, policy and the (mis)education of Black children

David Gillborn

Whereas the Queen's majesty, tendering the good and welfare of her own natural subjects, greatly distressed in these hard times of dearth, is highly discontented to understand the great number of Negroes and blackamoors which (as she is informed) are crept into this realm . . . who are fostered and relieved here, to the great annoyance of her own liege people who want the relief which these people consume . . . hath given especial commandment that the said kind of people shall be with all speed avoided and discharged out of this her majesty's dominions . . .

Royal Proclamation of 1601 (File and Power 1981, pp. 6–7)

There is a common assumption that Britain was somehow ethnically homogeneous before the major post-war migrations from the Caribbean and Indian subcontinent in the mid twentieth century. In fact, Britain has *always* been ethnically diverse and, as the quotation above demonstrates, racism has a long history too. In this chapter, my focus is upon the most recent part of that history; specifically, how has education policy sought to respond to Britain's ethnically diverse population?[1] My aim is to identify broadly the changing landscapes of education policy: unfortunately, the continuities are strong. Indeed, I will argue that despite changes in terminology, even the most recent policy moves give little or no cause for optimism that racism is finally to be addressed seriously in education policy.[2]

Sally Tomlinson (1977) produced the first serious attempt to chart the position of 'race' issues in British education policy. Since then numerous writers have produced their own versions, almost all borrowing terms from Tomlinson's original.[3] This approach typically categorises changing perspectives and actions via a series of 'models' or 'phases'. This has its dangers, not least glossing over contradictions and resistance in an attempt to describe (create?) neat categories. The problem is visible in the wide variety of terms used by authors, sometimes choosing to highlight different trends and periods. As with previous attempts, my policy map is necessarily incomplete: the start/end dates are not precise and there are points of opposition and counter-developments where national trends contrasted dramatically with local practice in some areas. My hope is that by looking back, we can better understand current approaches and future possibilities.

HISTORY OF POST-WAR ISSUES OF RACE AND EDUCATION

Ignorance and neglect (1945 to the late 1950s)

The term 'ignorance and neglect' is James Lynch's (1986: 42) description of the early post-war period. The initial education policy response to migration from the Caribbean and Indian subcontinent was to do nothing. Others have variously referred to the same period as one of 'laissez-faire' disregard (Massey 1991: 9) or 'inaction' (Rose *et al.* 1969 in Massey, 1991).

Assimilation (late 1950s to the late 1960s)

In 1958 'riots' in Nottingham and Notting Hill, London, saw white racist attacks on migrant communities misrepresented in the press as demanding action on the 'colour problem', while politicians on both sides of the House of Commons sought to excuse the actions of convicted whites (Ramdin 1987: 208–10). 'Racial' diversity was, therefore, presented as a threat to order and the migrant communities (victims of white racist violence) were projected as a 'problem'. Policy responses at this point were characterised first, by action to severely restrict Black and Asian migration; and second, by the policy goal of assimilationism. Tomlinson, for example, points to the view of the Commonwealth Immigrants Advisory Council, who in 1964, stated that 'A national system cannot be expected to perpetuate the different values of immigrant groups' (Tomlinson 1977: 3). This view fuelled attempts to assimilate minorities into the majority culture (or at least the official version of it) and can be seen most clearly in the policies that prioritised teaching the English language and the physical dispersal of 'immigrant' children to minimise their numbers in any single class/school – a policy that left many children and young people especially vulnerable to racist attacks (cf. Dhondy 1982).[4] The overriding policy objective here was to protect the stability of the system and placate the 'fears' of white racist communities and parents: a circular from the then Department of Education and Science (DES), makes explicit the priorities of the period:

> *It will be helpful if the parents of non-immigrant children can see that practical measures have been taken to deal with the problems in their schools, and that the progress of their own children is not being restricted by the undue preoccupation of the teaching staff with the linguistic and other difficulties of immigrant children.*
>
> (DES circular 7/65, quoted in Swann 1985: 194, original emphasis)

Integration (1966 to late 1970s)

Roy Jenkins (then Labour Home Secretary) famously advocated, in a 1966 speech, 'not a flattening process of assimilation but equal opportunity, accompanied by cultural diversity, in an atmosphere of mutual tolerance' (quoted in Mullard 1982: 125). This was important symbolically for acknowledging the contemporary existence of marked *in*equalities of opportunity, and for apparently withdrawing support for assumptions of white cultural superiority that had argued the need to 'absorb'/destroy ethnic differences. This period saw some important steps forward, not least the passing of the Race Relations Act (1976) and establishment of the Commission for Racial Equality (CRE). Nevertheless, educational work tended to assume a patronising and exoticised approach to teaching about 'race' and assumed the need to build 'compensatory' programmes to make good the supposed cultural deficits of minority pupils (Massey 1991: 11–12). It has been said that during this period 'emphasis was on life *styles* rather than life *chances*' (Lynch 1986: 41, emphasis added), a statement that draws attention to the publication of curricular materials that frequently reflected and reinforced crude stereotypes of minorities as at best exotic and strange, at worst as backward and primitive, and always as alien. The 'problem', therefore, was still seen as residing in the minority communities themselves; a position that continued to absolve the education system of responsibility. 'Tolerance' and 'diversity' emerged as new watchwords (that are still in vogue today) but essentially, protection of the status quo remained the key driving force in policy (just as in assimilationism).

Cultural pluralism and multiculturalism (late 1970s to late 1980s)

This period saw the rhetoric of cultural pluralism assume widespread support (across political parties). Like the other 'phases' there was a borrowing (in more or less altered forms) of some of the key concepts and terms of previous periods. So, for example, 'diversity' and 'tolerance' continued to feature prominently in the discourse, but importantly notions of liberal pluralism were at their height and began to find expression in official policy. An official committee of inquiry was established to examine the education of ethnic minority pupils (cf. Rampton 1981; Swann 1985) and its analysis traded on a 'radical' or 'strong' perspective that used differences in group outcome as indicative of inequalities of opportunity. The recommendations of the Rampton and Swann reports were highly criticised, from the political right and left. Nevertheless, the reports marked something of a watershed in public policy on 'race' and education in Britain by first, rejecting IQist notions of innate intellectual differences between 'races', and second, stating that teachers (in their expectations and actions toward pupils and parents) might actively be implicated in the creation of 'race' inequality. These advances, however, were highly constrained: not only did the Conservative government of the day reject the committee's most important recommendations (see below) but its chairman, Lord Swann, prepared a personal summary that barely even mentioned 'racism'.

Despite the changed nature of the public policy debate at this time, in education much work continued to trade on superficial 'positive images' stereotypes of the type Barry Troyna devastatingly described as the *3S's* – saris, samosas and steel bands (see Troyna and Carrington 1990: 20). As the phrase encapsulated, the concern was with a shallow 'celebration' of difference, in a context where issues of power and racism were conspicuously ignored or silenced. This was the very point pursued by anti-racists who sought to place issues of power at centre stage.

ANTI-RACIST COUNTER-CULTURAL DEVELOPMENTS

I noted earlier that a danger of labelling the past via a series of 'phases' is that counter trends and points of resistance can be glossed over. One of the most important such 'moments' in British education policy concerns the development of anti-racist analyses and pedagogies. Against the wider thrust of public policy, this period saw key developments on the anti-racist front, symbolised by the establishment of several prominent pressure groups (including the National Antiracist Movement in Education and All London Teachers Against Racism and Fascism: see Gaine 1995: 42–4; Massey 1991: 15–17). Despite its presentation in the media and parts of academia as a Marxist ideology of revolution (cf. Flew 1984; Palmer 1986), anti-racism was never tightly defined as a single theory or pedagogic approach. Much anti-racist work traded on a critique of previous approaches, only rarely venturing into the realms of suggested classroom practice. Godfrey Brandt's *The Realization of Anti-racist Teaching* (1986) stood out as a distinctive attempt to synthesise anti-racist critique and pedagogy. Brandt's work, as much as anyone's, captured the spirit of anti-racism at this point. He positioned liberal multiculturalism (with its fascination for 'positive images' and curricular change) as 'the Trojan horse of institutional racism' (p. 117) and argued that anti-racism differed fundamentally. In particular he argued that anti-racism should accord a central role to the 'experience and articulations of the Black community' (p. 119) and be characterised by an oppositional form. This involved an analysis that focused on power and the need to challenge dominant conceptions of knowledge and pedagogy. Nevertheless, anti-racism took a dynamic and varied form such that 'there was no body of thought called anti-racism, no orthodoxy or dogma, no manual of strategy and tactics, no demonology' (Sivanandan 1988: 147).

In many ways anti-racism reached a zenith, so far as education policy was concerned, with the work of the Inner London Education Authority (ILEA). Several local authorities, mostly serving large metropolitan areas, adopted anti-racist policies but the Greater London Council (GLC) and the ILEA (London's education authority) were at the forefront of public campaigns to advance anti-racist issues. In hindsight it is certainly true that the GLC and ILEA made mistakes. This version of 'municipal anti-racism' (Gilroy 1987) has subsequently been subject to numerous critiques, including those of left intellectuals who question both the conceptualisation and execution of public anti-racism for trading on essentialised notions of difference and for oversimplifying the complex politics of 'race' and racism (cf. Gilroy 1987, 1990; Modood 1992; Modood *et al.* 1996). Nevertheless, the GLC and ILEA led the way so far as anti-racist public policy was concerned; ILEA's Research and Statistics branch, for example, made concerted efforts to analyse and understand racialised patterns of success and failure in the capital's schools. Ultimately both the GLC and ILEA paid the price for their counter-cultural stance in their abolition at the hands of a Thatcher government.

An inquiry into a racist murder at Burnage High School in Manchester (Macdonald *et al.* 1989) also became entangled in the wider racialised politics of the time. The report's authors, all active in combating racism, argued publicly that 'the work of all schools should be informed by a policy that recognises the pernicious and all-pervasive nature of racism in the lives of students, teachers and parents, black and white, and the need to confront it' (Macdonald *et al.* 1989: xxiv). Nevertheless, this message was lost amid a torrent of distorted press coverage that misrepresented the particular criticisms that the panel had made of anti-racism as practised at Burnage. Rather than being recognised as a vital step forward in the attempt to identify workable and critical anti-oppressive strategies, the report was falsely presented as an attack on anti-racism *per se*; as 'signalling the failure of the anti-racist project in education' (Rattansi 1992: 11). Although anti-racist school practice is far from dead, therefore, the late 1980s and early 1990s witnessed many attacks on anti-racism (from left as well as right) and it undoubtedly suffered a retreat in many areas (cf. Gillborn 1995).

Although anti-racist initiatives were a vital part of this time period they never reached a widespread position of citation (let alone genuine influence). While multiculturalist and anti-racist advocates fought it out in meetings, on committees and in the pages of books and journals, it was only ever a modest version of multi-culturalism that achieved the status necessary for characterising the period as a whole. The peak for liberal pluralist multiculturalism was the publication of the Swann Report (1985) which, despite attempts to integrate anti-racist sensitivities, remained largely wedded to (and stands as an exemplar for) the cultural pluralist/ multicultural sensibilities of the period. Even as this period reached its peak, however, its destruction was in sight: signalled most obviously in the dismissive response of the Conservative government of the day. Speaking as the Swann Report was presented to Parliament, the then Secretary of State for Education, Keith Joseph, repeated the historic refusal of British governments to take serious targeted action on the inequalities endured by minority communities and their children:

> under-achievement is not confined to the ethnic minorities . . . [Our] policies apply to all pupils irrespective of ethnic origin. As they bear fruit, ethnic minority pupils will share in the benefit.
>
> (quoted in Gillborn 1990: 166)

It was Joseph's rejection of the report's principal recommendations, rather than the Swann Report itself, that set the tone for future policy in this field.

Thatcherism: The new racism and colour-blind policy (mid 1980s–1997)

This period was dominated by what Martin Barker (1981) characterised as 'the new racism'; a perspective that asserts a strong cultural homogeneity among the majority population as a basis for privileging the views, needs and assumptions of that group over minority communities. The focus on *'race'* and *superiority* of older times was replaced by a discourse that stressed *culture* and *difference*:

> You do not need to think of yourself as superior – you do not even need to dislike or blame those who are so different from you – in order to say that the presence of these aliens constitutes a threat to our way of life.
>
> (Barker 1981: 18)

This strand in Conservative ideology is strongly associated with Margaret Thatcher but as an overriding policy force it did not come to dominate until well into her reign as Prime Minister. However, elements of this same perspective outlived her occupancy of No.10 Downing Street and could still be seen in the speeches and policy programmes of both main parties as they fought the 1997 general election (cf. Gillborn 1999a). The period was characterised by ferocious individualism; as a prop for the pursuit and acquisition of individual wealth and power, but also as a refusal of wider state responsibilities and diversity around class and ethnic interests. The tone of the period is perhaps best captured by Thatcher's statement that there is 'no such thing as society' (cf. Thatcher 1993: 626).

The period witnessed a strong assertion of national homogeneity, where the interests of the majority *have* to come first, not through any supposed superiority (as in the assimilationist phase) but simply because *we* are 'different' and, after all, it's *our* country (cf. Ansell 1997; Barker 1981; Gillborn 1995).[5] In education, this phase is characterised by two events: first, its rise is clear in the rejection of the Swann Report (above), and second, the subsequent publication of the initial consultation on the National Curriculum, in 1987, which made no mention of cultural diversity. The period ended with the Tories' election defeat in May 1997.

Education policy in this period was characterised by *equiphobia* (Myers 1990) wedded to market economics and the tyranny of 'standards' discourse. This was seen most graphically in the sweeping education reforms of the decade (e.g. the introduction of the National Curriculum, testing regimes, and opting out of local authority control), each one pursued vigorously, with no reference to cultural diversity and with complete disregard (often contempt) for the likely consequences for minority pupils, parents and communities. 'Colour-blindness' (an obstinate refusal to consider ethnic diversity despite a wealth of evidence that minorities are *not* sharing equally) became the officially sanctioned approach. During his final year as Prime Minister, for example, John Major openly fixed colour-blindness as official government policy:

> Few things would inflame racial tension more than trying to bias systems in favour of one colour – a reverse discrimination that fuels resentment. An artificial bias would damage the harmony we treasure. Equality under the law – yes; equality of opportunity and reward – yes. These promote harmony.
>
> Policy must be colour blind – it must just tackle disadvantage. Faced by British citizens, whatever their background might be.
>
> (Major 1997: 7)

And what would this look like in education? More of the same market policies:

But how do you achieve equality of opportunity?

It begins with education.

Over the last few years we've opened up our schools so parents – and taxpayers – can see how well they're performing. That hasn't always made comfortable reading. Too often bad schools are found where we need good schools the most – in areas where education is a life line of hope . . . Testing children on the basic skills, and giving parents the results. Inspecting schools on a regular basis. And, when it's really necessary, closing down failing schools. . . . Specialist schools, grant-maintained schools, city technology colleges and – yes, if parents want them – grammar schools. This is the choice we're opening up.'

(ibid.: 7–8)

Under successive Conservative administrations, therefore, 'race' inequalities were removed from the agenda; subsumed amid other issues; and denied legitimacy as a topic for concerted action.

During this period, of course, there was also a running contest for influence between different factions *within* right-wing ideology, most obviously between the neo-liberals and the neo-conservatives (cf. Whitty 1992, 1997). The influence of both factions can be detected in the overall shape of the Tories' reforms, with the neo-liberal pursuit of market-driven reform somewhat tempered by the neo-conservative requirement to retain a core entitlement and 'National' Curriculum. The latter strand of neo-conservative thought was also apparent in the Tories' repeated refusal to grant state funding to Islamic schools. The latter area is one where an incoming Labour administration made an immediate difference (see below); but just how different is New Labour's approach to 'race' and education policy?

Naive multiculturalism: New Labour, old inequalities (1997–)

At the time of writing Tony Blair's self-styled 'New' Labour has not yet enjoyed a full term in office; it is early to be talking about a new phase in the politics of 'race' and education in Britain. Nevertheless, the first Labour government for eighteen years quickly established an approach very different (in some ways) to that of its Conservative predecessors. In other, quite fundamental respects, the parallels with previous approaches are distressingly strong.

EQUALITY OF OPPORTUNITY AND THE NAMING OF ETHNIC DIVERSITY

Once in office New Labour's first White Paper, *Excellence in Schools* (published just 67 days after the general election), proclaimed 'the Government's core commitment to equality of opportunity and high standards for all' (DfEE 1997: 3). The ritual concern with 'standards' (measured in a crude form) was a clear legacy from the previous policy phase, but the focus on equality of opportunity contrasted sharply with the Conservatives' open hostility to equity (see Gillborn 1995: 32). A further significant break with Tory education discourse was Labour's readiness openly to acknowledge *ethnic* inequalities in attainment and opportunity. The 1997 White Paper, for example, included several discreet references to inequalities of experience and outcome by ethnicity. The main body of the document carried a section entitled 'Ethnic minority pupils' that referred, among other things, to inequalities in achievement and offered modest commitments to consult on ethnic monitoring and 'best practice' in multi-ethnic schools (DfEE 1997: 34–5). In a document of more than 80 pages, the provision of a few paragraphs is, at best, a small beginning. In fact, *Excellence in Schools* set a pattern that was repeated later by another flagship policy document, the first report of the new Social Exclusion Unit (SEU) which, once again, took education as its first theme. Like the White Paper, the SEU's first report acknowledged the importance of racialised inequalities: in this case, the massive over-representation of Black students among those expelled from school.[6] Additionally, a wider review of academic research (Gillborn and Gipps 1996) was cited, including the view that white teachers might actively be involved in producing the inequalities via a range of differential expectations and responses to pupil behaviour.

These moves represented a significant break with previous policy but, in isolation, they proved inadequate. In both documents, the discussions of ethnic inequalities were separate from the rest of the analysis and did not impinge on the arguments feeding into the wider formulation of policy. Consequently, an understanding of racism and 'race' inequality remained almost completely absent from how the principal policy issues were conceived. As a result, policy continued to pursue colour-blind targets. This is important because the lessons of education policy since 1988 are clear: where equity is not monitored, and crude notions of league table 'standards' are prioritised, the outcome is frequently a *worsening* of existing inequality. In the decade following the 1988 Act, for example, there was a dramatic rise in the proportion of young people ending compulsory schooling with five or more higher grade (A*–C) passes in their General Certificate of Secondary Education (GCSE) examinations: from around 30 per cent in 1988 to just over 46 per cent in 1998. At the same time, however, the inequality in attainment between white and Black pupils worsened. In 1985 only 7 per cent of Black students attained five or more higher grades, compared with 21 per cent of whites (a gap of 14 percentage points). By 1996 the gap had grown to 22 percentage points, with 23 per cent of Black, and 45 per cent of whites attaining the same level (Commission for Racial Equality 1998; Drew 1995; Gillborn and Youdell 1998 p. 226).

FUNDING SEPARATE SCHOOLS: EQUALITY OF ACCESS OR STATE-SPONSORED SEGREGATION?

New Labour's commitment to 'equality of opportunity' was important, in view of the Conservatives' disdain for the notion, but their actions on 'race' and education remained firmly locked into a superficial and weak understanding of equity.[7] Although inequalities in experience and attainment have been openly acknowledged and described as unacceptable (see above on Black attainment and exclusions), the only binding targets established were those dealing in colour-blind terms; there were no specific targets for raising minority attainment nor reducing Black exclusions per se. In contrast, there was early action on the question of access and entitlement. After a decade of refusals by successive Conservative governments, within a year of its election Labour had granted state funding to Islamic schools: the Islamia primary in London (which first applied for state support in 1986) and the Al Furqan primary in Birmingham (which began moves in 1994). In granting the applications the Secretary of State for Education and Employment reportedly emphasised the technical merit of the applications, rather than any ideological points:

> Mr Blunkett said the schools had demonstrated that they 'will comply with the statutory provisions governing all maintained schools, such as delivering the national curriculum and offering equal access to boys and girls'.
>
> (Lepkowska 1998: 18)

It is interesting that equal opportunities, in terms of gender and access, were mentioned but not, apparently, any of the related issues that the decision raised concerning religious segregation. This is especially surprising in view of the controversy that had, until then, dogged these debates. For example, the last major inquiry into relevant issues, as part of the Rampton/Swann committee's work, could not agree a unanimous view. The committee argued that:

> The establishment of 'separate' schools would fail to tackle many of the underlying concerns of the communities and might exacerbate the very feelings of rejection which they are seeking to overcome.
>
> (Swann 1985: 519)

They saw 'a situation in which groups of children are taught exclusively by teachers of the same ethnic group' as undesirable for 'the children, the minority community' and 'society as a whole' (ibid.). Furthermore, a majority of the committee argued that existing anomalies in the funding of certain religious schools in Britain should be reconsidered as part of a review of the relevant sections of the 1944 Education Act (Swann 1985: 514). Six members of the committee, however, dissented from this position. They argued that:

> it is unjust at the present time not to recommend that positive assistance should be given to ethnic minority communities who wish to establish voluntary aided schools in accordance with the 1944 Act.
>
> (Swann 1985: 515)

Labour's decision on this issue went almost completely unremarked. There is insufficient space here to debate the pros or cons of any particular position in the separate schools debate; rather, for our purposes, it is significant that such a pivotal change passed without any explicit commentary by the government. It may be that the decisions were made purely on technical grounds of adequacy of teaching, management, curriculum etc. Alternatively (or additionally) the decisions may have been an attempt to extend formal equality of opportunity (of access and provision) to previously excluded minority communities. In any case, it is highly significant that such precedents were set without any attempt publicly to debate the implications in terms of social/educational policy, 'race' inequality and ethnic diversity. It is in this way that New Labour's approach can be characterised as 'naive multiculturalism'. There is a concern with a weak notion of equal opportunity (in terms of access) but a failure to engage with deeper structural forms of inequality. A further element of naive multiculturalism can be seen in Labour's response to the Stephen Lawrence inquiry, which presented an opportunity for anti-racist change, but was finally used in education as a platform for limited curricular moves.

THE STEPHEN LAWRENCE INQUIRY

The publication of the Stephen Lawrence Inquiry (Macpherson 1999) heralded a brief but highly significant period when the issue of racism in public institutions was placed high on the political and media agenda. Although the police service was at the centre of the Lawrence inquiry itself, other public services (especially education) were also implicated in its findings. The Department for Education and Employment (DfEE)'s response was quick and disappointing. There were strong echoes of Keith Joseph's dismissal of Swann (see above) in the department's assertion that steps were already being taken to address the issues. On the day that the report was published a DfEE press statement quoted David Blunkett on social justice in education:

> This is about how we treat each other and, importantly, how we learn to respect ourselves and one another as citizens . . . That is why we are promoting the teaching of citizenship at school, to help children learn to grow up in a society that cares and to have real equality of opportunity for all.
>
> (DfEE 1999: 1)

The prominence given to citizenship education was a worrying sign. Citizenship emerged as a key curricular issue during the years of Conservative reform and, for a while, became an area around which much multicultural and anti-racist work seemed to coalesce (Taylor 1992). Unfortunately, citizenship education, with its traditional emphasis on formal notions of pluralism and 'tolerance', does not necessarily provide a sound home for critical anti-racist developments (Gillborn 1995). Certainly, there is no evidence that work on citizenship can actually penetrate the school as whole (see Whitty 1992). Nevertheless, David Blunkett's emphasis on citizenship was retained and strengthened in the government's formal response to the Lawrence inquiry (Home Office 1999). As the *Times Educational Supplement* noted, 'in practice the plan will mean few changes in schools' (*TES*, 26 March 1999, p. 4).

In fact, the education-related parts of the 'action plan' involved little or no new action; they simply repackaged existing provision and policies. In relation to suggested changes in the National Curriculum, for example, it stated:

> The Department [for Education and Employment] has taken a number of actions to date. The National Curriculum addresses and values the diverse nature of British society.
>
> (Home Office, 1999)

The arrogance of this assertion is breathtaking. Macpherson had questioned the adequacy of the National Curriculum for a multi-ethnic society but was met simply with an apparent reassurance that things were fine. The section continued with explicit references to a few none-core subject areas (history; geography; music; art; personal, social and health education) before stating that teachers had already been granted sufficient 'flexibility':

> all subject documents are designed to provide teachers with flexibility to tailor their teaching to stimulate and challenge all pupils, whatever their ethnic origin or social background.
>
> (ibid.)

The section continued with heavy emphasis on citizenship education, talking about diversity and understanding but making no reference at all to racism or anti-racism:

> *we will ensure that citizenship has a prominent place in the revised National Curriculum and that provision builds on existing good practice* . . . developing pupils' knowledge and understanding of different beliefs and cultures, including an appreciation of diversity.
>
> (ibid., original emphasis)

The potential for a return to the worst kind of multiculturalism (characteristic of earlier phases) was clear: racism was left unexamined and unopposed, substituting for any anti-racist intent, a concern with 'understanding'. This theme continued in the department's talk of 'mutual respect and tolerance' in relation to guidance on good behaviour, and a restatement of policies already in place (prior to Macpherson) such as measures on truancy and exclusion, including provision for more on-site units. Finally, the government trumpeted 'the new "*Excellence in Cities*" initiative' which it claimed 'will bring enormous benefits to children living in inner city areas, including those from minority ethnic communities'. Again, note the way that Black students were subsumed into another category (inner-city children) almost as an afterthought.

CONCLUSIONS

Those who cannot remember the past are condemned to repeat it.

George Santayana (1863–1952)

The late 1980s, the 1990s and the start of the twenty-first century witnessed a succession of education reforms that left no publicly funded school untouched. In terms of ethnic diversity and racism, however, little of substance has changed. Although there are pockets of good anti-racist practice, at the national level it is clear that 'race' equality has never been a major concern. Despite its renewed commitment to 'equality of opportunity' and the fine words that met the publication of the Lawrence Inquiry, for example, New Labour has failed to break decisively with the traditional policy neglect in this field. Perhaps the one area where ethnic diversity *has* been addressed differently, in relation to funding for minority religious schools, is also the area where little or no public debate has taken place.

If national policy makers are serious about race equality they should consider moving away from some of the tried and failed approaches of the past. In this chapter, several have emerged. The approach that subsumes 'race' beneath other categories of action was clear in Keith Joseph's rejection of the Swann Report (in 1985) and the same tactic emerged in the DfEE's response to the Lawrence Inquiry (1999). A concern for 'tolerance' and 'understanding' has long been a feature of policy discourse but, without clear and targeted anti-racist action, the lessons of the past are that such an approach is at best limited, at worst tokenistic. The marketising zeal of recent Conservative administrations has been replaced by New Labour's programme of social inclusion, but both have refused to set specific targets for minority attainment while prioritising crude and exclusionary 'standards' that appeal to tabloid sensitivities but leave ethnic inequalities to worsen. Racism and 'race' inequality are long established traits of the British education system; there is little reason for optimism that they will remain anything except a minority concern for the foreseeable future.

NOTES

1   Parts of this argument have been developed elsewhere, including Blair *et al.* (1999) and Gillborn (1999b). In this paper the word 'race' is presented in inverted commas to denote its socially constructed nature (cf. Gillborn 1990).
2   Throughout this paper I use 'racialised' to refer to patterns of experience and outcome that are strongly associated with differences in ethnic origin. The term 'racism' is used here to denote social processes and differences in outcome that result in the disproportionate disadvantage of one or more minority ethnic groups.
3   The most frequently cited addition to this literature is undoubtedly Chris Mullard's essay 'Multicultural Education in Britain: from Assimilation to Cultural Pluralism' (Mullard 1982).
4   Dispersal was again embraced as a policy tool, in the late 1990s, by a Labour government keen to placate popular racist sentiments about asylum seekers.

5   Interestingly, similar themes of the rights and sensitivities of natural (white) subjects can be seen in the proclamation of 1601 quoted at the beginning of this chapter.
6   One study revealed that children of Black Caribbean ethnic origin were almost six times more likely to be expelled than their white counterparts (Gillborn and Gipps 1996: 52–3).
7   There have been many attempts to formulate definitions of equality of opportunity in education. Briefly, 'weak' versions tend to stress questions of access (concerning formal conditions) rather than substantive differences in attainment and experience, which are central to 'strong' versions of the concept: see Foster, Gomm and Hammersley 1996; Gillborn and Youdell 2000; Halsey, Heath and Ridge 1980; Valli, Cooper and Frankes 1997).

REFERENCES

Ansell, A.E. (1997) *New Right, New Racism: Race and Reaction in the United States and Britain*, London: Macmillan.

Barker, M. (1981) *The New Racism: Conservatives and the Ideology of the Tribe*, London: Junction Books.

Blair, M., Gillborn, D., Kemp, S. and MacDonald, J. (1999) 'Institutional racism, education and the Stephen Lawrence Inquiry', *Education and Social Justice*, 1, 3, pp. 6–15.

Brandt, G.L. (1986) *The Realization of Anti-racist Teaching*, Lewes: Falmer.

Commission for Racial Equality/Runnymede Trust (1993) 'The debate so far', Conference paper 9, *Choice, Diversity, Equality: Implications of the Education Bill*, A Working Conference, 30 January.

Commission for Racial Equality (1998) *Education and Training in Britain*, London: CRE.

Commonwealth Immigrants Advisory Council (1964) *Second Report*. Cmd 2458, London: HMSO.

Department for Education and Employment (DfEE) (1997) *Excellence in Schools*. Cm 3681. London: The Stationery Office.

Department for Education and Employment (DfEE)(1999) 'Ethnic minority pupils must have the opportunity to fulfil their potential – Blunkett', *Press Release 90/99*, London: DfEE.

Dhondy, F. (1982) 'Who's afraid of ghetto schools?', in Dhondy, F., Beese, B. and Hassan, L. (eds) *The Black Explosion in British Schools*, London: Race Today Publications.

Drew, D. (1995) *'Race', Education and Work: the Statistics of Inequality*, Aldershot: Avebury.

File, N. and Power, C. (1981) *Black Settlers in Britain 1555–1958*, London: Heinemann.

Flew, A. (1984) *Education, Race and Revolution*, London: Centre for Policy Studies.

Foster, P., Gomm, R. and Hammersley, M. (1996) *Constructing Educational Inequality*, London: Falmer.

Gaine, C. (1995) *Still No Problem Here*, Stoke on Trent: Trentham.

Gillborn, D. (1990) *'Race', Ethnicity and Education: Teaching and Learning in Multi-Ethnic Schools*, London: Routledge.

Gillborn, D. (1995) *Racism and Antiracism in Real Schools: theory . policy . practice*, Buckingham: Open University Press.

Gillborn, D. (1999a) 'Race, nation and education: New Labour and the new racism', in Jack Demaine (ed.) *Education Policy and Contemporary Politics*, London: Macmillan, pp. 82–102.

Gillborn, D. (1999b) 'Fifty years of failure: "race" and education policy in Britain', in Annette Hayton (ed.) *Tackling Disaffection and Social Exclusion: Education Perspectives and Policies*, London: Kogan Page, pp. 135–55.

Gillborn, D. and Gipps, C. (1996) *Recent Research on the Achievements of Ethnic Minority Pupils*, Report for the Office for Standards in Education, London: HMSO.

Gillborn, D. and Youdell, D. (1998) ' "Raising standards" and deepening inequality: league tables and selection in multi-ethnic secondary schools', Paper presented at the annual meeting of the American Educational Research Association, 13–17 April, San Diego.

Gillborn, D. and Youdell, D. (2000) *Rationing Education: Policy, Practice, Reform and Equity*, Buckingham: Open University Press.

Gilroy, P. (1987) *There Ain't No Black in the Union Jack*, London: Hutchinson.

Gilroy, P. (1990) 'The end of anti-racism', *New Community*, **17**, 1, pp. 71–83.

Halsey, A.H., Heath, A.F and Ridge, J.M. (1980) *Origins and Destinations: Family, Class, and Education in Modern Britain*, Oxford: Clarendon Press.

Home Office (1999) *Stephen Lawrence Inquiry: Home Secretary's Action Plan*, London: Home Office. Available at http://homeoffice.gov.uk/ppd/oppu/slpages.pdf

Lepkowska, D. (1998) 'Muslims gain equality of funding', *Times Educational Supplement*, 16 January, p. 18.

Lynch, J. (1986) *Multicultural Education: Principles and Practice*, London: Routledge and Kegan Paul.

Macdonald, I., Bhavnani, R., Khan, L. and John, G. (1989) *Murder in the Playground: The Report of the Macdonald Inquiry into Racism and Racial Violence in Manchester Schools*, London: Longsight.

Macpherson, W. (1999) *The Stephen Lawrence Inquiry*. CM 4262-I. London: The Stationery Office.

Major, J. (1997) *Britain – The Best Place in the World*, text of a speech to the Commonwealth Institute, 18 January. London: Conservative Central Office.

Massey, I. (1991) *More Than Skin Deep*, London: Hodder and Stoughton.

Modood, T. (1992) *Not Easy Being British: Colour, Culture and Citizenship*. Stoke-on-Trent: Runnymede Trust and Trentham Books.

Modood, T., Banton, M., Cohen, P., Gillborn, D. and Shukra, K. (1996) 'The changing context of "race" in Britain: a symposium', *Patterns of Prejudice*, **30**, 1, pp. 3–42.

Mullard, C. (1982) 'Multiracial education in Britain: from assimilation to cultural pluralism', in Tierney, J. (ed.) (1982) *Race, Migration and Schooling*, London: Holt, Rinehart and Winston, pp. 120–33.

Myers, K. (1990) 'Review of "Equal Opportunities in the New Era" ', *Education*, **5**, October, p. 295.

Palmer, F. (ed.) (1986) *Anti-Racism – An Assault on Education and Value*, London: Sherwood Press.

Ramdin, R. (1987) *The Making of the Black Working Class in Britain*, Aldershot: Westwood House.

Rampton, A. (1981) *West Indian Children in Our Schools*, Cmnd 8273, London: HMSO.

Rattansi, A. (1992) 'Changing the subject? racism, culture and education', in Donald, J. and Rattansi, A. (eds) (1992) *'Race', Culture and Difference*, London: Sage, pp. 11–48.

Rose, E.J.B., Deakin, N., Abrams, M., Jackson, V., Peston, M., Vanags, A.H., Cohen, B., Gaitskell, J. and Ward, P. (1969) *Colour and Citizenship*, Oxford: Oxford University Press.

Sivanandan, A. (1988) 'Left, Right and Burnage', *New Statesman*, 27 May, Reprinted in Sivanandan, A. (1990) *Communities of Resistance: Writings on Black Struggles for Socialism*. London: Verso, pp. 145–52.

Social Exclusion Unit (1998) *Truancy and School Exclusion Report by the Social Exclusion Unit*, Cm 3957, London: SEU.

Swann, Lord (1985) *Education for All: Final Report of the Committee of Inquiry into the Education of Children from Ethnic Minority Groups*, Cmnd 9453, London: HMSO.

Taylor, M.J. (1992) *Multicultural Antiracist Education after ERA: Concerns, Constraints and Challenges*, Slough: National Foundation for Educational Research.

Thatcher, M. (1993) *The Downing Street Years*, London: Harper Collins.

Times Educational Supplement (1999) 26 March: 4.

Tomlinson, S. (1977) 'Race and education in Britain 1960–77: an overview of the literature', *Sage Race Relations Abstracts*, **2**, 4, pp. 3–33.

Troyna, B. and Carrington, B. (1990) *Education, Racism and Reform*, London: Routledge.

Valli, L., Cooper, D. and Frankes, L. (1997) 'Professional development schools and equity: a critical analysis of rhetoric and research', in Apple, M.W. (ed.) *Review of Research in Education*, Volume 22, Washington DC: American Educational Research Association, pp. 251–304.

Whitty, G. (1992) 'Education, economy and national culture' in Bocock, R. and Thompson, K. (eds) *Social and Cultural Forms of Modernity*, Oxford: Polity.

Whitty, G. (1997) 'Creating quasi-markets in education: a review of recent research on parental choice and school autonomy in three countries', in Apple, M.W. (ed.) *Review of Research in Education*, Volume 22, Washington DC: American Educational Research Association, pp. 3–47.

2 The education of Black children: Why do some schools do better than others?

Maud Blair

INTRODUCTION

The literature on the schooling and education of black[1] children in Britain is extensive. With few exceptions (Channer 1996; Nehaul 1996, Blair and Bowne 1998), most of what has been written has focused on issues of underachievement, over-representation in suspensions and expulsions, early drop-out rates in the USA etc. This focus on the negative is not at all surprising. Black parents over the years have campaigned for better education for their children, have run their own supplementary schools to improve their children's chances, have tried to influence policy and practice in schools and have generally been vocal and active in their attempts to challenge discriminatory and unfair practices faced by black children and to reverse the continuing high levels of under-performance of black children in public examinations. Writers on the subject have tried to share their understandings of the nature and causes of these disadvantages, but despite the research, the community campaigns, the efforts of multiculturalists and antiracists, little seems to have changed over the decades and black and other minority children continue on aggregate to underperform in standardised tests compared to their white peers (Gillborn and Gipps, 1996).

A number of theories have been put forward to explain this situation. One explanation, the cultural dissonance explanation (Driver 1979), holds that white teachers[2] do not understand the cultures of black children and therefore misinterpret their behaviour and impose sanctions more frequently or more harshly on black children leading to conflict and disaffection with school. Black children in a white racist society are deemed, therefore, to suffer from low self-esteem, especially if the curriculum either does not reflect their cultures and interests or these are represented negatively in curriculum materials (Green 1982). Another theory, closely allied to cultural dissonance, is that teachers do not understand the learning styles of black children and therefore the teaching and learning experiences of black young people are negatively affected. For black children to succeed, it is argued, it becomes necessary for them to reject their own black identities and think and act white (Fordham and Ogbu 1986; Fordham 1996). There is also the argument that black children are aware that the job market does not operate in their favour and so they see little point in putting a lot of effort into academic work (Ogbu 1988). Others have sought explanations in the children themselves, arguing that certain 'racial' groups are intellectually inferior to others (Jensen 1969; Eysenck 1971; Hernstein and Murray 1994) or that black children behave more badly and are therefore justifiably placed in lower academic sets (Foster 1990). But the explanation that has been widely put forward both in Britain and in the USA is that racism – structural, institutional and individual – has been the main cause of the negative experiences of schooling of black and other minority children. In Britain, researchers have pointed to the disproportionate levels of reprimands and disciplinary measures that are routinely taken against black children in the classroom (Tizzard *et al.* 1988; Mortimore *et al.* 1988; Gillborn 1990; Wright 1992; Connolly 1995), and in particular the unfair and unjust manner in which black students are disciplined.

> Perhaps even more significant than the frequency of criticism and controlling statements which Afro-Caribbean pupils received was the fact that they were often singled out for criticism even though several pupils of different ethnic origins were engaged in the same behaviour. . . . In sum, Afro-Caribbean pupils were not only criticised more often than their white peers, but the same behaviour in a white pupil might not bring about criticism at all.
>
> (Gillborn 1990: 30)

That black children were more likely to be placed into lower sets and streams was also observed (Foster 1990; Wright 1987). Although Foster argued that black students deserved their placement in lower sets because of their higher incidence of poor and disruptive behaviour, the evidence in favour of the racism and discrimination explanation has been overwhelming.

Some writers, however, have also argued for a more complex understanding of the political and social positioning of black children in schools (Rattansi 1992; Scott-Jones 1996) and of black males in particular (Noguera 1997). Referring to the (damaging) effects of discrimination on black students which some writers have highlighted, Scott-Jones declares that

> There is no recognition (by some researchers) of the possibility of a range of reactions to discrimination on the part of students. There is no acknowledgment of the possibility that some students respond to discrimination with an increased determination to do well in school.
>
> (Scott-Jones 1996)

Scott-Jones further argues that the way schools are organised may not be suitable for adolescents, especially those transferring from elementary to middle/secondary school. Others have pointed to the way that schools neglect the role of peer group pressure on adolescents as well as the importance of taking account of the adolescent's natural desire for independence at a time of confusing emotional and physical changes associated with growing up (Cullingford and Morrison 1997; Hargreaves *et al.* 1996; Measor and Woods 1984).

The factors which exist to complicate and confound our understanding of the educational experience of black students, therefore, are many and varied. In an attempt to answer the question posed in the title of this paper, I will argue that there are essentially three major factors which allow some secondary schools in Britain to succeed with black students where others have failed. The first is an understanding by the adults in the school of the *political and social concerns* of their students, and the willingness and courage to address these, however uncomfortable or difficult. Teachers need to know and understand their students individually in order to assist their daily interactions and cater for them as individuals, and also as members of groups in order to be familiar with some of the wider issues that affect students as members of the wider society. The second is adult understanding of and empathy with the *needs and concerns of adolescents*. There is a need for teachers to be in tune with the particular age-group of students they teach in order to cater appropriately for them. The third is the school's willingness to *work with parents as genuine partners* in the pursuit of a socially and academically rewarding experience for students. In their attempts to understand their students as individuals, teachers need to form *meaningful* partnerships with parents, partnerships which recognise that parents are the primary carers of children, and, especially where the teachers are white, that there are issues which affect minority ethnic group students' lives which they cannot grasp unless they deliberately seek that knowledge. Parents are well placed to provide that information.

The focus on black students in this paper comes from the belief that if a school is willing to honestly address the issues that beset minority ethnic groups (for example black or Gypsy Traveller students) it is more likely to embrace the issues that exist for dominant groups, whereas schools that take a 'colour-blind' approach are more likely to interpret students' needs as meaning white students' needs, an approach which not only misses the diversity and complexity of students' lives, but also marginalises them (Blair *et al.* 1998). Instead of creating a warm and welcoming environment for black and minority ethnic group students and their parents, 'colour-blind' schools are more likely to develop a 'racially hot' environment marked not only by resentment and conflict but by disaffection and more likely than not, 'underachievement'. Education in such schools is for black communities, no longer, as Noguera states,

> . . . the most viable path to social mobility, (but) serves as a primary agent for reproducing their marginality. (1997: 220)

In order to illustrate my theories, I draw on research evidence from a study carried out by the Open University during 1997 for the Department for Education and Employment (DfEE). Most of the examples are drawn from one of the 18 schools which were involved in the study.

A SCHOOL THAT IS SUCCESSFUL FOR BLACK
STUDENTS? LIKE FINDING A NEEDLE IN A HAYSTACK

School effectiveness has been defined in the literature in measurable terms to mean success in standardised test scores, and more precisely in secondary schools in Britain, to mean acquiring grades A* to C. In seeking schools where students performed well in standardised tests, we began in our study by drawing on the Office for Standards in Education (OFSTED) lists of the General Certificate of Secondary Education (GCSE) results and highlighted those schools which not only performed well in the league tables, but also had a workable figure of a minimum of 10 per cent of black students. The study also covered Bangladeshi and Pakistani students, but this paper focuses entirely on black students largely because the school from which I draw my examples had less than 2 per cent students of South Asian origin. The issues for these groups of students (important though they are regardless of the numbers in the school) also differ in some important respects from those of black students, though my general theories outlined above apply to all students whatever their ethnic group.

Having selected schools which appeared on the OFSTED lists to be academically successful, we visited these schools in order to ascertain the level of success of the black (and South Asian) students. It was not so surprising to us to discover that schools which seemed on the face of it to be successful, were in fact only successful for some of their students. There is an assumption in the literature that an effective school is likely to combine a number of important factors. These are that the school has strong leadership, is well-organised, the staff are united and share a vision, there is a positive ethos, and that there are high expectations of students (Smith and Tomlinson 1989; Nuttall and Goldstein 1989; Reynolds and Cuttance 1992). Smith and Tomlinson (1989) concluded that a school which was 'effective' was likely to be effective for all its students, including minority ethnic group students. However, many so-called 'effective' schools operate in a 'colour-blind' manner which assumes that all students have the same needs and are affected by the same issues. One school in our study, which would qualify as 'effective' by the criteria above, provides an interesting example. A brief look at the ethos and the question of academic success serves to illustrate the point.

In relation to the school ethos, the level of negativity that existed in this school amongst the black students, and amongst the black boys in particular, indicated that their concerns were either not known or not heeded. The students were so pleased to be able to talk about what schooling was like for them, that a group of them asked for a further interview after school because, after my one hour with them in which they gave several examples of racism, especially by specific members of staff, one boy declared that I had not 'heard the half of it'. This state of affairs was not confined to this one school alone but existed for nearly all the black boys interviewed and a significant number of the girls in all the schools, with the exception of the one, Northern Catholic School, from which I draw my examples of 'success'.

Academically, black girls in the school given in the example above appeared, on the face of it, to perform as well and sometimes better than their white male and female peers. However, even this was deceptive. When the category 'black girls' was further broken down into the different ethnic groups (African, African-Caribbean, 'mixed-race'), we found that a school which seemed successful for all black girls was in fact only successful for African and dual ethnicity ('mixed-race') girls. African-Caribbean girls did not do well. The general impression in Britain is also that African students, male and female, generally do well and sometimes better than white students in public examinations. In this apparently successful school (and others), black boys (including African boys) achieved significantly lower grades than their white peers. Furthermore, this level of 'underachievement' was not confined to that one year but, according to the figures, or to the headteachers' statements, applied to at least two or three years previously. This situation was no different for our exemplar school (Northern Catholic) except in the question of steady improvement of black students' results. In this school, black girls from different ethnic groups did well and although the results for the black boys were still by and large lower than for other student groups, they had shown steady improvement over the previous three years. In the year of the study, black girls achieved on average the highest scores for science, followed by black boys, and black boys came second to the white boys in mathematics.

There were therefore no schools in our study which could be said to be equally successful for all their students, least of all for the black students. We decided therefore, that rather than search for the proverbial needle in the haystack, we would examine the factors that led to the steady progress by black students in Northern Catholic School. The school was no different in size from two other Catholic schools (approximately 700 students and approximately 30 per cent black students) and only different in class composition from the one mentioned above, which had more African, dual ethnicity and middle-class black students. It was not by any means a 'highflying' school in terms of its position in the national league tables. It is at any rate commonly accepted that league tables do not and cannot measure accurately a school's actual achievement because of the complexities of schooling, of the environment and because of the diverse concerns of schools. As we state in Blair and Bourne (1998: 69),

> 'good systems' do not necessarily by themselves guarantee successful attainment for all groups of students, nor do league table measurements currently take into account value-added factors and the hard work put in by teachers who want to provide a curriculum that is relevant to a very diverse student intake.

League tables which tell us the percentage of students who obtained high grades in their examinations do not tell us *which* students received these grades and can therefore mask the failure of schools in relation to particular groups of students. A factor which stood out for Northern Catholic School was that there was a qualitatively different response from the black students at this school about their experience of schooling, and as mentioned, black students were making more progress academically than in any of the other schools with a comparable intake.

HOW A SCHOOL CAN MAKE A DIFFERENCE

On the whole, schools in Britain have not succeeded, despite attempts by the multi-cultural and antiracist movements, in creating environments in which black students as a whole feel the sense of belonging which comes with acceptance of who they are. But in order to accept and respect students' identities, it is necessary to know them and to understand them. This seems to be a particularly tall order in an environment which is ethnically, linguistically and religiously diverse. However, it is this overall student-centred culture and philosophy within the school that is at the root of 'effectiveness' for all students. To achieve such an environment requires a culture change which goes beyond well-meaning policy or statements of intent. Changing a school's culture cannot be done overnight but requires courage and patience, and most of all a deep sense of commitment and a genuine desire to provide equality of opportunity for all students. This last point is a particular challenge at a time in British education when greater tensions are being created between the personal and social needs of students and what Hargreaves *et al.* (1996: 6) describe as the 'traditional, judgmental, fact-centred systems of assessment and evaluation'. In the following sections I describe those issues which were found to be essential for creating a positive learning environment for black students.

UNDERSTANDING THE ISSUES AND CONCERNS OF BLACK STUDENTS

An examination of the literature which focuses on issues of 'race', ethnicity and education in British schools reveals an interesting and important fact – that black secondary school students, regardless of where they are in the country or what school they attend, seem to speak with one voice about the nature of their experience of schooling. Our own interviews with black students confirmed what many researchers have documented: that black students feel they are unfairly treated by teachers (i.e. 'picked on'); they believe that teachers often operate with racial stereotypes which are demeaning; that this outlook on the part of teachers affects their attitudes to black students; that teachers have low expectations of them; that teachers discriminate against them; that they do not treat them with respect; and (a complaint common to all students) that teachers do not listen to them, and also that teachers always 'stick up for and support each other' (Wright 1987, Mac an Ghaill 1988; Gillborn 1990; Mirza 1992; Connolly 1995).

Listening to and respecting students

At Northern Catholic, the school decided that in order to deal with the serious problem of black student alienation it was important to listen to the grievances that were brought to them by students, and then find strategies for developing a culture which created a positive learning environment for black students. Listening to students meant actively attempting to understand things from their point of view. The headteacher listened to both the perspective of the students and that of the teachers about what they thought caused the poor behaviour and poor relations within the school. It was important for the students to know that the headteacher would not always 'stick up for teachers', especially when they were wrong. Complaints of racism were never dismissed as a symptom of the 'chip on the shoulder', but were properly investigated and, especially where a teacher had been unaware of the racial nature of their actions, this was explained so that the teacher could see the effects of their actions on the students. This non-judgemental approach was found to be necessary because of the complex nature of racism which can sometimes be unintended, unconscious and unacknowledged (Mac an Ghaill 1988; Gillborn 1997). In contrast, in another school, the black student who reported to the headteacher that he had been treated by his teacher in a racially discriminatory way was questioned about his own attitudes to school, told about his history of poor behaviour and then accused of 'reverse racism'. There was in this school a high level of disaffection amongst the black students, especially the boys, who were also disproportionately affected by exclusions.

An aspect of listening to students and respecting their point of view related, at Northern Catholic, to the manner in which information was gathered and used. It was not enough to have a mission statement which pronounced equality of treatment for all. It was important, as the deputy headteacher stated, that it was made clear to students that they would be believed unless, after investigation, the facts proved to be different. This approach was just as supportive to teachers, who realised that this was not a licence for students to make false accusations or try to gain an advantage, but was inherently about creating a fair and just system. If teachers respected students' rights to be heard, and in the process learnt about the issues that affected students and why, this was more likely to improve relationships within the school than an approach which was authoritarian and dismissive of students' concerns. Teachers were thus encouraged to reflect on their words and actions to understand how these were viewed by students. They were also encouraged to discuss with students rather than immediately resort to punishment when certain types of behaviour were unacceptable. In this way, a culture of mutual respect was developed and one in which black students felt assured that their concerns mattered to the school, would be investigated and appropriate action taken. The deputy head stated that:

> The key to good relations in our school is that we take time to listen to students. We give them a fair hearing. If students feel that you will listen to them and investigate things properly, and sometimes you spend a lot of time listening to something you knew all the time, but the bottom line is, they know you will listen to them.

Respecting student cultures

One of the concerns that black students have is that their histories are excluded from what is considered to be valuable knowledge in the school curriculum. Not only is it excluded, moreover, but what exists is sometimes found to be eurocentric or racist. The restrictions placed on the school curriculum by the demands of the National Curriculum inhibit attempts by schools to place the histories and cultures of minority ethnic groups within the mainstream academic subject area. The feeling of marginalisation of black students was recognised at Northern Catholic, and attempts were made to meet this concern by the introduction within the Personal and Social Education (PSE) programme of a six week course in Afrikan Studies which was taken by all students in the school. This was later followed by a six week course of Irish Studies to reflect another major ethnic group in the school.

The initial introduction of Afrikan Studies was, as can be expected, controversial and greeted with less than enthusiasm from some members of staff and parents. It clearly required courage and perseverance, not only in ensuring that the course was introduced but in gradually persuading staff that it was important and useful. The strategies that were used for addressing staff concerns are discussed below.

UNDERSTANDING AND RESPONDING TO ADOLESCENTS

Hargreaves *et al.* (1996) contend that secondary schools have not traditionally been responsive to the needs of adolescents or taken heed of changes in the wider society. A factor that is often omitted in research, and certainly one that seems to be absent in teachers' dealings with black students, is that their identities go beyond the question of 'race' or ethnicity to embrace those factors which they share with all young people, namely, the fact of growing up. It is often assumed that when individual black boys misbehave, it is a factor of their 'race' rather than of their adolescence. It seems likely that this would lead teachers to treat black students differently from white students and explain the pervasive feeling amongst black young people that they are treated unfairly. It is also assumed that in order to create a positive learning environment for black young people, one need only address questions of racism and discrimination and ignore the need to understand black young people *as young people*.

A vital component of teacher education should be to help teachers understand the ways and the needs of adolescents. Many writers have pointed to this phase of development as being particularly difficult for the young people themselves. Adolescents, as Hargreaves *et al.* (1996) put it, 'are complex, diverse, and unpredictable'. These characteristics are part of young people's attempts to grow and become more independent. Writing over 20 years ago, Curtis and Bidwell (1977: 41) stated that,

> although some parents and teachers are sensitive to the ways they assist youth to achieve independence, much opinion seems to be critical of the struggle for independence. This is surprising since this ultimate independence is necessary for the continuance of society.

In many schools, this quest for independence is punished rather than harnessed for the benefit of the young people themselves and the school. In some schools in our study, however, staff showed sensitivity and an ability to engage constructively with the dilemmas of youth. They understood the pressures of the peer group and attempted to work with this rather than condemn it. In these schools, suspensions and expulsions were few or non-existent because staff took an approach which was empathetic rather than hostile towards young people.

Head of year (Southern International School):

> We very rarely permanently exclude. A student would have to have done something horrendous for it to get to the stage of a permanent exclusion. It's very rare, for example, in a case of violence, for students to go home not having made up. We talk through problems with students and help them find alternative ways of dealing with situations.

At Northern Catholic, the head of the school understood and responded to what one headteacher described as 'the fantastically strong stereotypes in the society of what people think black boys are like'. These stereotypes included the belief that where black boys were gathered in a group, there were likely to be drugs or they were preparing to do something antisocial like 'mugging'; that black males are violent and threatening; that they have no interest in education and therefore 'underachieve'; and generally that black males spelt 'trouble'. The headteacher of Northern Catholic School made it clear to the black students that she understood what they had to face, and assured them that such attitudes towards them by teachers would not be tolerated. But, whilst she offered her full support to the students, she also tried to ensure that they took responsibility for themselves and others around them. It was made clear, for example, that a change in the school culture could not occur without their full co-operation and contribution. Furthermore, not only were they encouraged to take responsibility for themselves, but also to play their part in the community, for example, helping to organise a youth conference.

There was thus an understanding that black students were not only adolescents with all the problems of adolescents, but that they were adolescents who were situated differently from their white peers both within the culture of the school and of the wider society. It was wrong therefore to compartmentalise their experiences into either 'race', or youth; it was necessary to see and appreciate the complexity of their experiences as young-black-males/females. In their dealings with all adolescents, the school worked with peer group leaders to provide examples for others in relation to both behaviour and academic achievement.

> We work through individuals to reverse the trend amongst boys which says that to be an achiever is not cool. One African-Caribbean boy . . . is a very bright boy but became more involved with the social side of life and was underachieving. So I called him and told him he was turning out to be the equivalent of a 'dumb blonde' – tall and good-looking but with nothing. He's

very popular with the girls. I asked him if there was a particular girl that he liked and he said, 'Ella'. So I said, 'She's not going to want you if you are not going to be of a similar academic status. Your good looks aren't going to last forever. You can't get through on that charm and that smile. The kind of girls you like are not going to be interested if you're on the dole.' He knew exactly what I meant. He didn't like to be compared to the dumb blonde. Now he's one of our role models and we have great hopes for him.

The headteacher's appeal to the young man's masculinity is clearly problematic in its ignorance of the dynamics of both gender and disability, and is an issue that needs to be resolved. The point being made here, however, is that it was recognised that giving students equality of opportunity was not a question of 'take it or leave it'. Adolescent boys, with their need for peer group approval and facing the challenge that working hard at school is 'soft', are unlikely to take up opportunities for extra classes or revision work. One teacher pointed out that boys of this age tend to be 'immature learners' and need to be given extra encouragement to take up such opportunities. This also applied to students who were alienated or had other reasons for not taking up opportunities where they occurred. Often, it was the personal interest shown in such an individual by a teacher that could make all the difference.

> **Student**: (Mrs B.) called me to the office the other day and she says, 'I've seen a spark and I don't want it to die. You've got the ability and you can do it. Do you mind me mentoring you? When you get your coursework, show me; when it's finished, show me.' She wants to monitor everything – my attendance, my punctuality, and I will gladly go along with that because I know that she is doing it because she really cares. She is a really good teacher.

PARTNERSHIPS WITH PARENTS

As stated at the beginning of this chapter, black parents have been engaged in an ongoing struggle to secure the educational rights of their children in British schools. One reason for this ongoing struggle has been the failure of schools to relate to minority ethnic group parents with respect, and the tendency also to hold stereotypical attitudes towards them. Discussions with black parents reveal very similar concerns to those of their children (Blair and Bourne 1998). Parents have complained about teachers making assumptions about their personal characteristics on the basis of stereotypes about black people. Teachers sometimes assume that black parents are aggressive and this makes them feel intimidated, thus hindering their ability to relate to black parents. One parent stated:

> Most (black) people were born in this country, went to school in this country, and half of these teachers, we used to play with them. So why are they finding us so aggressive?

Amongst the stereotypes held by teachers is an assumption that black parents are not interested in their children's education because they do not always attend 'Open Evenings' where parents meet with teachers to discuss the children's progress. Such arrangements, say parents, are often a waste of time because teachers do not give them quality information about academic progress but focus on behaviour, or else they report that the children are 'doing fine' when this is not reflected in the children's work.

> Usually when I go to Parents' Evenings, it's like, 'Well, she is doing fine'. It is such a generalisation. I want specifics, and they don't seem to be able to give me specifics. You know, I'll say, 'How is she doing in the particular subject?' and they say, 'Fine'. I mean that is why a lot of us are walking the streets because everything was 'fine' at the Parents' Evening.

Parents also report being 'fobbed off' by the school when they want to take up a concern, and that when they do go to the school, they are treated with disrespect not always by the teachers themselves, but sometimes by reception staff. Parents talk about being 'talked down to' by teachers and generally treated, on the basis of their colour and class, as second-class citizens.

How do schools that are 'successful' for black students avoid these mistakes? As with students, the most effective ways of gaining the parents' support and co-operation was to listen to their concerns, consult them about and give them a voice on important issues, both pastoral and academic, and perhaps most importantly, show them respect by acting on their concerns and not merely involving them in a tokenistic way. At Northern Catholic School, an Association of Black Parents and Parents of Black Children was formed. They met in the school and discussed the issues relating to the education of their children, issues which they wanted to take up with the school. These were then reported to the headteacher, or, through the governor representative, to the board of governors. Availing the parents of the school in this way, and then taking up their concerns, also helped to create an environment in which previously disempowered parents felt more confident to join the school's governing body and take an active part in decisions made about and for the school. The headteacher also made it her business to try to understand the issues for the black communities by involving herself in community affairs and getting to know the communities from which the students came. She forged strong relationships with people in the black community. Through this personal education, she understood that her role in the education of black students did not begin and end at the school gate. She understood that black people, young and old, were subject to police harassment and intimidation and she was sometimes called upon by black families to vouch for their children's character where these children came before the law. She also helped and advised parents to find legal support where students in the school were called before the criminal justice system. This intimate understanding of the political issues which beset the lives of the students and their parents gained this headteacher the respect and trust of the black parents. One parent said this of her:

(Black) parents have the confidence to come to her as a friend. She is seen as a friend in arms, struggling together for the good of their children.

The general policy in the school towards the parents was to have a genuine 'Open door'.

> We say to parents that if your child comes home with something and you are asking yourself, 'Should I ring the school?' We say, 'Ring. Don't think anything is too trivial'. We encourage parents to be open, to see if there is anything about the work, the quality of the work, is there too much work, or is there something about the way the teacher may have treated the child in class. We are open enough to say, 'come in and tell us'.

The parents were also closely consulted and involved in policy decisions. When the school was drawing up its anti-racist policy, leading members of the black community were asked to comment on the draft produced. This was then circulated to all parents with children in the school for further comments, then given to the school's governing body for endorsement, before it was finally written up. A similar procedure was taken for the anti-sexist policy.

The interest in the lives and concerns of the black students was an indication of this headteacher's concern for all the students in her school, a concern which was well demonstrated in the support she gave to an 'at risk' Irish boy who finally left school with good credentials. This approach was quite different from that of headteachers in other schools where issues of concern to black students and their parents were often considered 'too sensitive' (see also Hayden 1997), or attempts to address them were seen as 'pandering to minority interests'. What was generally not recognised in schools was that the disadvantaged position of minority group students was part of the wider systemic disadvantages which are experienced by members of minority groups. Instead, the tendency in schools was to blame students and their families for any failures, and to avoid critical thinking or reflection about the school's role in creating or perpetuating such 'failures'.

STRATEGIES FOR INVOLVING TEACHERS IN SCHOOL CHANGE

Attempting to change a school is a difficult and slow process because, as Hargreaves *et al.* state,

> educational change is not just a technical process of managerial efficiency, or a cultural one of understanding and involvement. It is a political and para-doxical process as well . . . educational change which promises to benefit all students . . . threatens many entrenched interests.
>
> (Hargreaves *et al.* 1996: 163)

General change is difficult enough, but entrenched interests are particularly threatened when the type of change required involves an examination of and deep reflection on one's own beliefs and value systems. The half-hearted and sometimes failed attempts in the 1970s and 80s to implement multicultural and antiracist education bear witness to this difficulty (Troyna, 1992). But change is difficult because it is also about

> transforming sophisticated relationships not simple behaviours, in complex classroom situations and organizational systems, whose purpose and direction are politically compounded and contested.
>
> (Hargreaves *et al.* 1996: 168)

At Northern Catholic, the headteacher recognised the potential difficulty of convincing teachers that change was needed, and that this change had to embrace the whole philosophy and culture of the school and not just the disciplinary measures taken against misbehaving students. She was convinced that not only were there gross injustices being perpetrated against the black students with particular reference to the black boys, she was sure that no single strategy would be sufficient to change the climate of hostility and conflict in which the black students and teachers were engaged. She needed to be sensitive to the grievances brought to her by the black students as well as take account of the sensitivities of teachers whose very identity as professionals was threatened.

The strategy adopted embraced both multicultural and antiracist methods. On the one hand, a course on Afrikan Studies was introduced, initially outside school hours and attended voluntarily by students, and then as part of the compulsory Personal, Social Education (PSE) programme in which all students took part. This strategy, which was interpreted by some teachers and parents as favouring black students, met with some opposition. To address this, meetings were organised in order to discuss the basic philosophy of the school and to gain a unified understanding of what equality of opportunity meant in practical terms. It was also explained that unless the issues which affected the black students could be effectively tackled, the relationships in the school would continue to negatively affect the whole of the school community, and black students would continue to 'underachieve' in relation to other students. The headteacher stated,

> I've been quite outright in saying that whatever strategies we use to help black students raises the achievement of the white students and of the whole school because if there is a social problem, it helps to change the atmosphere.

Teachers were encouraged to discuss their fears and misgivings and to ask questions in a climate of openness and honesty in a non-judgemental environment. Parents too were invited to express their feelings and to come to the school if they had questions or wanted to discuss the implications of the Afrikan Studies programme. Alongside the implementation of the Afrikan Studies programme, teachers received in-service education on issues of equality of opportunity.

Another strategy was to get teachers and students to define together what they wanted from their school. As a Catholic school, Year 9 Tutors and their students (12–13 year olds) took 'retreats' together every year, and this was an occasion for all to learn about better communication, conflict resolution, the school's educational and moral mission, and for teachers to get to know their students and 'bond' together outside the normal routines and environment of the school. Out of these meetings and 'retreats' emerged a Code of Behaviour for the whole school and one which applied to the staff as much as it did the students. This Code of Behaviour defined what was acceptable and not acceptable behaviour and, importantly, provided guidelines for resolving difficulties in a respectful and conflict-free environment.

The process of gaining the co-operation of teachers was a long and, according to the headteacher, a hard one. It took six years before she began to feel that there was much more of a united front in the school. The black students were given assurances that racism and unfair treatment against them would not be tolerated and that they had the ear of senior management in the school if they had any grievances. All parents were given the assurance that if their children had a serious grievance, this would be heard by senior management, and together with the parents, the complaint would be investigated and something would be done about it.

The political rationale for addressing the concerns of groups and not only of individuals was explained to the teachers, who were informed that such action applied to all students regardless of ethnicity. These combined strategies, and the headteacher's perseverance in the face of sometimes very strong opposition, finally seemed to pay off so that it was the teachers themselves who were at last able to appreciate the benefits of the more peaceful environment in which they were working. Black students began to feel confident that the one issue which most affected them, that of being racially discriminated against, would at last be taken seriously. A further benefit, which the open discussions and the ability to engage with controversial and difficult subjects allowed the school to do, was to address the issues that affected adolescents as adolescents without the clutter of racial stereotypes. The level of mutual trust that developed enabled the school to introduce changes that were of benefit to the whole school community. Teachers were able to develop an understanding of not only black students' needs but the needs of all students, and to experience the benefits of this for their own teaching.

CONCLUSION

The case of Northern Catholic High School is an illustration and not a template for what can be done to change the schooling experiences of black students. Every school operates within its own context and with its own set of problems and issues. That the problems faced by black students in British schools are not confined to specific areas of the country, and that they are just as likely to apply in situations of low as well as high black student population, have been well demonstrated in research. The example of Northern Catholic should therefore offer some encouragement. Black students need to know that they are not only welcome and wanted in the school, but that they will be treated fairly, their cultures will be respected, the political issues that beset them as black people will be understood and form part of the school's sensitivities and responsibilities toward them. They need to know that their particular needs will be recognised as complex and comprising their ethnic and 'racial' identities as well as their needs as 'children' or young people, but also that their differences will be appreciated.

A major criterion in achieving this kind of positive environment for black and all students is teachers who are willing to learn and genuinely understand the issues that affect their students.

Hargreaves *et al.* (1996: 6) state that

> Change is most effective, not when it is seen as a problem to be fixed, an anomaly to be ironed out, or a fire to be extinguished. Particular changes are more likely to be implemented in schools where teachers are committed to norms of continuous improvement as part of their overall professional obligations.

Regretfully, changes relating to 'race' and ethnicity are usually regarded as 'a problem to be fixed' and 'an anomaly to be ironed out'. This was undoubtedly the case for many teachers at Northern Catholic. What was needed was not only strong and determined leadership and a clear vision of what was right for the school, but enough teachers who were committed 'to the norms of continuous improvement' to create the momentum for change and provide the support needed for this to be effective. The extent to which the united 'Catholic' philosophy helped the process is open to speculation. The most important 'mission' was that of ensuring that none of the students who attended this school, and none of their parents, should feel in any way marginalised or discriminated against. To achieve this requires from any senior management in a school the ability to throw off the 'baggage' of assumptions that we all carry and which play such an important part in influencing how we see others and how we relate to them (see for example Sleeter 1994).

What is needed, as one headteacher said, is the ability to create in a school a 'we' ethos and not an ethos of 'them' and 'us' which divides teachers from students and black from white. Unfortunately, black students in many schools are consciously or unconsciously experienced as 'Other' (Blair 1994). Changing this situation is the real challenge facing teachers who not only care about their students but genuinely want to make a difference to their lives.

NOTES

1   I use the term 'black' here to refer to people of African descent whether they be from Africa or the Caribbean. The term is also used to refer to people of dual heritage where one parent is of African descent.

2   Approximately 98 per cent of teachers in British schools are white. Most black children will therefore be taught by white teachers, and some might never have a black teacher throughout their schooling. In writing about 'teachers', therefore, it is assumed in this paper that the teachers are white.

REFERENCES

Blair, M. (1994) 'Black teachers, black students and education markets', *Cambridge Journal of Education*, Vol. 24, pp. 277–91.

Blair, M., Bourne, J. with Coffin, C., Creese, A. and Kenner, C. (1998) *Making the Difference: Teaching and Learning Strategies in Successful Multi-ethnic Schools*, London: DfEE.

Channer, Y. (1996) *I Am a Promise: The Schooling Achievement of British African-Caribbeans*, Stoke-on-Trent: Trentham Books.

Connolly, P. (1995) 'Racism, masculine peer-group relations and the schooling of African/Caribbean infant boys', *British Journal of Sociology of Education*, **16**, 2, pp. 75–92.

Cullingford, C. and Morrison, J. (1997) 'Peer group pressure within and outside school', *British Educational Research Journal*, **23**, 1, pp. 61–80.

Curtis, T.E. and Bidwell, W.W. (1977) *Curriculum and Instruction for Emerging Adolescents*, New York: Addison Wesley.

Driver, G. (1979) 'Classroom stress and school achievement: West Indian adolescents and their Teachers', in Saifullah Khan, V. (ed.) *Minority Families in Britain: Support and Stress*, London: Macmillan.

Egglestone, S.J., Dunn, D.K. and Anjali, M. (1985) *Education for Some: The Educational and Vocational Experiences of 15–18 Year Old Members of Minority Ethnic Groups*, Stoke-on-Trent: Trentham.

Eysenck, H.J. (1971) *Race, Intelligence and Education*, London: Temple Smith.

Fordham, S. and Ogbu, J. (1986) 'Black students' school success: coping with the burden of "acting white"', *The Urban Review*, **18**, 3, pp. 1–31.

Fordham, S. (1996) *Blacked Out: Dilemmas of Race, Identity and Success at Capitol High*, Chicago: University of Chicago Press.

Foster, P. (1990) *Policy and Practice in Multicultural and Antiracist Education*, London: Routledge.

Gillborn, D. (1990) *'Race', Ethnicity and Education*, London: Unwin and Hyman.

Gillborn, D. (1997) 'Young, black and failed by school: the market, education reform and black students', *International Journal of Inclusive Education*, **1**, 1, pp. 6587.

Gillborn, D. and Gipps, C. (1996) *Recent Research on the Achievement of Ethnic Minority Pupils*, London: HMSO.

Green, D. (1982) Teachers' influence on the self-concept of different ethnic groups, unpublished Ph.D. thesis, cited in Troyna, B. (1993) *Racism and Education*, Buckingham: Open University Press.

Hargreaves, A., Earl, L. and Ryan, J. (1996) *Schooling for Change: Re-inventing Education for Early Adolescents*, London: Falmer.

Hayden, C. (1997) *Children Excluded from Primary School: Debates, Evidence, Responses*, Buckingham: Open University Press.

Herrstein, R.A. and Murray, C. (1994) *The Bell Curve: Intelligence and Class Structure in American Life*, New York: The Free Press.

Jensen, D. (1969) 'How much can we boost IQ and scholastic achievement?', *Harvard Educational Review*, **39**, 1, pp. 1–23.

Mac an Ghaill, M. (1988) *Young, Gifted and Black: Student–Teacher Relations in the Schooling of Black Youth*, Milton Keynes: Open University Press.

Measor, L. and Woods, P. (1984) *Changing Schools*, Milton Keynes: Open University Press.

Mirza, H. (1992) *Young, Female and Black*, London: Routledge.

Mortimore, P., Sammons, P., Stoll, P., Lewis, D. and Ecob, R. (1988) *School Matters: The Junior Years*, Wells: Open Books.

Nehaul, K. (1996) *The Schooling of Children of Caribbean Heritage*, Stoke-on-Trent: Trentham.

Noguera, P. (1997) 'Reconsidering the "Crisis" of the Black Male in America', *Journal of Social Justice*, **24**, 2, pp. 147–64.

Nuttall, D. and Goldstein, H. (1989) 'Differential school effectiveness', *International Journal of Educational Research*, **13**, pp. 769–76.

Ogbu, J. (1988) 'Understanding cultural diversity and learning', *Educational Researcher*, **21**, 8, pp. 5–14.

Rattansi, A. (1992) 'Changing the subject? Racism, culture and education', in Donald, J. and Rattansi, A., *'Race', Culture and Difference*, London: Sage.

Reynolds, D. and Cuttance, P. (1992) *School Effectiveness: Research, Policy and Practice*, London: Cassell.

Scott-Jones, D. (1996) 'Motivation and Achievement: Implication of Minority Status', Discussion Paper presented at the annual meeting of the American Education Research Association, NY, April.

Sleeter, C. (1994) 'How white teachers construct race', in McCarthy, C. and Crichlow, W., *Race, Identity and Representation in Education*, London: Routledge.

Smith, D. and Tomlinson, S. (1989) *The School Effect: a Study of Multiracial Comprehensiveness*, London: Policy Studies Institute.

Tizzard, B., Blatchford, P., Burke, J., Farquhar, C. and Plewis, I. (1988) *Young Children at School in the Inner City*, Hove: Lawrence Erlbaum Associates.

Troyna, B. (1992) 'Can you see the join? A historical analysis of multicultural and antiracist education policies', in Gill, D., Mayor, B. and Blair, M. *Racism in Education: Structures and Strategies*, London: Sage.

Wright, C. (1987) 'Black students–white teachers', in Troyna, B. (ed.) *Racial Inequality in Education*, London: Routledge.

Wright, C. (1992) 'Early education: multiracial primary school classrooms', in Gill, D., Mayor, B. and Blair, M. (eds) *Racism in Education: Structures and Strategies*, London: Sage.

3 Academic disidentification: unravelling underachievement among Black boys

Jason W. Osborne

INTRODUCTION

Educational and psychological research has long noted that students of African or Caribbean descent (collectively referred to here as Black) tend to experience poor academic outcomes relative to White majority students. This trend persists even after controlling for exogenous variables such as socioeconomic status, prior academic preparedness, and family structure (for a recent overview of this research, see Steele 1997). There are numerous explanations for these trends in the literature, including differences in cognitive style (e.g. Shade 1982), aversion to intellectual competition (Howard and Hammond 1985), language barriers and general cultural differences (e.g. Jacob and Jordan 1993) and even genetics (Herrnstein and Murray 1994). However, as authors such as Steele (1997) have pointed out, these theories tend not to be very satisfying. For example, if cultural differences are the culprit, why do children who emigrate from cultures drastically different from ours (e.g. Middle Eastern countries, Asian countries) often do better than Black children who come from families and communities with cultures that are arguably more similar to those of the majority White culture? Why do African immigrants (children not born into the majority White culture) do better in school than African-descended children born into the majority White culture? It is questions such as these that tend to make genetics and lingual/cultural theories unsatisfying. Other observations also raise interesting questions. For example, the Black White gap is not static, nor is it present at the beginning of schooling. The gap between White and minority students widens by as much as two grade levels by sixth grade (e.g. Alexander and Entwhistle 1988; Valencia 1991, 1997).

Recently, theories focusing on social psychological factors have emerged in the literature to raise and attempt to answer some of these questions. Specifically, Claude Steele's stereotype threat theory, John Ogbu's cultural ecological theory, and Majors and Billson's cool pose theory all focus on social psychological and cultural factors that cause Black students to psychologically withdraw from (disidentify, selectively devalue) school. These three theories all examine the same problem from slightly different angles, yet all seem to come to similar conclusions – that it is difficult for students of color to view themselves as good students, to define the self through academics, to value academics while still maintaining the integrity of the self.

This is exceedingly important, as individuals who are unable to define themselves through academics, to identify with academics, are more likely to experience adverse academic outcomes (e.g. withdrawal from school, poor grades). This view is supported by a growing number of empirical studies. More importantly, this perspective on the academic disparity between White and Black students provides clear avenues for impacting and ameliorating this problem.

THEORETICAL PERSPECTIVES ON UNDERACHIEVEMENT AMONG BLACK BOYS

Stereotype threat

Steele (1992, 1997) has attempted to understand the chronic underperformance of disadvantaged minority students through examining the socio-cognitive dynamics of schooling and the academic environment, specifically the effects of negative group stereotypes. Steele argued that schooling and the school environment is aversive to members of groups for whom there are negative group stereotypes long before the achievement gap manifests because of negative stereotypes concerning the intellectual ability of group members. While most students experience some anxiety over being negatively evaluated, students who belong to groups with a negative intellectual stereotype not only risk personal embarrassment and failure but also risk confirming the negative group stereotype. This, he argued, leads to increased anxiety for these students, which depresses performance at every level of preparation.

Steele further argued that being continually immersed in an aversive environment can contribute to what he called 'disidentification', the selective devaluing of academics. There is a rich tradition in psychology, dating back to William James (1890/1950) of viewing humans as motivated to view themselves in a positive light. Many theories of self-esteem state that performance in a domain will affect the self-esteem only to the extent that that domain is valued, or central, to the self-concept. Domains that are devalued have little impact on the overall self-esteem, and domains that are highly valued have a great deal of impact on self-esteem. Further, individuals appear to be extremely facile in their ability to alter which domains they perceive as central in order to maintain a certain positivity of self-esteem. Several authors have argued that individuals are particularly likely to selectively devalue domains for which their group, or they personally, fare poorly and selectively value domains for which their group, or they personally, fare relatively well (e.g. Crocker and Major 1989; Major and Schmader 1998; Tesser 1988). For example, Taylor and Brown (1988) reported that individuals tend to value those domains which they fare well in, Tesser and Campbell (1980) reported experimental evidence for selective devaluing in response to relatively poor performance, and Tesser, Millar and Moore (1988) reported heightened negative affect in response to poor performance on a valued dimension compared to a devalued dimension (for a more thorough discussion, see Major and Schmader 1998).

Thus, according to this perspective, there are two good reasons why Black students should disidentify, or selectively devalue academics: to reduce anxiety and improve self-esteem by eliminating a source of negative evaluation – academics. Ironically, this self-protective strategy should increase the likelihood of disidentified students experiencing adverse academic outcomes. Students who are more identified with academics should be more motivated to succeed because their self-esteem is directly linked to academic performance. In contrast, students not identified with academics should be less motivated to succeed because there is no contingency between academic outcomes and self-esteem – good performance is not rewarding, and poor performance is not punishing, leaving those who have disidentified with no compelling incentives to expend effort in academic endeavors. These disidentified individuals may therefore be at higher risk for academic problems, especially poor grades and dropping out, but also absenteeism, truancy, and delinquency (see also Finn 1989; Hindelang 1973; Newmann 1981).

Steele further argued that disidentification is not a normal state of affairs for Black students, that they do not begin schooling disidentified (a point empirically supported by Osborne 1995, 1997a). On the contrary, he argued that all students begin schooling strongly identified with academics, and that there must be something in the educational environment (what he termed 'unwise schooling' in homage to Goffman) to cause students to become disidentified.

Ogbu's Cultural-Ecological Perspective

While many authors tend to lump disadvantaged minority students together, Ogbu (e.g. 1997) has made an argument that not all minority groups are equal. He separates minority groups into two groups: those in a country or society voluntarily (immigrant or voluntary minorities) and those that have been subjugated and/or brought into a society against their will (involuntary or non-immigrant minorities). In the United States, for example, Asian and some Latino (e.g. Cuban) populations are examples of the former, while Black, Native-American, and other Latino (e.g. Puerto Rican) populations are examples of the latter. Ogbu argued that the social realities for students from these two groups are very different and, as such, lead to different outcomes. Involuntary minorities tend to develop a social or collective identity that is in opposition to the social identity of the dominant group (Whites). Thus, while voluntary minority students are able to view education as a path to success in their newly adopted country, Black students tend to view education as a system controlled by the group that subjugated them, their oppressors. School is seen as an inappropriate aspect of 'proper' Black identity (see Fordham and Ogbu 1986). Black children are instead encouraged to value other aspects of society, usually whatever is in opposition to White values, as appropriate for themselves. Ogbu labels this 'cultural inversion'.

This cultural inversion arose initially, he argues, to serve boundary-maintaining and coping functions under subordination. Today, inversions remain because there are few incentives to give them up while members of these groups still feel subjugated and oppressed. In the specific example of school learning, members of involuntary minority groups might consciously or unconsciously interpret school learning as a displacement process detrimental to their social identity, sense of security, and self-worth. Furthermore, these minority groups have observed that even those who succeed in school are not fully accepted or rewarded in the same way that White students are. This, combined with peer pressure and cultural pressure not to 'act white' (e.g. Fordham and Ogbu 1986), may make a compelling force against identification with academics.

Conversely, Ogbu argues, voluntary minority students have a much easier time integrating academics into the self-concept and excelling at school. For these students, who have come to a culture willingly, education is generally seen as the route through which they are able to build a better future for themselves. While they tend to have greater lingual and cultural barriers to overcome than involuntary minority students, they tend to do better because they are able to identify with academics. There is no culture of opposition, no collective identity opposing excelling at school. In fact, in many of these communities there is significant peer and group pressure to excel, a situation in stark contrast to the group dynamics found in involuntary minority groups.

Thus, while voluntary minorities are able to identify with academics, involuntary minority students are less able to do so due to the social dynamics of their society.

Majors and Billson's cool pose

Ogbu's oppositional perspective is echoed by other authors, including Majors and Billson (1992). They argue that Black males adopt a 'cool pose', or a ritualized form of masculinity that allows that boy or man to cope and survive in an environment of social oppression and racism. According to Majors and Billson, cool pose allows the Black male to survive by projecting a front of emotionlessness, fearlessness, and aloofness that counters inner pain from damaged pride, poor self-confidence, and fragile social competence that comes from existing as a member of a subjugated group. Unfortunately, as with Steele's notion, cool pose depicts Black males as victims of their coping strategies. In terms of education, cool pose often leads to behaviors, such as flamboyant and non-conformist behavior, that often elicit punishment in school settings. Equally unfortunately, the development of a cool self-concept appears to be incompatible with a hard-driving, motivated, identified student. Thus, Black boys, according to this perspective, adopt a strategy for coping with group membership that appears to be incompatible with identification with academics.

Summary

While these theories seek to understand the problem of Black student under-achievement from different perspectives, all three seem to imply that Black students, as well as other students of color, are at high risk for academic disidentification. It may be that Black students are at disproportionately higher risk due to the extremely negative way society tends to view them. This increased level of disidentification, in turn, is likely to be a significant contributing factor to academic problems, including under-performance, withdrawal from school, delinquency, and other undesirable academic outcomes.

EMPIRICAL EVIDENCE

Recently, several studies have provided evidence supporting the notions that: (a) Black students (specifically Black boys) are more likely to experience academic disidentification, (b) disidentification is a developmental process, (c) identification with academics is related to academic outcomes, and (d) the social dynamics of the environment (e.g. salience of stigma vulnerability) can adversely affect academic performance.

Black boys are more likely to disidentify than other students

One of the central tenets of this chapter is that, for a variety of possible reasons delineated by Steele, Ogbu, Majors and Billson, Fordham, and others, Black students, especially Black males, are more likely to experience academic disidentification (detaching of self-esteem from academic outcomes) than Whites. Implicit in this statement is the assertion that students from other involuntary minority groups are also likely to experience this outcome. An important corollary to this is that academic disidentification is expected to be developmental in nature, increasing over time.

Osborne (1995, 1997a) tested this assertion within the context of a large database that is representative of the population of American students, the National Education Longitudinal Survey of 1988 (National Center for Educational Statistics 1992). In this study identification with academics was operationalized at the group level as the correlation between global self-esteem (the Rosenberg Self-View Inventory, Rosenberg 1965) and academic outcomes (achievement tests and cumulative grades). The results of these studies were striking. As presented in Figure 3.1, at the beginning of the study (eighth grade), all groups studied (White, Latino, and Black boys and girls) were significantly identified with academics (all correlations ranging from $r = .22$ to .27, all $p < .001$). However, by tenth grade the correlations for Black boys had dropped dramatically and significantly to $r = .07$, while all other groups remained substantially the same. By twelfth grade the correlations for Black boys had dropped to $r = -.02$, while the correlations for other groups again remained highly significant. Note that socioeconomic status was partialled out of these correlations, and that controlling for locus of control did not substantially change the results.

Other studies also support this assertion. For example, Osborne, Major and Crocker (1992) found experimental support for Steele's hypothesis that the self-esteem and affect of Black college students is less reactive to academic feedback than that of Whites, even when that feedback is explicitly presented as diagnostic

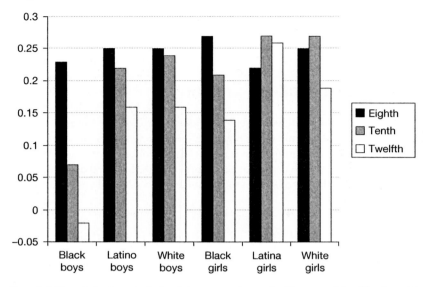

Figure 3.1 Trends in the correlation between grades and self-esteem: Identification with academics

of a students' academic potential and ability. In other cross-sectional studies, there have been lower correlations between self-esteem and academic outcomes for Blacks than Whites (Demo and Parker 1987; Hansford and Hattie 1982; Jordan 1981; Lay and Wakstein 1985; Rosenberg and Simmons 1972). Thus, these findings lend strong support to the argument that Black males are particularly at risk for academic disidentification.

Disidentification is a developmental process

The results from Osborne (1995, 1997a) support the notion that most students begin schooling identified with academics and learning. Even as late as eighth grade there is no evidence of relative group-level disidentification among any group, especially Black boys. While a more sensitive measure might detect the beginnings of disidentification earlier, the good news from these data is that, while the seeds of disidentification are undoubtedly sown much earlier, there is a long grace period within which we can work to prevent disidentification.

Identification with academics is related to academic outcomes

Another crucial piece to this puzzle is the assertion that disidentification will adversely affect academic outcomes. As discussed above, there is excellent theoretical support for this notion. Clear empirical evidence is more elusive, but available in limited fashions at this point. First, Osborne (1997b) showed that identification with academics predicted several academic outcomes in the context of a two-year prospective longitudinal study, such as cumulative grades, withdrawal or dismissal from school, as well as receipt of academic honors. Second, Osborne and Ravsch (2000) demonstrated that, within the NELS, a nationally representative sample of American students, withdrawal from school is related to identification with academics, especially for boys, and that even among the most at-risk students (students who are members of disadvantaged racial minority groups (Latino and Black), low in socioeconomic status, and poor academic outcomes), strong identification with academics was associated with remaining in school.

The social dynamics of the environment can influence academic outcomes

A final piece of this puzzle is why Black boys would be more likely to disidentify than other students. Steele (1992, 1997) argued that it is heightened anxiety associated with concern over confirming the stereotype of the group as intellectually inferior that drives this phenomenon. Osborne (in press) has found that state anxiety while testing explains up to 46 per cent of White–Black differences in test performance. Further, Steele and Aronson (1995) found that by experimentally reducing the perception of an academic task as diagnostic of ability (thus, in Steele's theoretical framework, reducing anxiety and stereotype threat), Black students expended more effort and performed at a higher level than their counterparts who were tested under 'normal' testing conditions. This study provides empirical support for a causal link to poorer academic outcomes (via reduced effort expenditure) because of disidentification. Thus, Steele and Aronson (1995, and other studies, summarised in Aronson, Quinn, and Spencer 1998) experimentally demonstrated that the social dynamics of the environment can drastically influence academic performance, and that Blacks are vulnerable to this effect, even in the absence of a task that is perceived to be diagnostic of ability.

Summary

While much work is left to be done, there appears to be very good initial support for the argument that Black boys underperform in academic arenas, relative to Whites, due at least in part to higher levels of academic disidentification. Specifically, there is evidence that Black males are particularly vulnerable to disidentification, that disidentification is linked to adverse academic outcomes including, but not limited to, poor grades and withdrawal from school, that disidentification is a developmental process that does not occur until exposure to years of schooling, and that concern over confirming the negative group stereotype is related to poor performance. Further, while the majority of these data come from studies done in the USA, it should be in no way limited to students within the USA. At the least, it should hold within Westernized, White-majority countries, and Gibson and Ogbu (1991) present evidence that caste-like minority groups around the world show poor academic outcomes relative to the majority population, including IQ scores, academic performance, withdrawal from school, and exhibition of behavioral problems. Examples of these groups include the Maoris of New Zealand, West Indians in the UK, the Baraku of Japan, and Oriental Jews in Israel. These findings make this line of inquiry all the more important.

DERAILING DISIDENTIFICATION

There appears to be convergence in these three theories discussed above. In all cases, there are social psychological forces turning Black boys away from being psychologically invested in educational achievement. All three authors present suggestions for reducing or reversing this effect, although they vary a great deal in terms of ease of implementation and scope of intervention necessary. One particularly hopeful sign is that research supports Steele's assertion that disidentification is a developmental process that occurs over years of schooling, thus giving a broad window of opportunity for derailing this process and allowing Black boys to remain identified. Another positive note is Osborne (2000) that shows students who remain identified with academics also tend to have better academic outcomes, regardless of race.

DERAILING DISIDENTIFICATION FROM A STEREOTYPE THREAT PERSPECTIVE

According to Steele's theory, there appear to be two things working together to cause disidentification in Black boys (aside from other, less remediable factors, such as low socioeconomic status, family expectations, and peer pressure): a salient negative group stereotype and anxiety over confirming the negative group stereotype on the part of the student (note that Steele and Aronson 1995 demonstrated that the student does not have to believe the stereotype in order for it to affect their performance). Steele (e.g. 1997) has argued that a true multicultural curriculum could help students of color find a place in education and reduce the stigma vulnerability that leads to disidentification. He argued that most so-called multicultural curricula are simply the traditional Eurocentric curricula with some ancillary information about people of color added on (a view supported by Grant and Sleeter 1985, who labelled this type of curriculum as ethnic studies). This approach to multicultural education separates and marginalizes members of these groups, often relegating them to special periods of time during which they are to be studied, but not at other times of the year (e.g. Black History Month). Steele (1992) argued that a true multicultural curriculum (where the contributions of people of colour are infused throughout the school curriculum, Grant and Sleeter 1985) would serve to diffuse stigma vulnerability and disidentification by making people of color less invisible in academia. Majors and Billson (1992) also explicitly support this intervention as a way to assist Black boys.

Steele (1997) also suggests changing remediation practices to improve identification with academics. In the US, at least, but I suspect in other countries as well, Black males are remediated at a rate much higher than whites. If one reflects on the message remediation sends a student, it is clear that, while well-meaning, it cannot help but exacerbate the problem of stigma vulnerability and disidentification. To students already fighting overt and subtle messages telling them they might be intellectually inferior, the authorities in the school send them the message that they are in dire peril, doomed to failure, unless they receive help. Theoretically, this should increase stigma vulnerability and the likelihood of disidentification.

Perhaps worse, one of the things that traditional remediation does is 'dumb down' the curriculum. Students are perceived as not being able to handle difficult 'mainstream' material, so the difficulty of schoolwork is reduced until it becomes unchallenging. From a self-esteem standpoint, this is a tragic turn – by eliminating the challenge to academics (and often, the possibility of failure), it eliminates the reward, the reason to stay ego-involved in schooling. An examination of what school-age students are engrossed in reveals a common theme of challenge and possible failure: sports, dating, peer relations, video games. These activities are difficult, and success is by no means certain. It seems that the potential for victory, the challenge, and the infrequent victories over long odds keep people hooked most effectively (a variable reinforcement schedule, for those Skinnerians reading this).

Accordingly, Steele (1997) suggests replacing the traditional model of remediation with a model of challenge, whereby students would be given challenging work in a supportive, collaborative environment. He argues that this conveys respect for their potential and shows that they are not 'regarded through the lens of an ability-demeaning stereotype' (p. 625). This makes sense, not only from the perspective of Stigma Vulnerability theory, but also from a motivational standpoint, discussed above. Challenging activities can be more ego-involving and rewarding than non-challenging activities. While these two aspects of schooling are most immediately obvious for intervention and attempts at preventing disidentification or facilitating re-identification, Steele (1997) discussed other strategies.

As many in Western countries view IQ and intelligence as genetic, stable, trait-like, and immalleable, belonging to a group with a stigma of intellectual inferiority is a daunting prospect. It becomes an intellectual caste system, especially if one buys into the genetic argument posited by Herrnstein and Murray (1994). Unfortunately, this may be closer to the layperson's view of intelligence than we would like to admit. Thus, promoting the idea of intelligence as malleable, expandable, and responsive to training (as in Jausovec 1994) could go a long way toward improving the motivation and optimism of students who belong to these groups, especially Black males.

One thing that multicultural curricula have been relatively successful at doing is providing role models. Black males need to see that Black males can be successful in academic domains, that they can become scientists, engineers, mathematicians, teachers, etc. The popular media are notoriously poor at allowing these role models to receive widespread attention. Here's an anecdotal example: when a recent article of mine (on this topic) was published (Osborne 1997a) there was a great deal of media attention in the US. One of the most widely-read newspapers in the US (*USA Today*) put a write-up of the findings on the front page of the Life section of their paper. It was not until I had shown it to many colleagues that one pointed out the irony of its presentation. Immediately above the story, in full color, was a picture of some professional basketball players, all Black males. Immediately below it was a picture, in full color, of a group of White doctors performing surgery. This reflects the messages prevalent in society. If you are White you have certain options and paths open to you. If you are Black, especially if you are a Black male, you have other options. More exposure to academic role models can help counteract the popular media's message, and it is something that individual teachers and administrators can do.

DERAILING DISIDENTIFICATION FROM A CULTURAL-ECOLOGICAL PERSPECTIVE

From Ogbu's perspective, it is not the social-cognitive aspects of the school environment that are leading to disidentification, but rather the social stratification and continuing subjugation of Blacks in the US and, presumably, other Western European nations. Thus, Ogbu suggests more community-oriented interventions. For example, Ogbu (1992) cites the observation that, while almost all segments of society verbalize the importance of academic achievement, voluntary minority and majority students often feel the sting of stigma associated with poor grades. In contrast, he argues, there is less community and family pressure to achieve good grades among involuntary minorities, with little social rejection or stigma attached to being a poor student or a dropout. In fact, peer pressure probably attaches stigma to academic excellence, in marked contrast to other segments of society. Involuntary minority students who excel at academics often must adopt self-presentational strategies in order to remain accepted as part of their peer group. Thus, he highlights changing community and family norms to emphasize academic achievement, celebrate those who excel in academics, and place pressure on those not doing well.

Second, Ogbu (1992) discusses different strategies students tend to use. He identified one, in particular, that should allow students to identify with academics, and excel, without losing their peer group or self-concept. He labelled this strategy 'accommodation without assimilation'. This strategy involves students' recognizing that they can participate in two cultural frames for different purposes without losing their own cultural identity or undermining their loyalty to their minority community. It also happens to be the strategy most often adopted by successful voluntary minority students. This essentially involves behaving according to school norms while at school and community norms while at home. These students are able to excel at school without paying the costs associated with completely adopting majority norms (for a thorough discussion of the costs associated with racelessness or 'acting White', see Fordham 1988).

To facilitate this process, Ogbu (1992) suggests that special counselling and related programs should help involuntary minority students to learn to separate attitudes and behaviors enhancing school success from those that lead to 'acting White', avoid interpreting the former as a threat to their social identity and group loyalty, and take responsibility for their own academic performance and school adjustment.

On the community level, Ogbu also suggests that community leaders and respected members need to model positive achievement behaviors and help children separate attitudes and behaviors that lead to academic success and behaviors that lead to loss of ethnic identity. Further, community members need to provide children with concrete evidence that academic achievement is valued and appreciated on the same level that other activities, such as sports and entertainment, are valued. On this note, Osborne (1997a) reported evidence that Black males tended to become increasingly identified with sports performance and peer popularity while they became disidentified with academics. This suggests that this particular argument and recommendation is a key component to reducing disidentification.

Finally, Ogbu (1992) suggests that the involuntary minority middle class need to remain active in their communities. The voluntary minority middle class retains strong ties with the communities they come from, in spite of often residing outside that community. These individuals tend to regard their accomplishments as community accomplishments, and vice-versa. In this community, the middle class provides concrete evidence that school success pays and is compatible with membership in the community. In contrast, members of involuntary minorities tend to view success as their ticket out of the community. In this case, success means leaving the community, which may make it a strong disincentive to strive for success. Perhaps more importantly, there are few examples of how academic success equates to personal and community success available to children in the involuntary minority communities. This may influence identification with academics as there is no perceived contingency between academic success and financial or personal outcomes.

COOL POSE AND DERAILING ACADEMIC DISIDENTIFICATION

Similar to Ogbu, Majors and Billson (1992) make a compelling argument that the self-protective 'cool pose' adopted by Black boys (and other involuntary minority males, probably) is responsible for academic disidentification. Many of the roots of cool pose seem to be similar to the social issues Ogbu discusses (perceived subjugation, etc.). In addition to recommendations discussed above (such as moving toward a true multicultural curriculum, and overhauling our notion of remediation), Majors and Billson (1992) focus on several other ideas for diffusing this need for self-protection that leads to disidentification. One of these suggestions is for Black students to receive more Afrocentric socialization (teaching values such as cooperation, mutual respect, commitment, and love of family, race, community, and nation). Majors and Billson argue that this is not an anti-White or oppositional ideology, but rather encourages a more collective focus that reflects the Black situation in Western European cultures more accurately than White values of individualism and competition. Majors and Billson also encourage closer linkages between high schools and postsecondary institutions to facilitate high school completion, such as the Upward Bound program has done.

SUMMARY

This chapter reviewed three theoretical perspectives (Steele's stereotype threat, Ogbu's cultural-ecological framework, and Majors and Billson's Cool Pose) that all suggest that certain disadvantaged minority students, Black boys in particular, are at higher risk for academic disidentification. There is evidence to support this perspective, although this is a fairly recent topic of discussion. Finally, authors' suggestions for improving the academic lives of Black boys (and other students in similar situations) were discussed, with particular attention paid to proposals that would inhibit disidentification or facilitate re-identification. Initial evidence (presented by Steele 1997) indicates that at least some of the interventions discussed above can be implemented successfully on small scales – individual teachers, schools, and school districts. Research by Steele and Aronson (1995) reinforces the fact that even small changes to the school or classroom environment can have large effects for the students. While much work remains to be done, these findings leave this author, at least, hopeful that we are on the brink of a more profound understanding of the factors influencing academic underachievement in minority groups, especially Black boys, and possibly being able to do something meaningful about it.

REFERENCES

Alexander, K. L. and Entwhistle, D. R. (1988) 'Achievement in the first two years of school: Patterns and processes', *Monographs of the Society for Research in Child Development*, **53**, 2.

Aronson, J., Quinn, D. M. and Spencer, S. J. (1998) 'Stereotype threat and the academic underperformance of minorities and women', in J. K. Swim and C. Stangor (eds) *Prejudice: The Target's Perspective*, New York: Academic Press.

Crocker, J. and Major, B. (1989) 'Social stigma and self-esteem: The self-protective properties of stigma', *Psychological Review*, **96**, 4, pp. 608–30.

Demo, D. H. and Parker, K.D. (1987) 'Academic achievement and self-esteem among African-American and White college students', *Journal of Social Psychology*, **127**, 4, pp. 345–55.

Finn, J. D. (1989) 'Withdrawing from school', *Review of Educational Research*, **59**, 2, pp. 117–42.

Fordham, S. (1988) 'Racelessness as a factor in Black students' school success: Pragmatic strategy or Pyrrhic victory?' *Harvard Educational Review*, **58**, pp. 54–84.

Fordham, S. and Ogbu, J. (1986) 'Black students' school success: Coping with the burden of "acting White"', *The Urban Review*, **18**, pp. 176–206.

Ghouri, N. (1998) 'Race chief attacks training negligence', *TES*, July 3.

Gibson, M. A. and Ogbu, J. U. (1991) *Minority Status and Schooling: A Comparative Study of Immigrant and Involuntary Minorities*, New York: Garland Publishing.

Grant, C. A. and Sleeter, C. E. (1985) 'The literature on multicultural education: Review and analysis', *Educational Review*, **37**, pp. 97–118.

Hansford, B. C. and Hattie, J. A. (1982) 'The relationship between self and achievement/ performance measures', *Review of Educational Research*, **52**, pp. 123–42.

Herrnstein, R. A. and Murray, C. (1994) *The Bell Curve*, New York: Grove Press.

Hindelang, M. J. (1973) 'Causes of delinquency: A partial replication and extension', *Social Problems*, **20**, pp. 471–87.

Howard, J. and Hammond, R. (1985) 'Rumors of inferiority', *The New Republic*, **193**, September 9, 17–21.

Jacob, E. and Jordan, C. (eds) (1993) *Minority Education: Anthropological Perspectives*, Norwood, NJ: Ablex.

James, W. (1890/1950) *The Principles of Psychology*, New York: Holt, Rinehart and Winston.

Jausovec, N. (1994) 'Can giftedness be taught?', *Roeper Review*, **16**, pp. 210–14.

Jordan, J. T. (1981) 'Self-concepts, motivation, and academic achievement of Black adolescents', *Journal of Educational Psychology*, **73**, pp. 509–17.

Lay, R. and Wakstein, J. (1985) 'Race, academic achievement, and self-concept of ability. 25th annual forum of the Association for Institutional Research', *Research in Higher Education*, **22**, 1, pp. 43–64.

Major, B. and Schmader, T. (1998) 'Coping with stigma through psychological disengagement', in J. K. Swim and C. Stangor (eds) *Prejudice: The Target's Perspective*, New York: Academic Press.

Majors, R. and Billson, J. M. (1992) *Cool Pose: The Dilemmas of Black Manhood in America*, New York: Lexington Books.

National Center for Educational Statistics (1992) *National Education Longitudinal Study of 1998 First Follow-up: Student Component Data File User's Manual*, US Department of Education, Office of Educational Research and Improvement.

Newmann, F. M. (1981) 'Reducing student alienation in high schools: Implications of theory', *Harvard Educational Review*, **51**, pp. 546–64.

Ogbu, J. U. (1992) 'Understanding cultural diversity and learning', *Educational Researcher*, **21**, pp. 5–14.

Ogbu, J. U. (1997) 'Understanding the school performance of urban blacks: Some essential background knowledge', in H. Walberg, O. Reyes and R. Weissberg (eds), *Children and Youth: Interdisciplinary Perspectives*, London: Sage Publications.

Osborne, J. W. (1995) 'Academics, self-esteem, and race: A look at the underlying assumptions of the disidentification hypothesis', *Personality and Social Psychology Bulletin*, **21**, 5, pp. 449–55.

Osborne, J. W. (1997a) 'Race and academic disidentification', *Journal of Educational Psychology*, **89**, pp. 728–35.

Osborne, J. W. (1997b) 'Identification with academics and academic success among community college students', *Community College Review*, **25**, pp. 59–67.

Osborne, J. W. and Rausch, J. (2001) Identification with academics and academic outcomes in secondary students. Paper presented at the national meeting of the American Education Research Association, Seattle, WA.

Osborne, J. W. (2001) 'Testing stereotype threat: Does anxiety explain race and sex differences in achievement?' *Contemporary Educational Psychology*.

Osborne, J. W., Major, B. and Crocker, J. (1992) 'Social stigma and reactions to academic feedback'. Poster presented at the annual meeting of the Eastern Psychological Association, Boston, March.

Rosenberg, M. (1965) *Society and the Adolescent Self-image*, Princeton, NJ: Princeton University Press.

Rosenberg, M. and Simmons, R. (1972) 'African-American and White self-esteem: The urban school child', Rose Monograph Series, Washington, DC: American Sociological Association.

Shade, B. (1982) 'Afro-American cognitive style: A variable in school success', *Review of Educational Research*, 52, pp. 219–44.

Steele, C. (1992) 'Race and the schooling of African-American Americans', *The Atlantic Monthly*, April, pp. 68–78.

Steele, C. (1997) 'A threat in the air: How stereotypes shape intellectual identity and performance', *American Psychologist*, **52**, pp. 613–29.

Steele, C.M. and Aronson, J. (1995) 'Stereotype threat and the intellectual test performance of African-Americans', *Journal of Personality and Social Psychology*, **69**, 5, pp. 797–811.

Taylor, S. E. and Brown, J. D. (1988) 'Illusion and well-being: A social psychological perspective on mental health', *Psychological Bulletin*, **103**, pp. 193–210.

Tesser, A. (1988) 'Toward a self-evaluation maintenance model of social behavior', in L. L. Berkowitz (ed.) *Advances in Experimental Social Psychology*, **21**, pp. 181–228, San Diego, CA: Academic Press.

Tesser, A. and Campbell, J. (1980) 'Self-definition: The impact of the relative performance and similarity of others', *Social Psychology Quarterly*, **43**, pp. 341–47.

Tesser, A., Millar, M. and Moore, J. (1988) 'Some affective consequences of social comparison and reflection processes: The pain and the pleasure of being close', *Journal of Personality and Social Psychology*, **54**, pp. 49–61.

Valencia, R. R. (1991) 'The plight of Chicano students: An overview of schooling conditions and outcomes', in R. R. Valencia (ed.) *Chicano School Failure and Success: Research and Policy Agendas for the 1990s* (pp. 3–26). The Stanford Series on Education and Public Policy, London: Falmer Press.

Valencia, R. R. (1997) 'Latinos and education: An overview of sociodemographic characteristics and schooling conditions and outcomes', in M. Barrera-Yepes (ed.) *Latino Education Issues: Conference Proceedings*. Princeton, NJ: Educational Testing Service.

Part II

Radical Black
approaches to education

4 The 'miseducation' of black children in the British educational system – towards an African-centred orientation to knowledge

Mekada Graham

INTRODUCTION

The schooling of black[1] children within the British educational system continues to be the focus of discontent and general dissatisfaction among black parents, professionals and communities. The inertia of the authorities to the increasing numbers of black[2] children cited in official school exclusion data parallels the 1960s, when high referral rates of black children to educationally subnormal schools were largely ignored by educational authorities (Coard 1971; CRE 1996; Social Exclusion Unit 1998; Department for Education and Employment 1997). At the same time black families are continually pathologised for the educational 'problems' of their children rather than pursuing a serious analysis of institutional structures and educational processes that sometimes result in their differential treatment. Research over the past decades has revealed the continued importance of racism and culture as central issues in the processes of educational delivery (Carby 1984; Dei 1999a; Gilborn 1995; Bourne, Bridges and Searle 1994; Wright 1985).

In response to continuing concerns expressed by black professionals, parents and communities in the way the educational system has failed many black children, educational authorities introduced multicultural and anti-racist approaches to schooling. Although these approaches have served a useful purpose in highlighting the dynamics of racism in the functions and operations of educational institutions, they fall short of examining alternative knowledge systems as critical pedagogy in working for educational and social change. One of the central tenets underpinning anti-racist education recognises the power relationships in society and the role of education in producing and reproducing racial, gendered and class-based inequalities. This analysis has largely been confined to the functions and operations of educational institutions and the infusion of acceptable cultural forms into the school curriculum.

In recent years, the meaning of race and the significance of the term have become extensively problematised. Consequently, anti-racist policies are increasingly perceived as a single-issue standpoint that encourages a hierarchical view of oppression. Critical theorists have argued that anti-racist policies and multicultural perspectives are being diluted within notions of multi-oppression to become almost meaningless or located within an equal opportunities framework (Sivanandan 1994; Dei 1999a). It has become customary among academic circles to deny the significance of race and difference in shaping the contexts for power and domination in society. Many educators and academics simply equate race with ethnicity to counter the importance of race in discussions about school exclusions. Yet, interestingly, but disturbingly 'race' is evoked in public and academic discussions about crime and the 'problem' of black young people. Despite the reluctance of many educators to engage in discussions about race, there can be no denial of the saliency of racism affecting the life chances, aspirations and opportunities of black young people in a racist culture (Dei 1999a).

The series of events that led to the Stephen Lawrence Inquiry (Macpherson 1999) and the subsequent Macpherson Report provide a stark example of institutional racism and its prevalence in British society. Moreover, the Macpherson Report substantiates what black people have been voicing for many years; racism permeates the structures and institutions of British society. This acknowledgement of institutional racism by the wider society raises important questions concerning anti-racist praxis, its place and future within education.

Anti-racist and multicultural approaches to education are steeped within assimilation and integration models that encapsulate adaptation and change to conventional knowledge in addressing the educational needs of black and minoritised children. An examination of the dominant model of anti-racist education draws attention to the failure of this approach to challenge the hegemonic nature of conventional knowledge production and its dissemination as a source of oppression. This area of dominance cannot be separated from the social, political and economic hegemony within the wider society. Alternative knowledge systems such as African-centred worldviews challenge the existing parameters of anti-racist education to embrace a broader remit in order to gain cultural inclusion across the spectrum of human knowledge.

An analysis of alternative knowledge systems draws attention to their continuing marginality in the processes of knowledge production and its dissemination. This exclusion becomes critical given the power imbalance between groups in society in the validation of knowledge and their access to knowledge dissemination (Dei 1999b). It is in this regard that over the past decades, a new generation of black scholars and educators have advanced an alternative system of knowing; African-centred worldviews that affirm the traditions, histories, experiences and visions of African people wherever they are located. African-centred worldviews acknowledge the multiplicity of world cultures and their contribution to the betterment of humanity. Thus, African-centred ways of knowing as an alternative inclusive intellectual paradigm offer the opportunity for students to see the world through the eyes of their African ancestry. These opportunities can assist in finding a way to stem the path of 'miseducation', disengagement and disaffection among some young black people and therefore, open 'up a new and transformed consciousness for all peoples, particularly those of African descent' (Dei 1994: 5).

The purpose of this chapter is three fold:

1) to examine briefly multicultural and anti-racist approaches to education and their failure to address the hegemonic nature of Eurocentric knowledge as the only valid way of knowing;

2) to provide a summary and discussion of African-centred worldviews and orientation to knowledge as the foundation of learning; and

3) to consider the role of cultural resource knowledge as an action-orientated communal strategy for social and educational change, and, moreover, the importance of community rites of passage programmes as a holistic educational strategy to assist in re-engaging young black people to education.

This chapter, therefore, seeks to establish the validity of cultural resource knowledge as an effective educational tool in responding to the needs of many black students for whom the current processes of schooling have undermined their subjectivities and lived experiences.

ANTI-RACIST AND MULTICULTURAL APPROACHES TO EDUCATION

The conventional models of race relations have underpinned anti-racist and multicultural approaches to education. Social science research during the 1950s and 1960s adopted a social anthropological model to the study of black people. Several studies (see Patterson 1963; Little 1947; Fitzherbert 1967) applied a 'scientific' rationale to assess the process of adjustment of black people into the British way of life. Mullard (1982) suggests the development of multiracial education models parallel broadly the social theories of assimilation, integration and cultural pluralism. He maintains that these strategies and methods fostered cultural subordination and political neutralisation of black communities to maintain as far as possible the dominant structure of institutions, values and beliefs. The aims and tasks of education were employed within the schooling process as 'the primary site for successful assimilation' (Carby 1984:185). Moreover, the presence of black children was perceived to be a problem for their white counterparts. This view was suggested in a DES circular 7/65, which stated 'the culture, language and religion of immigrant children not only impedes their progress, it also has a negative effect on their white counterparts'.

During the 1960s, educational authorities responded to the presence of black pupils by introducing bussing as a desirable arrangement not only for white pupils avoiding 'concentration in any particular area', but also in the interests of black pupils to assist their chances of assimilation. The assimilation model demanded that black people discard their cultural heritage, which defines their identities and lived experiences. This perspective was anchored in the belief of the superior value of Western culture and institutions (Mullard 1982).

The assimilation perspective ignored structural inequalities and racial discrimination was perceived as the result of individual attitudes and prejudice, just a quirk of some white people unfamiliar with their black neighbours (Rose and Deakin 1969). The notion of individual prejudice was placed high on the agenda of educational discourse alongside the possibility of educating away inequalities and prejudice. The assimilation model was further refined during the late 1960s to become integration, encapsulated in the often-quoted definition by government minister, Roy Jenkins (1966) 'by integration, I mean not a flattening process of assimilation but equal opportunities accompanied by cultural diversity in an atmosphere of mutual tolerance'.

Mullard (1982) argues that the integration model was in effect a more sophisticated liberal model of assimilation, thus the DES were able to reaffirm their commitment to the assimilation of black people through the educational system (Troyna and Cashmore 1982). The integration model was translated into educational discourse as a liberal humanistic approach. This approach proposed the acknowledgement of the history and cultures of black pupils as valuable only insofar as the understanding of their cultures would serve to promote better race relations. A Select Committee (1973) promptly rebutted the demand from black parents and teachers for black studies to be introduced into the school curriculum. Apparently, black studies was seen as divisive and had little to offer to wider education and better race relations. John (1976) sees that integration was predicated upon rejecting those areas of history and culture that were perceived in society's terms as not in accord with 'normal' values and practices. Thus, John (1976) identifies the contradictions inherent within the integration approach, which embraces assimilation and the rejection of cultural heritage. He recognises that cultural heritage is critical in securing the wellbeing of black pupils in order to survive the schooling process!

Anti-racist approaches to education – schooling attempts to get its 'house' in order

Multicultural and cultural diversity approaches to schooling were criticised for their refusal to address fundamental issues of racism within the educational system. Anti-racist approaches to education emerged as a reactive stance that purported to address the racial inequalities identified by black parents and teachers as a major factor in the underachievement and disaffection of black pupils. The anti-racist education movement propelled the debates about the 'individualised' racism of some teachers to examine institutional components of education that generated racial inequalities (Mullard, 1982). The underlying premise of anti-racist approaches to education recognises that 'racism is an integral element in a total social and economic system and in all its institutions' (Gill, Singh and Vance 1987: 124). The theoretical perspectives of anti-racism draw upon the experience of colonialisation and imperialism as the roots of racism and the propagation of racist ideology prevalent in wider society. The role of all educational institutions invites practices to dismantle structural oppression both through curriculum and in teaching directly about equality and social justice. Pressure groups such as the National Association for Multiracial Education (NAME) and All London Teachers Against Racism and Facism (ALTARF) emerged to campaign against racism in schools, and to provide support for teachers and parents and develop anti-racist teaching materials for all children.

The anti-racist approach to schooling developed as one of the key strategies in eradicating racist ideology and limiting the damage to all children, particularly black children. It is concerned with changing teachers' perceptions of black children and rooting out racism within the curriculum. Critics of anti-racist approaches to the school curriculum have sometimes centred upon the idea of 'tradition' and the loss of superiority fostered in literature that was often perceived as canons of received culture. For example, Enid Blyton's 'golliwog' stories have been sanitised so that the author's work can be returned to its 'rightful traditional' place. In recent years, however, there has been dissolution of anti-racist policies, as the meaning of 'race' has become extensively problematised in academic discourse and practices. Consequently, race is viewed as privileging a minority that invites a hierarchical view of oppression. Dei (1999a: 19) has alluded to the continuing saliency of race that 'shape and/or demarcate schools, communities, workplaces, social practices and lived experiences'. He contributes to the re-framing of anti-racist knowledge in articulating the interlocking and intersecting nature of social oppressions as well as an acknowledgement of the saliency of particular oppressions at given historical times. It is within this context that the saliency of race is linked to schooling in powerful ways.

The existing parameters of anti-racist approaches to education have failed to explore opportunities for enhancing and maximising the potential of black children in the validity of knowledge that stands in their histories, cultures, traditions and lived experiences. This approach assists in reconnecting disaffected pupils to educational processes as a valuable tool in effective learning outcomes for young black people.

Multicultural approaches to education – an expression of cultural oppression?

The introduction of multiculturalism in schools has generated a considerable amount of literature defining the contours of multicultural approaches to education. These perspectives have largely addressed cultural issues by adding items of 'cultural interest', such as music, dance and food. These items of cultural interest have become known as the three 'S's' – steel bands, saris and samosas. Bryan, Dadzie and Scafe (1985) discuss the problematic nature of this approach. Many schools embraced cultural interests that presented a multicultural atmosphere but no challenge to the underachievement of black children. Thus, schools appeared to be responding to the educational needs of black children but in reality this approach became another form of subtle social control.

The current multicultural debates have moved from a traditional approach about the infusion of acceptable 'cultural forms' within the school curriculum to questioning established assumptions about the ethnocentric nature of knowledge as the foundation for learning. This discussion draws attention to the historical dominance of Eurocentric knowledge as the only valid way of knowing and the ways in which they 'become so deeply embedded that they typically are seen as "natural" or appropriate norms rather than as historically evolved social constructions'

(Scheurich and Young 1997: 7). These historical pathways are important because European philosophies played a central role in the invention of racial hierarchy through 'codifying and institutionalising both the scientific and popular European perceptions of the human race' (Eke 1997: 5). Thus the history of racism within European social thought has served to subjugate the knowledge systems of people outside of Europe. Alongside these considerations the historical cultural denigration of Africa and its people continues to be a defining feature of British society.

Eric (quoted in Sewell 1997: 182) speaks to the problems faced by black pupils and their disengagement from schooling frequently located in alienation from the school curriculum.

> When I asked my history teacher why we keep having to learn about Henry VIII, he said because that is the way life is. I was tired of seeing white faces in all my books. We know nothing about the Caribbean or Africa. We don't even know about black people who lived in England. We might as well be white.

These problems are related similarly in other student narratives.

> 'We hear about (our) history as slavery. It's like Africa never existed until the white man came and civilised everybody'.
>   'I personally denied my blackness, because that is how I made it in the system. I look back . . . at the years that I have wasted . . . spending hours with things which are totally irrelevant to me and to what I want to do with my life as a black person.'
>
> (Swann Report 1985: 93–103)

In some cases black pupils are expressing anger at being placed in a position to deal with teachers who are ignorant of the achievements and contributions of societies outside of Europe, and in Africa in particular. These narratives give voice to various educational needs that are sometimes neglected within educational environment. Moreover, culturally based epistemologies have received little attention in the development of an inclusive curriculum that reflects the multicultural nature of British society. As Dei (1995: 164) explains: 'when a teacher gives voice and space to multicentric perspectives and other legitimate interpretations of human experiences, all students gain from knowing the complete account of events that have shaped growth and development'.

It is within this context that African-centred ways of knowing become relevant to educational discourse.

AFRICAN-CENTRED WAYS OF KNOWING

Widely respected black scholars have detailed the existence of traditional African-centred worldviews, and certain distinguishing cultural characteristics and beliefs that seem to continually prevail (Asante 1988; Diop 1978; Nobles 1985; Myers

1988). These generalised worldviews are consistent with cultural value systems that are cited at a deep structural level.

Traditional African philosophical assumptions – significant ways of knowing and understanding the world – survived the physical uprooting of African people through enslavement to remain an essential part of their ethos (Herskovitz 1958; Asante 1988; Nobles 1980). There are two main issues that have generated controversy surrounding the legitimacy of African-centred worldviews.

First, it is claimed that African people within the Diaspora are now so far removed from African cultural values and traditions (because of their forced removal from Africa and the experience of 400 years of enslavement) that they have become fully acculturalised. As a result of this process they have developed their own modern 'identities' based upon their lived experiences in Western societies. The subjugation of African identities has become more problematic than ever before as the 'modern' denigrates and dismisses the African past and the importance of its legacy in the lives of people of African descent. These challenges do not negate acknowledgement and recognition of the cultural diversity and shifting identities among African people. However, these explanations are all too easy to accept, particularly when African people within the Diaspora have been taught to separate themselves from Africa and Africans (Graham 2000).

Eminent black scholars have engaged in identification and analysis of African cultural value retention that is expressed in many forms through and within black existence. This evidence suggests that people of African descent tend to function within African-centred worldviews whatever their geographical location (Herskovitz 1958; Mbiti 1970; Schiele 1994). In other words, African social philosophies continue to inform the everyday social realities of black people in local communities.

African-centred ways of knowing offer a critique of the degradation and discard of the 'traditional' and 'culture' in the interest of the so-called 'modern' and the 'global age'. This approach embraces a space where historical truths, tradition, oratory, metaphysical and material cultures are empowering to black communities living in European societies. The affirmation of these knowledge systems provides a vehicle for affirming their humanity that resists the severing of their past, history and cultures from themselves. In addition, this space confers an opportunity to examine the African past, culture and tradition in order to learn from its sources of empowerment and disempowerment in assisting people to search for ways forward (Dei 1999b).

Second, historically, many black communities have represented themselves in ways that have been viewed as essentialised discourses. It has been proposed that these essentialist discourses proffer the meta-narratives inherent within European modernity.

Recent trends in postmodern theorising represent a challenge to the power, authority and centrality of conventional knowledge. Postmodern discourse represents a paradigm shift that rejects the simplified universal or grand narratives that construct an essentialised reality. This allows space for the experiences and forms of knowledge generated by those groups excluded along the lines of race, gender and class. Postmodern perspectives embrace the local, specific and the complexity of lived experiences that legitimise claims to knowledge. Whilst postmodern discourse has particular relevance in the production of knowledge and its dissemination of subjugated groups in society; postmodernity forms the world into an array of separate entities without connections or shared values or norms. This fragmentation and discontinuity becomes problematic for black communities where these aspects are part of a unified experience. It is this unified experience that embraces locally produced knowledge emanating from cultural histories, social interactions and the experience of daily life (Dei 1999b). It is within this context, that African-centred knowledge systems view the identity of self as extended so that self is viewed as multifaceted yet connected to the collective (Graham 1999). This understanding invites a critique of the postmodern project as essentially a product of European social thought characterised by a view of the modern as its frame of reference. What is more, the notion of the modern has historically been used to devalue and oppress people outside of Europe. West (1989: 91) asks the poignant question: 'does the postmodern debate seriously acknowledge the distinctive cultural and political practices of oppressed peoples?' These questions invite concern about notions of difference and whether postmodern debates strengthen social understanding of the cultural practices of oppressed peoples. It can be argued, therefore, that Eurocentric hegemony and racial bias extends to the postmodern debate and has been a feature of almost all critical approaches, including critical theory (see for example Scheurich and Young 1997; Stanfield 1994; Bell 1992).

In any event, dominant epistemologies and sources of knowledge are derived largely from Western European philosophical, historical, social, political, economic and cultural development and like all specialised knowledge 'reflect the interests and standpoint of its creator' (Hill Collins 1991: 201). Allowing space for other culturally based epistemologies remains somewhat problematic for European thought and can sometimes foster a strategic refusal on the part of some academics to engage in African-centred ways of knowing.

The following is a brief summary of the primary principles and values that underpin African-centred worldviews (Akbar 1976; Asante 1987; Myers 1988; Asante 1990; Schiele 1997).

The spiritual nature of human beings

Spirituality forms the cornerstone of the African-centred worldview and is the essence of human beings. Spirituality has been defined as 'the creative life-force, the very essence of all things that connects all human beings to each other' (Arewa 1998: xvii). Spirituality connects all elements of the universe – people, animals and inanimate objects are viewed as interconnected. Since they are dependent upon each other, they are, in essence, considered as one (Mbiti 1970; Nobles 1985).

The interconnectedness of all things

This worldview emphasises the interdependence of all the elements of the universe. The world, ideas and human beings are not dichotomised into either/or, mind/

body, and spirit/material. The interconnectedness of all things sees no separation between the material and the spiritual; 'reality is at one and inseparably spiritual and material' (Myers 1988: 24) as all reality (universe) begins from a single principle. Human beings are perceived as an integral part of nature, and living in harmony with the environment helps them to become at one with all reality. The interconnectedness of human beings spiritually is translated socially, so that the human being is never an isolated individual but always the person in the community. The community defines the person, as Mbiti (1970: 141) explains: 'I am because we are; and since we are, therefore I am'. To become aware of the cultural self is an important process that connects a person spiritually to others within a culture. Furthermore, self-knowledge within the context of one's cultural base and connection with others provides the basis for transformation, spiritual development and wellbeing.

Collective nature of identity

African-centred worldviews propose that the individual cannot be understood separately from other people because there is no perceptual separation of the individual from others (Myers 1988). From these assumptions of collective identity follows the emphasis upon human similarities or commonalities rather than upon individual differences. The collective nature of human beings entails collective responsibility for what happens to individuals. This ethos corresponds with Mbiti's (1970: 141) adage 'whatever happens to the individual happens to the whole group and whatever happens to the whole group happens to the individual'. These philosophical precepts are developed through the concept of personhood. Who you are, your personhood comes about through your relationship with the community.

Karenga (1997) proposes that personhood evolves through the process of becoming that negates the idea that personhood is achieved simply by existence. The process of being is marked by successive stages of integration or incorporation into the community. To promote personhood requires optimal emotional, physical, intellectual and spiritual health. These principles underlie the need to achieve harmony with the forces of life. King (1994: 20) outlines the process to achieving a harmonious way of living. He suggests the combination of co-operating with natural forces that influence events and experiences while at the same time 'taking responsibility for one's life by consciously choosing and negotiating the direction and paths one will follow'.

African-centred worldviews include the concept of balance. The task of all living things is to maintain balance in the face of adverse external forces. When this inner peace is compromised, the psychological, social and physical wellbeing of a person is threatened.

African-centred worldviews – cultural resource knowledge in black communities

For black communities, European societies can be a hostile place. It is important to understand the nature of this hostility they encounter, its institutions and social practices, in order to exercise agency in the choices made by individuals and their families (Dei 1999b). It is within this context that cultural heritage and ways of knowing become critical for the survival and wellbeing of black people and their communities.

African-centred ways of knowing derived from cultural heritage and lived experiences are important sites of empowerment where cultural connections are made relevant to everyday experiences. Dei (1999b: 9) suggests that cultural resource knowledge provides the vehicle for affirming humanity and resistance in the severing of the past, history and cultures from black communities themselves. This knowledge is often spoken about as 'freedom from mental slavery'. This confers the space where falsehoods that have been told about black people can be challenged and through this process knowledge can be used to assist families and young people in finding solutions to problems in their everyday lives. It is through this understanding that black communities exercise intellectual agency in engaging in a process of reclamation and revitalisation of knowledge systems such as African-centred worldviews. These ways of knowing maintain a connection with the spiritual as well as material realms of life. This spiritual dimension of knowledge 'gives power and strength in physical communication as a means of connecting the inner strength and character to the outer existence and collective identity' (Dei 1999b: 6).

African-centred ways of knowing constitute the maintenance of cultural autonomy as a powerful resource in affirming the authority of communities. Cultural resource knowledge assists people in framing their life worlds and their experience in the Diaspora. A discussion about black communities often invites a critique about the notion of a black community or communities. It has been suggested that a black community does not exist. These assertions often relate to conventional ideas of community as a static uniformed entity. However, according to Dei (1999b) community can refer to a mode of resistance, and can be a form of critical discussion and change. Thus, with this understanding the fact that some individuals may indicate that they are not part of a black community is no reason to deny that one exists.

The role of African-centred cultural knowledge as a mode of resistance has been pivotal in dislodging strategies of domination in the subjugation of the histories, cultures and experiences of black communities. For example, the emergence of supplementary schools provided the vehicle for black parents to mobilise community resources and exercise intellectual agency in their children's education. Black parents felt that racism within the educational system conspired to provide an environment that was hostile to their children's learning and was ultimately responsible for the underachievement, disengagement and disaffection of their children. Dove (1995) in her research asked parents to indicate why they sent their children to supplementary schools. The following is a brief summary of their responses.

- To improve their children's academic performance;
- To receive more cultural learning;
- To receive more exposure to positive images of black people;
- To access more support for children and parents;
- To keep children off the streets and involved in something positive;
- To build children's confidence

Parents believed that supplementary schools provided their children with a better education albeit on a part-time basis in contrast to full time state schooling. It is within the context of community that African-centred knowledge has become an important tool in the education of black children. This approach confers the maintenance of a cultural heritage that challenges the dominant definition of knowledge proffered by European cultures. Thus, this space affirms the energies required in maintaining cultural elements and products and the creation of knowledge through experiences in daily life. African-centred knowledge presents education through a worldview that is integrated within communities. In this way, learning is conveyed to the younger generation by elders as an integrated part of a community's social, spiritual/ancestral and natural environment (Dei 1999b). Therefore, many supplementary schools provide a multifaceted approach including enhancing and improving children's academic performance, exposure to an African-centred orientation to knowledge, spiritual values, and character building and facilitating intergenerational unity.

Over the past decades there has been a growing momentum towards African-centred knowledge as a theory of social change in the regeneration of black communities. These strategies are articulated through the popularity of Kwanzaa and rites of passage programmes that embrace a Caribbean past and a critical reading of African social philosophies. African-centred knowledge has been utilised by communities to assist in the institutionalisation of their cultural values beyond the scope of family and friends. In this way, rites of passage programmes are action-orientated social practices assisting young black people in affirming African values through patterns of interpreting realities outside of Eurocentric constructs that often place black people within a consciousness of racism and oppression. This approach gives opportunities for black young people to connect and create a way of being and thinking that is congruent with African cultural values. The broader context of education as an integrated part of communities provides the context in which rites of passage programmes become an important tool to stem the path of disaffection and underachievement among young black people in the British educational system.

COMMUNITY RITES OF PASSAGE PROGRAMMES –
EDUCATING THROUGH CULTURAL RESOURCE
KNOWLEDGE

It has been argued that most Western societies have abandoned adolescent rites of passage as a model of transition into adulthood. Nevertheless, specific language expressions that define adolescence such as youth, teenager and juvenile remain in common usage. According to Stevens (1982), mainstream culture has abdicated responsibility for initiating young people. People have lost confidence about what constitute the values to be passed on and what people are being initiated for. For young black people the potentially difficult period of adolescence is often compounded through the experience of institutional and cultural racism that permeates most aspects of British society.

Black parents, elders and educators have been conscious of the need for an orderly process of maturation to nurture and develop the physical, intellectual, emotional and spiritual needs of young black people in order to prepare them for adulthood. Consequently, there has been a steady growth in community rites of passage programmes as a method of supporting transitional relationships. Moreover, these programmes encapsulate a broader context for education where the harmonious development on a personal, communal and spiritual level can take place (Graham 1987, 1999; Hill 1992; Obonna 1996). In this way, rites of passage programmes fulfil an important role in assisting young black people in the transition to adulthood. They bring together families and groups and communities to educate young people in order to connect spiritual values to the material world. As Dei (1999b: 20) explains, 'spirituality in education connects learners to the universal meaning of human existence . . . spirituality supplies the context of meaning for society and regulates thought and behaviour of individuals in everyday life'. Therefore, the complex linkages of the spiritual and emotional wellbeing of the individual are nurtured as an important dimension to assist in effective learning outcomes. Thus, the learner shares in a sense of community and belonging within a broader context of education that is not constrained by the classroom but located within an integrated community process.

African-centred ways of knowing embrace the concept of personhood through the process of becoming that is achieved through understanding and appreciating self, community, co-operation, purpose, creativity and spirituality. The spiritual/ancestral realms of personhood can assist in the nurturing and emotional wellbeing of young people. In this way, young people are accorded the challenge to grow, change and develop grounded in the moral, intellectual and social virtues and ideals integrated within the context of local communities.

African-centred rites of passage programmes draw upon value systems enshrined in the Nguzo Saba or seven princples (Karenga 1977, 1997).

The Nguzo Saba
Umoja (unity)
To strive for and maintain unity in the family, community and nation.
Kujichagulia (self-determination)
To define ourselves, name ourselves, create for ourselves and speak for ourselves
Ujima (collective work and responsibility)
To build and maintain our community together and our brothers' and sisters' problems are our problems and to solve them together
Ujamaa (co-operative economics)
Mutual financial interdependence, shared resources, balance

Nia (purpose)

To make our collective vocation the building and developing of our community and to be in harmony with our spiritual purpose

Kuumba (creativity)

To do always as much as we can, in the way that we can, in order to leave our community more beautiful than we inherited it.

Imani (faith)

To believe with all our hearts in our parents, our teachers and our people.

There are several forms of rites of passage programmes:

- Community based rites of passage. These programmes offer short-term inter-generational rites of passage experience for young people to assist in the passage to the threshold of adulthood.
- Church based rites of passage programmes. The black churches play an important role in supporting major transitional relationships. These programmes have been developed alongside church orientated youth programmes.
- Therapeutic rites of passage programmes. These programmes have been developed as social work interventions that seek to educate and support young people involved in self-destructive behaviours.
- Family support rites of passage programmes. The focus for these programmes has been on providing family support in the transition into adulthood and includes young people, adults and elders.

Warfield-Coppock (1990) has advocated an organised community based approach to restoring socialisation processes consistent with African philosophies adapted for modern society. The reclamation and reconstitution of these cultural products has been advanced and applied by black scholars and practitioners on the continent of Africa as well as throughout the Diaspora (Mutisya 1996; Hill 1992; Obonna 1996). African-centred knowledge systems provide the theoretical underpinning to these action-orientated programmes. In addition, they also include local cultural knowledge and experiences concerning the social realities of everyday living. This is because it is within local communities that cultural resource knowledge is nurtured and cultural connections made relevant in everyday lives.

Rites of passage programmes play an important role in intergenerational unity. Historically, elders played a pivotal role in the socialisation and education of children, affirming the adage 'wisdom embraces knowledge'. They provided the linchpin for the generations comprised of adults, children and ancestors (Wilcox 1998). Diallo and Hall (1989: 44) consider the features of elderhood that contributed to the maintenance and forward flow of community.

> Grandparents form the circle of elders. They represent the world of knowledge and constitute the supreme council of the village. To avoid the anger of the ancestors, with whom they can communicate through rituals and divination, they are supposed to know all the prohibitions and how to remedy any

violations of a social taboo. They are wise and move thoughtfully. They are walking books of know how.

The shaping of adults was well understood in traditional African communities as the stages of human development leading to the end of life were viewed as a continuous expansion, in which the physical body, the mind and the consciousness were continually opening and widening. These opportunities for young people to engage in a voyage of self-discovery and affirmation assist in nurturing their emotional, spiritual and intellectual wellbeing. This approach facilitates intergenerational communication that ensures the peaceful transition towards adulthood and creates an understanding of the role of each generation in society (Boateng 1990).

This action-orientated approach to integrated education calls for the active involvement of communities, groups and families in the schooling process. Education and schooling must serve the needs of local communities. This requires meaningful partnerships with groups, organisations and families. Some black young people seem to lack a sense of connection and identification with schools. This alienation can sometimes be located in the negation of black pupils' lived experiences in communities. This situation is often compounded by the exclusion of African-centred cultures and epistemologies in learning environments. These considerations invite new directions. New directions require innovative strategies that suggest an examination of the ways in which African-centred perspectives can be integrated into the learning process. Hill (1992), a leading pioneer in the rites of passage movement, has developed specific educational programmes that have been effectively employed in classrooms in state schooling. Hill (1992) has successfully integrated community cultural knowledge into local schools to assist in reconnecting black young people with education. These linkages serve to strengthen and support institutions within black communities. This approach does not mean a complete rejection of all mainstream education has to offer. As Dei (1994: 20) asserts: 'on the contrary, it calls on the African scholar to utilise the best of what mainstream has to offer through a review of its paradigms, viewpoints, and methods as a basis to critique contemporary society on issues of social justice, racism and white privilege'.

CONCLUSION

The social and emotional cost of disaffection, disengagement and alienation among young black people presents an important challenge to educators to actualise the prevailing discourse of social justice and equity in education and schooling. This requires an urgent re-thinking in the way education and schooling responds to the educational needs of young people. At the same time, there are growing demands from black parents for educators to fulfil their responsibility in addressing the educational needs of young black people. Black parents are concerned about the consistent failure of the educational system to educate their children. Educators must listen to young black people and their experiences of schooling in order to engage in practical action to reconnect young black people to education. As a first step, schools must recognise the validity of all knowledge and appreciate the variety of perspectives that contribute to our understanding of human existence. This is to ensure that education serves the needs of people in local communities so that their concerns about the historical distortions of black peoples' lives and experiences are addressed. In this way, African-centred perspectives can make an important contribution in supporting an inclusive school curriculum that seeks to address the power imbalance in what constitutes valid knowledge. This approach can assist in the re-engagement of young black people and their sense of connectedness and identification with schools. Young black people must see themselves represented in the school system. I believe links with community organisations and groups through the integration of rites of passage programmes into the classroom can ensure meaningful partnerships with the wider black community. Such involvement can assist in creating new directions in the education of black children.

ACKNOWLEDGEMENT

I would like to thank Dr Martin Hewitt, Senior Lecturer, University of Hertfordshire, for his useful comments on an earlier draft of this chapter.

NOTES

1   I use the term African and black interchangeably to refer to all peoples who trace some ancestral and cultural affinity to continental Africa (i.e. peoples of African descent and all those who define themselves as black/African).
2   The over representation of black children in official school exclusion data refers to children of African and African-Caribbean descent.

REFERENCES

Abarry, A. and Assante, M. (1995) *African Intellectual Heritage: a Book of Sources*, Philadelphia: Temple University Press.
Akbar, N. (1976) 'Rhythmic patterns in African personality' in King, L. and Dixon V. and Nobles W. (eds) *African Philosophy: Assumptions and Paradigms for Research on Black People*, Los Angeles, CA: Fanon Research Development Center.
Akbar, N. (1985) 'Our destiny: Authors of a scientific revolution' in McAdoo, H. and J. McAdoo (eds) *Black Children: Social Psychological and Educational Environments*, Newbury Park, CA: Sage Publications.
Arewa, C. S. (1998) *Opening to Spirit: Contacting the Healing Power of the Chakras and Honouring African Spirituality*, London: Thorsons.
Asante, M. (1987) *The Afrocentric Idea*, Philadelphia, PA: Temple University Press.
Asante, M (1988) *Afrocentricity: The Theory of Social Change*, Trenton, NJ: Africa World Press.
Asante, M. (1990) *Kemet, Afrocentricity and Knowledge*, Trenton, NJ: Africa World Press.
Asante, M. (1994) 'Afrocentricity, race and reason', *Race and Reason*, Autumn edition, pp. 20–2.

Bell, D. (1992) *Faces at the Bottom of the Well: The Permanence of Racism*, New York: Basic Books.

Boateng, F. (1990) 'African traditional education: a tool for intergenerational communication', in Asante, M. K. and Asante, K. W. (eds) *African Culture: The Rhythms of Unity*, Trenton: Africa World Press.

Bourne, J. Bridges, L. and Searle, C. (eds) (1994) *Outcast England: How Schools Exclude Black Children*, London: Institute of Race Relations.

Brown, P. (1995) 'Educational achievement in a multiethnic society: the case for an Afrocentric model', *The International Journal of Africana Studies*, **1** and **2**, pp. 100–20.

Bryan, B., Dadzie, S. and Scafe, S. (1985) *The Heart of the Race: Black Women's Lives in Britain*, London: Virago.

Carby, H. (1984) 'Schooling in Babylon' in Hall *et al.* (eds) *The Empire Strikes Back*, CCCS, London: Hutchinson.

Coard, B. (1971) *How the West Indian Child is Made Educationally Subnormal*, London: New Beacon Books.

Commission for Racial Equality (1996) *Exclusion from School: The Public Cost*, London: CRE.

Dei, G. (1994) 'Afrocentricity: a cornerstone of pedagogy', *Anthropology and Education Quarterly*, **25**, 1, pp. 3–28.

Dei, G. (1995) 'African studies in Canada, problems and challenges', *Journal of Black Studies*, **26**, 2, pp. 153–71.

Dei, G. (1999a) 'The denial of difference: reframing anti-racist praxis', *Race, Ethnicity and Education*, **2**, 1, pp. 17–37.

Dei, G. (1999b) 'Rethinking the role of Indigenous Knowledges in the academy', Public lecture, Department of Sociology and Equity Studies in Education, OISE: University of Toronto.

Department for Education and Employment (1997) *Permanent Exclusions from Schools in England 1995/96*, London: DfEE.

DES (1965) *The Education of Immigrants*, Circular 7/65, London: HMSO.

DES (1985) *Education for All* (Swann Report), London: HMSO.

Diallo, Y. and Hall, M. (1989) *The Healing Drum: African Wisdom Teachings*, VT: Destiny Books.

Diop, C. (1978) *The Cultural Unity of Black Africa*, Chicago, IL: Third World Press.

Dove, N (1995) 'The emergence of black supplementary schools as forms of resistance to racism in the United Kingdom' in Shujaa, M. J. (ed.) *Too Much Schooling, Too Little Education, A Paradox of Black Life in White Societies*, Trenton, NJ: Africa World Press.

Eze, E. (1997) *Race and the Enlightenment*, Oxford: Blackwell Publishers Ltd.

Fitzherbert, K. (1967) *West Indian Children in London*, London: Bell and Sons.

Gill, D., Singh, E. and Vance, M. (1987) 'Multicultural versus anti-racist science: biology' in Gill, D. and Levidow, L. (eds) *Anti-racist Science Teaching*, London: Free Association Books.

Gillborn, D. (1995) *Racism and Antiracism in Real Schools*, Open University Press: Buckinghamshire.

Graham, M. (1987) Exploring Black Families: Rites of Passage (Unpublished practice report).

Graham, M. (1999) 'The African-centred worldview: developing a paradigm for social work', *British Journal of Social Work*, **29**, 2, pp. 252–67.

Graham, M. (2000) 'Honouring social work principles – exploring the connections between anti-racist social work and African-centred worldview', *Social Work Education*, **19**, 5, pp. 423–34.

Graham, M. (in press) *Social Work and African-centred Worldviews*, BASW, Birmingham, UK: Venture Press.

Herskovitz, M. J. (1958) *The Myth of the Negro Past*, Boston, MA: Beacon Press.

Hill, P. (1992) *Coming of Age: African American Male Rites of Passage*, Chicago, IL: African Images.

Hill, P. (1998) *The Journey (Adolescent Rites of Passage) Youth Workbook*, East Cleveland, OH: National Rites of Passage Institute.

Hilliard, A. (1985) 'Kemetic concepts in education', *Journal of African Civilisations*, **6**, 2, pp. 133–53.

Hill Collins, P. (1991) *Black Feminist Thought*, London: Routledge.

Jenkins, R. (1966) Address given by the Home Secretary to a meeting of the Voluntary Liaison Committee, London: NCCI.

John, G. (1976) Quoted in British Council of Churches, *The New Black Presence in Britain: A Christian Security*, London: BBC Publications.

Karenga, M. (1977) *Kwanzaa, Origin, Concepts, Practice*, Los Angeles, CA: Kawaida Publications.

Karenga, M. (1993) *Introduction to Black Studies* (2nd edn), Los Angeles, CA: University of Sankore Press.

Karenga, M. (1997) *Kwanzaa: A Celebration of Family, Community and Culture*, Los Angeles, CA: University of Sankore Press.

King, A. E. (1994) 'An Afrocentric cultural awareness program for incarcerated African-American males', *Journal of Multicultural Social Work*, **3**, 4, pp. 17–28.

Little, K. (1947) *Negroes in Britain: A Study of Race Relations in English Society*, London: Routledge Kegan and Paul.

Macpherson, W. (1999) *Stephen Lawrence Inquiry*, Report of an inquiry by Sir William Macpherson of Cluny, London: TSO, Cm 4262.

Mbiti, J. (1970) *African Religions and Philosophy*, Garden City, NY: Anchor Books.

Mullard, C. (1982) 'From assimilation to cultural pluralism', in Tierney J. (ed.) *Race, Migration and Schooling*, Eastbourne, Sussex: Holt Rinehart and Winston.

Mutisya, P. (1996) 'Demythologisation and demystification of African initiation rites', *Journal of Black Studies*, **27**, 1, pp. 94–103.

Myers, L. (1988) *Understanding an Afrocentric World View: Introduction to Optimal Psychology*, Dubuque, IA: Kendall.

Nobles, W. (1980) 'African philosophy: foundations for black psychology', in Jones, R. (ed.) *Black Psychology*, New York: Harper and Row.

Nobles, W. (1985) *Africanity and the Black Family*, Oakland, CA: Black Family Institute Publications.

Obonna, P. (1996) *Education of the Black Child Conferences, Rites of Passage Programmes*, Manchester: Kemetic Guidance Group.

Patterson, S. (1963) *Dark Strangers*, London: Tavistock Publications.

Rose, E. and Deakin, N. (1969) *Colour and Citizenship, A Report on British Race Relations*, Oxford: Oxford University Press.

Scheurich, J. and Young, M. (1997) 'Colouring epistemologies: are our research epistemologies racially biased?', *Educational Researcher*, **26**, 4.

Schiele, J. (1994) 'Afrocentricity as an alternative worldview for equality', *Journal of Progressive Human Services*, **5**, 1, pp. 5–25.

Schiele, J. (1997) 'The contour and meaning of Afrocentric social work', *Journal of Black Studies*, **27**, 6, pp. 800–19.

Select Committee (1973) 'Race relations and immigration', *Education Report*, London: HMSO.

Sewell, T. (1997) *Black Masculinities and Schooling – How Black Boys Survive Modern Schooling*, Stoke-on-Trent: Trentham Books.

Sivanandan, A. (1994) 'Introduction', in Bourne, J., Bridges, L. and Searle, C., *Outcast England: How Schools Exclude Black Children*, London: Institute of Race Relations.

Social Exclusion Unit (1998) *Truancy and School Exclusion Report*, London: HMSO.

Stanfield, J. H. (1994) 'Ethnic modeling in qualitative research', in Denzin, N. and Lincoln, Y. (eds) *Handbook of Qualitative Inquiry*, Newbury Park, CA: Sage.

Stevens, A. (1982) *Archetypes: A Natural History of the Self*, New York: William Morrow.

Swann Report (1985) London: HMSO.

Troyna, B. and Cashmore, E. (1982) *Black Youth in Crisis*, London: Allen Unwin.

Warfield-Coppock, N. (1990) *Afrocentric Theory and Applications: Adolescent Rites of Passage*, Washington DC: Baobab Associates.

West, C. (1989) 'Black culture and post-modernism', in Kruger, B. and Mariani, P., *Remaking History*, Dia Art Foundation, Seattle, WA: Bay Press.

Wilcox, D. (1998) 'The Rites of Passage Process for African American Youth: Perspectives of Eight Elders', unpublished PhD thesis, Ohio: Kent State University.

Williams, C. (1987) *The Destruction of Black Civilisations: Great Issues of a Race from 4500 BC to 2000 AD*, Chicago, IL: Third World Press.

Wright, C. (1985) 'Who succeeds at school and who decides?', *Multicultural Teaching*, **4**, 1, pp. 17–22.

5   Lessons from America: the African American Immersion Schools experiment[1]

Diane S. Pollard and Cheryl S. Ajirotutu

INTRODUCTION

For a number of years, public elementary and secondary schools in the United States have been perceived as being in a state of crisis and calls for educational reform have been widespread. In urban public schools, particularly, where student populations tend to be most heterogeneous, there is widespread evidence that students who are not White and middle class are not faring well, academically, personally, or socially (Fine 1991; Fine and Weis 1993). Among African American students, school failure rates have reached critical proportions. A variety of indices ranging from standardized test scores to behavioral reports indicate that public schools across the United States are failing to educate African American children effectively. Nationally, calls for alternatives to this situation have been raised, and in some cases, bold and unique responses have been attempted.

In one large, urban Mid-western school district, two African American Immersion Schools were established as an alternative to stem the tide of school failure among students of this group. These schools were envisioned as using African and African American history and culture as the medium for transmitting academic and social skills to their students. The decision to establish these schools sparked controversy both nationally and locally. Some of their detractors described them as a return to segregation (*New York Times*, 22 January 1991). However, others noted that African centered educational institutions had long existed as viable educational models in the independent and private school sectors. Much of the controversy surrounding the two African American Immersion Schools that are the focus of this chapter seemed to stem from their establishment within the public school arena.

As initial planning for these schools took place, there was recognition of a need for a systematic documentation, and evaluation of their implementation and outcomes. In response to this need, the authors of this chapter designed and implemented the African American Immersion Schools Evaluation Project. This project is a six year, longitudinal study of these particular African American Immersion Schools. The project has documented and evaluated the first five years of operation in each of the schools. This chapter provides a description of highlights of the implementation of the African American Immersion Schools, summarizes selected findings from our longitudinal study, and discusses the implications of this particular educational reform for culturally based educational reforms nationally and internationally.

The establishment of the African American Immersion Schools in Milwaukee is of significant importance for school reform on both national and international levels. Major demographic changes in urban communities have had profound implications for schools. It was projected that the 50 largest cities in the United States will have school populations in which the majority of students are non-European American by the year 2000 (Frierson 1990). In many communities a significant proportion of these students are, or will be, African Americans. Given the alarming failure of public schools to prepare African American children for tomorrow's world, the need for alternative models was clearly evident. Similarly, other countries, such as Canada, England, South Africa, and New Zealand, are struggling to educate increasingly diverse student populations effectively. Thus, the African American Immersion Schools discussed in this chapter may be informative for these international efforts.

BRIEF OVERVIEW OF RELATED LITERATURE

In the United States, as in other societies, schools are powerful agencies of social-ization. They are major institutions of cultural transmission in which students learn the values, beliefs, and processes by which one mediates relationships and interactions (Kimball 1991; Spindler and Spindler 1991). Schools are expected to provide a bridge between the private world of the family and the broader social world through both socialisation and by teaching students the technical and academic skills they would need to be productive members of that world (Elkin and Handel 1989).

In many countries, the prevalent view of education was that one culture must be accepted as standard and dominant (Johnson 1992). For many, the historical and contemporary experiences of Europeans and European Americans has been presented as dominant and as the monocultural standard for academic, personal, and social socialisation. This European centered perspective has had a number of implications. First, it allowed educational institutions to ignore group differences in social and cultural background. Second, it attributed academic performance entirely to individual or family factors and paid scant attention to broader political, economic, cultural, and structural issues in the society. Third, this perspective tended to spawn interventions, which were narrow in focus and limited in scope (Comer and Haynes 1991).

This Eurocentric perspective on education has been challenged. First, a number of researchers have demonstrated that group or cultural factors are an integral part of the schooling and learning processes (Allen and Boykin 1992; Bell 1994). Second, some researchers have indicated that the assumptions that African American children perform poorly in school because of personal deficits are simply not borne out (Graham 1994; Mboya 1986). Furthermore some researchers have argued that many of the problems experienced by poor African American families and children are the result of structural dislocations in the society and related changes in economic and social opportunities rather than because of interpersonal problems internal to families. Finally, there is evidence that educational interventions that focus primarily on changing individuals in a short period of time are not effective strategies, particularly in the arena of school reform (Jones-Wilson 1989; Wehlage, Smith and Lipman 1992). Rather, some researchers have argued that educational interventions which take into account and build upon the cultural perspectives students bring to the school setting may be more influential (Whaley 1993; Jagers and Mock 1993; Ladson-Billings 1995). Finally several researchers have argued that culturally based educational reform requires changes in all aspects of school functioning (Hoover 1992; Lee 1992; Wehlage, Smith and Lipman 1992).

In summary, these particular African American Immersion Schools, as part of a large public school system were charged with continuing to serve the same academic and socialisation function as any other schools. The assumption underlying their establishment was that the infusion of African and African American culture, history and contemporary experiences throughout the curricular and extracurricular activities would help the schools perform these functions more effectively. In turn, this would lead to more positive academic, personal and social outcomes for students.

A DESCRIPTION OF THE AFRICAN AMERICAN IMMERSION SCHOOLS

Background

In 1989 the school board of a large Mid-western city established a task force to make recommendations regarding the educational and social crises involving African American males in its schools. This task force, which consisted of representatives from the schools, higher education, business and the community spent approximately six months analysing data concerning the academic and social situation of African American males locally and nationally. As a result of its deliberations, the task force made a series of recommendations to the school board, one of which was to establish two African centered schools, one elementary and one at the middle school level. These recommendations were accepted by the school board and an Implementation Committee was established to develop specific plans to put these schools into place. It should be noted that although the original Task Force focused on African American males, an early decision was that these particular schools serve both male and female students. The African American Immersion elementary school was opened in the fall of 1991 and the middle school opened at the beginning of the 1992 school year.

The African American Immersion Schools Evaluation Project, co-directed by the authors of this chapter, began its documentation and evaluation activities shortly before the inception of the elementary school in 1991. This research project had an interdisciplinary, holistic, participatory focus. The longitudinal study covered the initial five years of implementation at each school. It employed qualitative and quantitative methods aimed at: describing and explaining the changes that occurred at the two schools, evaluating the outcomes of these changes, and identifying information obtained from these schools that could be useful to other educational settings with similar populations.

Overview of major findings

As two of the first *public* schools to implement African centered educational models on a school-wide basis in the United States, these two schools shared some common characteristics. First, they had no peer institutions on which to model their new programmes. As a result the staffs had to simultaneously develop and implement new curricular strategies incorporating African and African American culture. Staff development, therefore was a key ingredient in the creation of these African centered educational models. Recognizing this, the district established a requirement that staff complete 18 university-level credits in African and African American history and culture within the first three years of their tenure at the schools. Second, as part of a large public school district, the schools also were required to meet the same educational requirements and goals as all other schools in the district. Thus the African centered aspect was grafted onto existing district wide curricular mandates and the schools were subject to the vicissitudes of being part of a large bureaucratic organization. Third, the majority of students served by these schools were from low income communities which had suffered the ravages of economic devastation. This population was similar to that in most of the schools in this district. One characteristic of it was high student mobility. The large number of students entering and leaving the schools each year blunted the educational impact of this reform effort.

On the other hand, our research revealed that the two African centered schools were implemented under significantly different conditions. These differences were related both to the characteristics of the students served and to characteristics of the organizational climate at the two schools. Therefore, the major findings must be discussed within the unique context found in each school.

The elementary school

This school served students from early through middle childhood; i.e. children from approximately ages 3 to 11. Most of the children were from the neighborhood surrounding the school and although student mobility was fairly high, some students were second generation pupils at the same school. The school was characterized by significant staff stability; the principal and a majority of the teachers had worked there for several years before the school was designated as an African American Immersion School and they chose to remain throughout the initial five years that it implemented this model. Perhaps as a result of their history of working together, this staff was able to establish a shared vision of what the school should be fairly soon after the school began to implement its African centered model. Several key ingredients supported the development of this vision.

One important ingredient concerned the administrative management strategies established at the school. The principal employed several key management strategies, which supported the transition to an African American Immersion School. For example, one strategy involved restructuring the school day to allow teachers at each grade level to have a common meeting time for planning. These teacher groups, called families, used their planning time to work collaboratively to design curriculum, evaluate students, and identify and share resources. Having this time allowed these teachers to work together to create appropriate culturally based learning experiences for their students.

Some examples of other key ingredients, which supported the development of an African centered educational model at the elementary school were:

1   an emphasis on staff development in which staff members took collective responsibility to meet the requirement of 18 college-level credits in African and African American history and culture soon after the African centered orientation was implemented at the school,
2   staff involvement in curriculum development and reform which resulted in the development and infusion of an African centered curricular focus across subject areas throughout the school, and
3   the institutionalisation of several school-wide activities developed to disseminate African and African American culture and history as important and valued knowledge.

Furthermore, some of these school wide activities were designed to include African American adults who have been successful in a wide variety of activities in the city as purveyors of knowledge and culture for the students.

A major impetus for the establishment of the African American Immersion Schools was to provide an alternative to traditional practices, which were failing to educate African American students effectively. This failure was most evident in measures of student academic performance. Accordingly a major aspect of the African American Immersion Schools Evaluation Project focused on student outcomes. We assessed changes in students' academic performance in two ways: (1) through a review of within school changes over the project period and (2) through a comparison of student performance in the African American Immersion schools and other comparable schools.

Using data generated by the school district, we assessed differences in academic performance in the elementary school over the five year period of the evaluation project. We documented differences in performance for different groups of students at a designated grade level. Performance was assessed via both local and national standardized tests. The analyses of these data revealed overall improvements in student outcomes in reading and writing and a more mixed pattern in mathematics performance. In addition, the authors of this chapter assessed changes in five aspects of cognitive abilities of two groups of students longitudinally using the Structure of Intellects test battery (Meeker 1987). Overall there was consistent gain in the five measures of cognitive abilities tested.

Our second assessment of student outcomes involved a comparison of student performance at this elementary school with other schools serving similar populations. Thirteen such schools in the city were compared with respect to overall school performance on district administered measures through the five years of the evaluation project. Our analyses of these data indicated that the African American Immersion elementary school generally improved or maintained its relative standing compared to the other schools in the city, which served similar student populations.

Finally, we assessed student outcomes in terms of the students' perceptions of this particular school. Annually, we interviewed a group of students who we followed longitudinally through the five year period of the evaluation project. A summary of the responses of 32 of these students to the question: 'What do you like most about your school?' revealed that students overwhelmingly described their experiences at the school in positive terms.

The middle school

An understanding of the events which occurred at the middle school over the initial five years that it implemented an African centered orientation must be based on two important contextual factors. One of these factors is germane to middle schools generally; the other is specific to this school.

Generally, middle schools have a relatively recent history in the United States. They were established as a result of dissatisfaction with the degree to which high schools, and later junior high schools, were unsuccessful in meeting the developmental needs of young adolescents and helping them make the transition from elementary to secondary school. Realizing that early adolescence is a time of rapid and major developmental change, middle schools were theoretically designed to provide a milieu that would recognize and accommodate these developmental changes and, at the same time, support academic growth. This required specific curricular, staff development and organizational strategies (Cuban 1992; National Middle School Association 1995). The provision of academic and social support is particularly crucial for African American young adolescents who must cope with the additional pressures related to their oppressed status within the dominant society (Spencer and Dornbusch 1990).

With respect to the African American Immersion middle school which was studied in this project, several specific factors converged to present significant challenges to the development of a coherent African centered educational model. One of these factors involved administrative turnovers. Soon after the announcement that the school was to become an African American Immersion School, the principal left. A new principal was assigned to the school one year prior to the inception of the Immersion program. At the end of the first year of the African American Immersion program, this principal was replaced and another principal was put in place. This principal brought in new assistant principals. Some of this turnover was initiated by the district administration while the rest was a result of interactions internal to the school. A second and related factor was a high level of staff mobility and instability. When it was announced that the school would become an African American Immersion School, teachers had the option to remain or request a transfer to another school. Unlike the elementary school, where most of the teachers chose to remain, a significant number left and were replaced with teachers new to the building. The phenomenon of teacher turnover persisted throughout the five years of the Evaluation Project. Two factors seemed to have contributed to the turnover in regular staff. First, many of the teachers failed to fulfill the requirement to take the 18 college level credits in African and African American history and culture which was in place for all teachers at the African American Immersion Schools. Second, recurring personnel issues between staff and the administration led many teachers to request transfers out of the building. Teacher mobility was heightened by instability because during that same time, the building was staffed by a large number of substitute teachers. It was not until the fourth year that this school operated as an African American Immersion School that the building was fully staffed with permanent teachers. In addition to high administrative and staff mobility, this school had one of the highest levels of student mobility in the district.

These internal patterns of instability were exacerbated by several external challenges to the very existence of the school during its initial, five year period as an African American Immersion School. These challenges ranged from reactions to the history of low student achievement, which had preceded this school's conversion to an African centered model to attacks on the idea of Afrocentric schooling, generally. These challenges contributed considerably to internal turbulence at the school during its third and fourth years. It is interesting to note that this occurred during the period when the problem of staff instability was declining. Unfortunately, however, the new staff, which included a large number of people committed to the idea of developing and implementing an African centered educational program, had to focus their energy and attention to reacting to these challenges.

As a result of these factors, administrators and staff at the African American Immersion middle school were not able to develop a shared vision of an African centered educational program for young adolescents. Consequently, during the first five years of implementation, staff did not gel into a collaborative, cohesive group and curriculum development did not take place on a consistent or a school wide basis. Some individual staff members created viable curriculum projects, and periodically, small groups of staff were able to come together to develop short term cross disciplinary curricular projects with strong, age appropriate, African centered themes; however, these efforts tended to be isolated and because of high staff turnover, all too often, the efforts were sometimes short lived.

The lack of a shared vision for the school was also reflected in the general school climate. While there were periodic efforts to establish a school climate that fostered learning within an African centered cultural milieu, these tended to be uneven and incomplete. For example, during the first year the school functioned as an African American Immersion School, a number of Afrocultural themes were identified with the notion that they would undergird school wide curricular and extra-curricular activities. However, over the five year period of the Evaluation Project, these themes diminished in importance and utilization.

Despite the general failure to implement major organizational and curriculum reform in this school, efforts to encourage parent involvement were somewhat more successful. Perhaps because this became an important priority for this school, a parent center was established in the school and parents became an important part of the school governance structure by the fourth and fifth years it operated as an African American Immersion School.

As with the elementary school, a major issue for the establishment of an African centered model at the middle school level concerned the traditional school program's failure to educate African American early adolescents effectively. Thus the academic outcomes of these students was of paramount interest. We analyzed the middle school data using the same strategies as those used for the elementary school. First, using district generated data, we assessed differences in student performance within the school during the five year period of the African American Immersion Schools Evaluation Project. Second, we used the same data to compare this middle school with two other middle schools which served somewhat similar student populations. Finally, we reviewed a sample of student responses to their experiences at the school. Our assessments using district data were restricted considerably in this case, however, because during the five year period that we documented and evaluated this school, the district mandated a number of changes in the assessment tools they used. As a result we were unable to obtain a consistent year-to-year measure of school performance over time. We were able to assess changes over some two and three year periods when the district used the same assessment tools.

Despite this problem, we were able to draw some conclusions about student outcomes during this school's initial five years of operation as an African American Immersion school. Overall student outcomes showed a mixed pattern during this period. This was evident in both behavioral and academic indices. For example, in some behavioral areas such as attendance, mobility and suspension rates, there was improvement over time both within the school and in comparison to similar schools. However, truancy rates remained relatively unchanged over this period. Similarly, with respect to academic performance, some areas such as overall grade point average and scores on standardized tests in writing and language increased. However, in other areas, such as reading and maths, overall declines were evident during the five year period. The comparisons of this school with other schools serving similar student populations also indicated mixed patterns. Although the three schools changed in relative standing during the periods that we were able to assess student performance from year to year, these changes tended to be inconsistent over time.

In contrast to the mixed pattern shown in student performance, the results of our annual interviews with a longitudinal sample of students from this school showed relatively positive perceptions of the school. Almost all of the students who responded to the interviews felt positive about their experiences at the school. In addition, these students felt that the opportunity to learn about African and African American history and culture would be beneficial to them both personally and socially.

SUMMARY AND CONCLUSIONS

The schools which were the subject of this study represented a bold initiative in school reform. This particular district was one of the first *public school districts* in the United States to establish African centered schools as an attempt to provide an alternative to educational models which were failing to educate African American children in urban settings effectively. In addition, to our knowledge, these are the only schools of this type which have been accompanied by a long term, holistic documentation and evaluation study. This study has analyzed both the types of changes necessary as a school attempts to transform its cultural base and the types of student outcomes which result from such change.

Our data clearly reveal that the implementation of an African centered model differed significantly in these two schools. Aside from obvious differences such as the developmental stage of the children served, we argue that important contextual factors accounted for the differences found. Specifically, the two schools differed in administrative management styles, in staff stability, and in the external reactions to them. These differences led to quite different kinds of staff development and curriculum reform efforts. These mitigating factors, we argue, may be reflected in the differences in student outcomes, which were described earlier in this chapter.

Our thorough documentation of these schools leads us to conclude that African centered educational programs can be viable entities within the public school sector as they have been in private school venues. However, in the public school arena, several important components are necessary if these types of schools are to survive and flourish.

1   An African centered model requires an administrative staff that can facilitate, reinforce and, most importantly articulate a clear vision for the school. Furthermore, this vision should be shared by a majority of school staff and made evident to students, parents and the community.
2   Staff stability is another key foundation underlying the successful implementation of an African centered educational program. Because the execution of programs such as this often involves simultaneously developing and implementing organizational and curricular materials, it is essential that staff are present over time to see changes through. In addition, staff stability is supportive to students.
3   Staff development is another key ingredient for the development of a successful African centered programme. In most cases, today's teachers have been grounded in European and European American orientations to history and culture. As a result they have little of the knowledge required to develop other centered educational models. Staff development therefore must become a mandate. Furthermore, this must be supported by the school and district administrations as well as the teachers.
4   Parent and community involvement should be encouraged and facilitated. This involvement helps students link the material learning in school to their

communities. The students' abilities to recognize these linkages should lead to positive academic, personal, and social outcomes.

5   The implementation of an African centered educational model in the public school sector requires the support of the school district. While specific types of support may vary with different situations, it is important that the district pay careful attention to the school's attempts to develop and maintain a program and reinforce, not undermine, those efforts.

Throughout the world, societies and their educational institutions which were once dominated by European and European American people are being challenged by increased diversity in their student population and society in general. Unfortunately, all too often schools have resisted the inevitable need to reform in order to meet this challenge. In practice this has resulted in denying students of color the kinds of educational experiences necessary to ensure their academic success. In the United States, African centered educational models have been proposed as an alternative to the public schools' failure to educate African American children effectively. The schools described in this study were among the first public schools to attempt to implement such African centered models. Our documentation and evaluation study suggests that, under certain conditions, similar culturally based school models may be worthy of consideration in other European dominated countries where children of African descent are part of the school population. However, key issues undergirding this viability include administrative and staff accountability and commitment as well as district and community level support. The data obtained from these schools suggest that further efforts to implement African centered models in public school settings must attend to these issues early and often.

NOTE

1   Portions of this chapter were taken from the following: Five Year Report: Dr. Martin Luther King, Jr. Elementary School and Five Year Report: Malcolm X Academy by Diane S. Pollard and Cheryl S. Ajirotutu. AAIS Evaluation Project.

REFERENCES

Allen, B. A. and Boykin, A. W. (1992) 'African American children and the educational process: Alleviating cultural discontinuity through prescriptive pedagogy', *School Psychology Review*, **21**, 4, pp. 586–96.

Bell, Y. R. (1994) 'A culturally sensitive analysis of black learning style', *Journal of Black Psychology*, **20**, 1, pp. 47–61.

Comer, J. P. and Haynes, N. M. (1991) 'Meeting the needs of black children in public schools: A school reform challenge', in C. V. Willie, A. M. Garibaldi, and W. L. Reed, (eds) *The Education of African Americans*, New York: Auburn House, pp. 67–71.

Cuban, L. (1992) 'What happens to reforms that last? The case of the junior high school', *American Educational Research Journal*, **29**, 2, pp. 227–51.

Elkin, F. and Handel, G. (1989) *The Child and Society: The Process of Socialization*, New York: Random House.

Fine, M. (1991) *Framing Dropouts: Notes on the Politics of an Urban High School*, Albany, NY: SUNY Press.

Fine, M. and Weis, L. (1993) *Beyond Silenced Voices: Class, Race and Gender in United States Schools*, Albany, NY: SUNY Press.

Frierson, H. T. Jr (1990) 'The situation of black educational researchers: continuation of a crisis', *Educational Researcher*, **19**, 2, pp. 12–17.

Graham, S. (1994) 'Motivation in African Americans', *Review of Educational Research*, **64**, 1, pp. 55–117.

Hoover, M. E. R. (1992) 'The Nairobi Day School: An African American independent school, 1966–1984', *Journal of Negro Education*, **61**, 2, pp. 201–10.

Jagers, R. J. and Mock, L. O. (1993) 'Culture and social outcomes among African American children: An Afrographic exploration', *Journal of Black Psychology*, **19**, 4, pp. 391–405.

Johnson, D. (1992) *Multiculturalism: In the Curriculum, in the Disciplines, and in Society*, New York: The Metropolitan Center for Educational Research, Development and Training. SEHNAP: New York University.

Jones-Wilson, F. C. (1989) 'Equity in education: A low priority in the school reform movement', in W. D. Smith and E. W. Chunn (eds) *Black Education: A Quest for Equity and Excellence*, New Brunswick, NJ: Transaction Publishers, pp. 28–35.

Kimball, S. (1991) *Culture and the Education Process*, New York: Teachers College Press.

Ladson-Billings, G. (1995) 'Toward a theory of culturally relevant pedagogy', *American Educational Research Journal*, **32**, 3, pp. 465–91.

Lee, C. D. (1992) 'Profile of an independent black institution: African centered education at work', *Journal of Negro Education*, **61**, 2, pp. 160–77.

Mboya, M. M. (1986) Black adolescents: A descriptive study of their self concept and academic achievement', *Adolescence*, **21**, 83, pp. 689–96.

Meeker, M. (1987) *A Curriculum for Developing Intelligence*, Vida, OR: SOI Systems.

National Middle School Association (1995) *This We Believe: Developmentally Responsive Middle Schools*, Columbus, OH: National Middle School Association.

New York Times, January 22, 1991: Editorial page.

Spencer, M. B. and Dornbusch, S. M. (1990) 'Challenges in studying minority youth', in S. S. Feldman and G. R. Elliott (eds) *At the Threshold: The Developing Adolescent*, Cambridge, MA: Harvard University Press, pp. 123–46.

Spindler, G. and Spindler, L. (1991) 'Reactions and worries', *Anthropology and Education Quarterly*, **22**, pp. 274–78.

Wehlage, G., Smith, G. and Lipman, P. (1992) 'Restructuring urban schools: The new futures experience', *American Educational Research Journal*, **29**, 1, pp. 51–93.

Whaley, A. L. (1993) 'Self esteem, cultural identity, and psychosocial adjustment in African American children', *Journal of Black Psychology*, **19**, 4, pp. 406–22.

6 Black supplementary schools: spaces of radical blackness

Diane Reay and Heidi Safia Mirza

INTRODUCTION

Black supplementary schools are set up by and for the black community, and are for the most part self-funding, organic grassroots organisations. These schools which are mainly run by women have a history that reaches back into the 1950s, ever since the first wave of post-war black migrants arrived and settled in Britain (Reay and Mirza 1997). Unlike the visible, established, voluntary-aided religious ethnic minority schools of the Jewish, Seventh Day Adventist or Muslim community, the schools are difficult to locate as they exist deep within the informal black community and supported by the black church networks. Rooted often, but not necessarily, in Methodism, Evangelicalism, Pentecostalism, Rastafarianism or the Afrocentrism of Garveyism, black supplementary schools are hidden away from the public 'gaze' of funders and local authorities. They quietly go about their business in community centres, church halls, empty classrooms, and even the front rooms of dedicated black people.

The schools are small concerns run after school, on Saturdays or Sundays. They are mainly, though not exclusively, for school aged pupils 5–16 years. Though some schools could have as few as five pupils, the average school caters for 30–40 pupils. However popular schools could have as many as 90 pupils. As little or no 'official' information is available on these schools, personal and social networks, 'word of mouth' and tracing ads in the black community press yielded our information. In our limited short term research we found 60 black supplementary schools in the Inner London and Greater London area where approximately 300,000 African-Caribbeans live (58.7 per cent of the black population). In Lambeth, one of the London boroughs where the black people make up almost 30 per cent of the population, we found twelve such schools.

However, this small scale study of African-Caribbean supplementary schooling focused on just four of the schools: three London based schools, Colibri, Community Connections and Ohemaa and one in a provincial city, Scarlet Ibis. To gather qualitative data we carried out participant observation in two of the schools and conducted in-depth interviews with seven black educators involved in running the schools, six women and one man. A repeat interview has recently been conducted with one of the female black educators. In addition, eight mothers whose children attended two of the supplementary schools were interviewed.

Although all four schools saw their clientele as primarily African-Caribbean this did not mean that the schools were mono-cultural in terms of their ethnic composition. As one of the black educators pointed out, the schools were culturally diverse in their intake. Only one school saw including white pupils as an acceptable part of their remit, but all accepted African and mixed race students and one had a small number of Asian pupils attending.

Our findings, arising as they do out of a very small scale investigation based on sixteen qualitative interviews and three days of participant observation, are necessarily exploratory and tentative. However, we hope to indicate through our data that black supplementary schools, despite their quiet conformist exterior, contain elements that are both subversive and affirming, providing spaces of radical blackness.

ACTIVISM, SOCIAL CAPITAL AND BLACK FEMALE VERSIONS OF COMMUNITY

The seven black educators, six women and one man, whose in-depth interviews form the main data for this study, had been involved in supplementary schooling for periods ranging from four to sixteen years. They had often started out as a member of a small group of black parents, talking in terms of themselves 'and a few other mothers getting together'. As Charity points out:

> It's mainly women who are the ones who are involved in education in this country. Within the Afro-Caribbean community it tends to be mainly women. In my family that was the case and at Colibri it was mainly women who came and that was fine. Obviously, there were a few fathers who were involved and there were a couple of men on the committee but it was mainly women.

Charity's narrative not only highlights the key contribution of women; it also presents a very different version of urban black community to those endemic in popular media and political discourses:

> There was a group of about six parents, who like myself as a black teacher, were dissatisfied with what was happening to black pupils. They felt if they had been in the Caribbean their children would be much further on academically and they decided something had to be done, schools weren't doing anything so it had to be them. I really wish someone had the time to chart the enormous amount of work they put in those first few years. It was immense. The school started off in someone's front room on Saturday mornings. The parents doing all the teaching themselves to start with and it was very much focused on what was their main concern; their children not being able to read and write properly. Then these parents found the group of children grew from 10 to 15 and soon it was 20 and at this point it was unmanageable running a Saturday school in someone's front room so they petitioned the council for accommodation

and finally got one of the council's derelict properties. They spent their spare time shovelling rubbish out of the room, tramps had been living there, doing building, repair work, getting groups of parents together to decorate. They pulled together and did all this work themselves, used the expertise they had to get the school on its feet and it was mainly the women organising things, making sure it got done, although in those early days quite a few men were involved as well.

As Charity's words indicate, these four black supplementary schools generate rich opportunities for contesting prevalent discourses about contemporary urban communities. There is none of the apathy, recalcitrance, fecklessness and aggression which permeate both popular and political discourses. Dominant discourses of the urban working class, both black and white, paint pictures of apathetic masses, the inactive and uninformed. Once named 'the underclass' by the socially and politically privileged, and now renamed the 'socially excluded' by the New Labour elite, these urban communities have been ritually pathologised as disengaged, disadvantaged and inherent underachievers (SEU 1998).

However Charity tells a very different story; one of effective agency. The agency she speaks of is not the individualised agency of the white middle classes (Jordan *et al.* 1994; Reay 1998a), but rather a collectivised agency grounded in communal responses to a mainstream educational system which is perceived to be failing black children. In her narrative, and that of Verna quoted below, we hear commitment, reciprocity and continuity:

> I really wanted to do Saturday school because so much was given to me when I was a child. I had so much positive input I wanted to give some of it back. I also wanted to challenge this government's views on community – that community isn't important. Not that I'm interested in politics. I keep my head down. My work is on the ground with children, doing my bit here and it has been rewarding, very rewarding. Children have gone through the school that others have given up on and they are doing very well. Matthew who was so very, very difficult when he came, could not sit down for more than thirty seconds, I see him now on his way to college. Perhaps it is alright, you know, that this is a stage. The school has done a great deal for a number of children. I can see the fruits of my labour.
>
> (Verna)

Verna is not 'interested in politics', rather her focus is intensive work 'on the ground with children'. She is engaged in, dare we say, a variant of motherwork (Hill Collins 1994), but one which, despite her protestations, ultimately has a political edge. Verna's text also speaks of community; a community grounded in her own labour. Community as a concept may be out of favour within academic circles (Young 1990), but all the women used the term extensively in their narratives as something they were not simply a part of but were also actively engaged in constructing through their work as educators. As Rose stated emphatically,

An important part of Saturday school is about creating community. That's part of what we're here for.

In order to make sense of the enormous chasm between popular and elite prejudices in relation to urban communities and the actual practices going on within them we need to inject a gendered analysis (see also Burlet and Reid 1998). So many successful communities across all fields of society are founded on women's invisible unpaid labour despite the high profile of *male* leaders. In her exemplary work on 'reading the community' Valerie Hey differentiates between male strategies of commandeering social resources and female strategies of constructing social capital in order to develop effective community links (Hey 1998). The black women educators had minimal possibilities of commandeering social resources. Rather, they all worked incredibly hard to generate a sense of community and develop social capital out of friends and neighbour social relationships. As Hey succinctly puts it 'There are at least two versions of community – his and hers' (Hey 1998: 2) and these six Saturday schools were all built on 'her version'.

Similarly Patricia Hill Collins makes a case for appreciating the specific nature of black female 'community connectedness'. She suggests we should rearticulate black women's experiences with Afrocentric feminist thought in order to challenge prevailing definitions of community. She writes:

> The definition of community implicit in the market model sees community as arbitrary and fragile, structured fundamentally by competition and domination. In contrast, Afrocentric models stress connections, caring, and personal accountability . . . Denied access to the podium, black women have been unable to spend time theorising about alternative conceptualisations of community. Instead through daily actions African American women have created alternative communities that empower.
>
> (Hill Collins 1990: 223)

Patricia Hill Collins shows that through re-conceptualising the work of mothers, women educators, church and union leaders, community power is not about domination as in the Eurocentric perspective, but about energy which is fostered by creative acts of resistance. Bourdieu has developed the concept of social capital which illuminates this point of gendered community participation. He perceives social capital as contacts and group memberships which, through the accumulation of exchanges, obligations and shared identities, provide actual or potential support and access to valued resources (Bourdieu 1993). Social capital is underpinned by practices of sociability which require specific skills and dispositions. However, we suggest that there are gender implications which Bourdieu ignores but which would point to a connection between social capital and Helga Nowotny's concept of emotional capital.

Nowotny develops the concept of emotional capital which she defines as 'knowledge, contacts and relations as well as the emotionally valued skills and assets, which hold within any social network characterised at least partly by affective ties'

(Nowotny 1981: 148). As Virginia Morrow points out, 'this concept should alert us to the invisibility of women's work in creating and sustaining social networks and hence social capital' (Morrow 1999: 10). The black women through their involvement in supplementary schooling were producing resources to compensate for perceived deficits in state educational provision and thereby enhancing the black community's stock of both social and cultural capital.

All six women were extensively involved in the wider black community, as well as the community they saw themselves as actively constructing through black supplementary schooling. They were all facilitating black parents' groups and working with local black arts and business collectives. Two of the women were involved in national black women's networks (Sudbury 1998). The social capital generated through such contacts was fed back into the schools, benefiting the pupils in a variety of ways; through additional funding, sponsorship and curriculum enhancement. For example in Scarlet Ibis a local black business had paid for computing equipment, while members of the black arts collective had volunteered their services and provided sessions on pottery making, set design and printing.

There are a variety of competing tensions within representations of black supplementary schools as forms of private sector schooling and evidence of black enterprise. They can be depicted as autonomous self sufficient organisations; part of a vibrant growing largely unacknowledged black enterprise culture which spans commerce, the voluntary sector, and arts and education fields. Aligned with such understandings of black supplementary schools are views of them as predominantly community self-help projects. Such representations coalesce around new right, and increasingly, New Labour emphases on enterprise and local initiatives. Yet at the same time, there are other images which cut across and powerfully contradict such representations, in particular, black supplementary schooling's association with the political Left's project of anti-racism and the rediscovery of marginalised groups' histories.

SPACES OF RADICAL BLACKNESS

> White bias is everywhere in education, everywhere except in Saturday school, that is.
>
> (Brenda)

Nancy Fraser writes about 'hidden' public spheres which have always existed, including women's voluntary associations and working class organisations. In earlier work (Reay and Mirza 1997) we have argued that there are commonalities between black supplementary schools and the socialist Sunday schools at the turn of the century. Both constitute 'counter-publics'. Whereas the socialist Sunday schools struggled to produce working class discourses to counter hegemonic middle class views on education, black groups in society have repeatedly found it necessary within a wider social context of white hegemony to form 'subaltern counter-publics':

in order to signal that they are parallel discursive arenas where members of subordinated social groups invent and circulate counterdiscourses, which in turn permit them to formulate oppositional interpretations of their identities, interests and needs.

(Fraser 1994: 84)

As Fraser goes on to argue, subaltern counter-publics provide spaces of discursive contestation, generating challenges to the discursive status quo. On the surface black supplementary schools appear as sites for conformist reinscriptions of dominant discourses, in particular, those of meritocracy and traditional pedagogy. Yet, there exist parallel spaces of contestation within supplementary schooling. In all four black supplementary schools could be found a reworking of dominant discursive notions of blackness. They demark the limits of white hegemony, offering a disruptive discursive space:

I think one of the things we really succeed in is giving the children a positive sense of self. We help them feel comfortable with their blackness when out there they are bound to come up against situations in which they are made to feel uncomfortable about being black.

(Verna)

As Verna's words exemplify, in black supplementary schools can be found a blackness neither vulnerable nor under threat; rather a blackness comfortable with itself. The sense of community evoked by black supplementary schooling aspires to a positive sense of blackness. Other black women educators also gave a sense of supplementary schools as spaces of blackness that held transformative potential for black children:

Our children have said that there's something special about being in an all black environment. It's difficult to explain – that they have this sense of being able to unwind, to be themselves, relax, so that's part of what we provide – a safe environment.

(Charity)

As spaces of blackness these four supplementary schools provided their black pupils with familiarity and a sense of centrality often missing from their experience of mainstream schooling. This feeling of comfortable centrality was one in which materiality (the all black context) and the discursive (the valorisation of blackness) were crucially intertwined:

The first time I took him to Saturday school it was amazing. We discussed the Saturday school a lot. I saw Saturday school as at times a black home, you know, feeling 'oh my god I can't cope with looking at a book', Oh Akin just go away and read and I knew that really was not fair to him, he should be able to be motivated all the time. I feel that if someone else is able to do that with him it would be great and I feel the Saturday school will develop that interest in him – the sort of things I'm not able to do because of the pressure on my time. When I came back with him from Saturday school Akin was jumping all over the place and saying 'Mum why can't I go to this school five days a week?' He loved it, he was really really excited. He said I know all about so and so and about so and so, all these people from Black history. He was fascinated and up to now if he's going to do Black history he's really excited.

(Cassie)

In Cassie's words we find a sense of black supplementary schooling as a space of belonging and collectivity. For Cassie black supplementary school represents another home with all the connotations of familiarity and safety that encapsulates. But at the same time she stresses the educational gains. It is both home and school, a combination black children rarely find in mainstream schooling. Black supplementary schools provide places and spaces where blackness becomes a positive and powerful identification in contrast to mainstream schooling where, regardless of how many anti-racist policies are written, blackness is still constructed, at best as marginal, at worst as pathological (Gillborn 1995).

As Verna's, Cassie's and Charity's words above illustrate, black supplementary schools provide alternative, autonomous spaces where teachers and pupils can create oppositional and empowering narratives of blackness. Signithia Fordham (1996) has written about the psychological costs incurred when black pupils attempt to achieve academically in mainstream schooling. Because dominant discursive constructions of intellectual ability conflate blackness with being less intelligent she argues that these black pupils are forced into a situation where they must 'act white' if they are to succeed, so as not to run the risk 'liquidating the self'. In contrast, these black supplementary schools were attempting to provide 'sacred black spaces' where children could achieve educationally and still 'act black'.

In recent work bell hooks expresses regret at the passing of separate black spaces, arguing that it has become fashionable to deny any need for black segregation in a world where black people are surrounded by whiteness:

In the past separate space meant down time, time for recovery and renewal. It was the time to dream resistance, time to theorise, plan, create strategies and go forward. The time to go forward is still upon us and we have long surrendered segregated spaces of radical opposition.

(hooks 1995: 6)

We argue that in black supplementary schooling lies the genesis of hooks' 'segregated spaces of radical opposition'; not in the sense of confrontational male agitation but in a more reflexive, discursive sense. The black women educators were all engaged in various ways in rewriting blackness as a positive social identity in its own right. Such reconstructions while not oppositional in any traditional sense are written against the grain of the dominant discursive constructions of blackness as a negative reflection of whiteness which still prevail across British society.

It could be argued that in a key sense black supplementary schools are a response to black people's continuing exclusion from mainstream public spheres which in turn is primarily a consequence of endemic social and institutional racism (Troyna 1993). Indeed all the black women educators talked about the racism their pupils and their parents encountered outside of the black communities:

> The kids meet so much racism in their everyday lives racism is definitely on the agenda here. We wouldn't be doing our duty by the kids if it wasn't.
>
> (Natasha)

Black supplementary schools as 'counter institutional buffers' (Hill Collins 1990) are not simply defensive institutions – the product of racial oppression which fosters historically concrete communities among black people and other racial and ethnic groups. The black supplementary school is much more than simply a reaction to racism. Like other black community spaces they do not just provide a respite from oppressive situations or retreat from their effects. Rather, as Patricia Hill Collins suggests:

> black female spheres of influence constitute potential sanctuaries where individual black women are nurtured in order to confront oppressive social institutions.
>
> (Hill Collins 1990: 223)

In creating a sanctuary in which the black child is recentred black women decentre the popular pervasive public myth of black underachievement and educational alienation. As radical educators black women challenge the knowledge claims, pedagogy, and praxis of the mainstream schooling, and harness their own radical version of education as a means of transforming their lives.

However the very thing – spaces of blackness – which makes black supplementary schools so inviting for black pupils and the women who create and nurture them constitutes its threat for the white majority. Unlike 'separatist' private independent white schools which are welcomed as standard bearers and examples of good educational practice, black supplementary schools as sites of black solidarity are openly perceived by the white majority as threatening (Tomlinson 1985).

This threat is conceived on a number of different levels, from crude fears of the 'rising up of the oppressed', to slightly more sophisticated critiques which accept the validity of black supplementary schooling yet criticise them as segregationalist and isolationist. At the heart of this white fear is the simple fact that within black supplementary schools lie powerful evocations of difference and 'otherness' that challenge white dominant hegemonic values. The variety of ways in which black supplementary schools are seen by both the educational establishment and the broader British public raises questions around power, normativity and the endemic terror and fear of blackness that lurks deep within the white psyche (Mirza 1998).

PEDAGOGIC APPROACHES IN BLACK SUPPLEMENTARY SCHOOLS

We have examined black supplementary schools as places for the inscription of positive black identities. Beyond this we also wish to look at pedagogic approaches within the four schools and how they relate to mainstream approaches. The four schools all emphasised Black history and Black studies as part of their curriculum offer:

> We focus on English and Maths but integrate Black studies into our curriculum offer. For example we'll do a project on black women writers and that will be part of our English curriculum.
>
> (Maxine)

But more than that, they offered a space for what Rose called 'thinking black':

> You know you've got a maths problem about money and you don't even think about it – it's how much do three yams cost not three pounds of carrots. It's as natural as that just thinking black.
>
> (Rose)

While we expected black supplementary schools to generate oppositional discourses on blackness to those prevalent in wider white society, we did not expect our black women educators to espouse child centred philosophies which ran counter to dominant views on pedagogy within the educational field (Reay 1998b). However, they did:

> Well we have to be versatile. For example with Shona who teaches here she uses different types of groupwork. She has this group who are very bright and sometimes they'll work together then sometimes she'll put them with the slower children so they can learn from them. We try different ways. And really it is about helping these children realise their learning potential because no matter what the experts say different children have different learning styles, so you can't just use one. You have to keep trying until you find one to suit the child. We are very conscious of that here. We think it's very important to match teaching styles to the child's learning needs.
>
> (Maxine)

and:

> I have a very strong philosophy of child centredness. I have always been very committed to supporting the child. In our society children often don't have a voice. I suppose parents might have expected Saturday school to be more formal, I mean we work in groups there is no sitting in rows but I believe in working in ways that are best for the child so there is a strong focus on three Rs

but also on making the work really interesting for the child, starting from where the child is and integrating things around culture and history.

(Verna)

We are not simply arguing that black supplementary schools are 'havens' of progressive educational practice. However, we suggest that they draw on complex, contradictory pedagogical strands within which child centredness remains an important component. This is particularly surprising during an historical period in which progressivism has been discredited and superseded within mainstream schooling by more teacher directed approaches which are increasingly reliant on textbooks and whole class teaching.

There is research which indicates that mainstream schooling practice, even during the supposed heyday of progressivism in the 1960s and 1970s, was rarely child centred (Galton *et al.* 1980; Galton 1989). Such evidence makes the responses of the black women educators even more unanticipated. The only one of our seven respondents to prioritise formal ways of teaching over child centred approaches was the one male in the sample but he too recognised the contradictions. He talked at length about the importance of differentiation but saw child centred approaches as too idealistic and time consuming. While the women's solution was a focus on meeting the needs of the individual child, Michael felt the only practical response was ability grouping.

However, the women's words need to be contextualised within a very real tension between the reinscription of traditional curricula through the strong focus on basic skills and the 3 Rs in all four schools, and competing progressive tendencies which prioritised children's initiative and creativity, and their autonomy as learners. All seven black educators were juggling difficult tensions between fitting in with mainstream and a clear conviction that they could meet the children's needs more effectively. For the black women educators there were additional tensions between parental demands and their own educational philosophies and between their often explicit focus on empowerment and the need to raise educational standards.

Our focus is on four schools and we cannot argue that they are typical of black supplementary schooling as a whole. As Sewell's research would seem to indicate, the field of supplementary schooling is characterised by heterogeneity and difference (Sewell 1996). However, we do argue that our data reveals strands of progressivism and child centredness in all four schools. For example all the schools had a regular circle time and a focus on Black studies, while two of the schools had a strong commitment to child centredness that infused all of the curriculum offer. Thus we can say in marked contrast to mainstream schooling, black supplementary schools demonstrate in their praxis that high standards, a child centred approach, and a relevant curriculum, for black as well as white children, are all possible to achieve.

CONCLUSION

In their implicit critique of pervasive unspoken whiteness of mainstream schooling, black supplementary schools put on the historical agenda new problems for society to solve. Black supplementary schools provide a 'sacred space of blackness' (Foley 1998) that enables the affirming of selfhood that the white majority take for granted in their privileged spaces of whiteness in mainstream schools. The black women educators were all engaged in various ways in rewriting blackness as a positive 'normative' social identity in its own right (see also Mirza 1997a; 1997b). Such reconstructions, while not oppositional in any traditional confrontational (masculine) sense, are written in opposition to the dominant discursive constructions of blackness as a negative reflection of whiteness which still prevail across British society.

The women were also reworking notions of community. The sense of community engendered through these black women's activities, embracing as it does an inter-dependency of the individual and the necessity of the communal, is very different from the traditional notion of community as defined through market forces. The mission of the four supplementary schools in our study is to integrate educational success with a commitment to remaining true to one's origins. On the surface black supplementary schools appear as sites for conformist reinscriptions of dominant discourses, in particular, those of meritocracy and traditional pedagogy. Yet, there exist parallel spaces of contestation within supplementary schooling in which goals of enabling young black people to achieve academically are combined with a simultaneous opposition to the system, an opposition which is encoded discursively rather than enacted antagonistically. Within the black supplementary schools in our study black women were working ceaselessly to create 'oppositional meaning' and facilitate social transformation through their sustained efforts in the three areas of community building, visions of blackness, and radical pedagogic practice.

REFERENCES

Bourdieu, P. (1993) *Sociology in Question*, London: Sage.
Burlet, Stacey and Reid, Helen (1998) 'A gendered uprising: political representation and minority ethnic communities', *Ethnic and Racial Studies* **21**, 2, pp. 270–87.
Foley, Douglas (1998) 'Review Symposium; Blacked Out: Dilemmas of Race, Identity and Success at Captial High', *Race Ethnicity and Education* **1**, 1, March pp. 131–35.
Fordham, Signithia (1996) *Blacked-Out: Dilemmas of Race, Identiy and Success at Capital High*, Chicago: University of Chicago Press.
Fraser, Nancy (1994) 'Rethinking the public sphere: a contribution to the critique of actually existing democracy', in H. A. Giroux and P. McLaren (eds) *Between Borders: Pedagogy and the Politics of Cultural Studies*, New York: Routledge, pp. 74–98.
Galton, M. (1989) *Teaching in the Primary School*, London: David Fulton Publishers.
Galton, M., Simon, B. and Croll, P. (1980) *Inside the Primary Classroom*, London: Routledge and Kegan Paul.
Gillborn, David (1995) *Racism and Anti-racism in Real Schools*, Buckingham: Open University Press.

Hey, V. (1998) 'Reading the community: A critique of some post/modern narratives about citizenship and civil society' in P. Bagguley and G. Hearn (eds) *Transforming the Political*, London: Macmillan.

Hill Collins, Patricia (1990) *Black Feminist Thought: Knowledge, Consciousness and the Politics of Empowerment*, London: Routledge.

Hill Collins, Patricia (1994) 'Shifting the center: race, class and feminist theorizing about Motherhood' in D. Bassin, M. Honey and M. M. Kaplan (eds) *Representations of Motherhood*, New Haven: Yale University Press.

hooks, bell (1995) *Killing Rage: Ending Racism*, London: Penguin Books.

Jordan, B., Redley, M. and James, S. (1994) *Putting the Family First: Identities, Decisions, Citizenship*, London: UCL Press.

Mirza, Heidi Safia (1997a) 'Black women in education; A collective movement for social change' in H. S. Mirza (ed.) *Black British Feminism*, London: Routledge.

Mirza, Heidi Safia (1997b) 'Mapping a genealogy of black British feminism' in H.S. Mirza *Black British Feminism*, London: Routledge.

Mirza, Heidi Safia (1998) 'Black masculinity and schooling: A black feminist response', *British Journal of Sociology of Education* (forthcoming).

Morrow, V. (1999) 'Conceptualising social capital in relation to health and well-being for children and young people: A critical review', *Sociological Review*, 47, pp. 744–65.

Nowotny, H. (1981) 'Women in public life in Austria' in Cynthia Fuchs Epstein and Rose Laub Coser (eds) *Access to Power: Cross-National Studies of Women and Elites*, London: George Allen and Unwin.

Reay, D. (1998a) *Class Work: Mothers' Involvement in Their Children's Primary Schooling*, London: University College Press.

Reay, D. (1998b) 'Setting the agenda: the growing impact of market forces on pupil grouping in British secondary schooling', *Journal of Curriculum Studies*, **30**, 5, pp. 545–58.

Reay, D. and Mirza, H. (1997) 'Uncovering genealogies of the margins: Black supplementary schooling', *British Journal of Sociology of Education*, **18**, 4 December pp. 477–99.

SEU (1998) *Bringing Britain Together: A National Strategy for Neighbourhood Renewal*, Report by the Social Exclusion Unit; Cmd 4045, London: HMSO.

Sewell, Tony (1996) *South London Supplementary/Heritage Schools: Shifting Out of Dominance*, Paper presented at British Educational Research Association Conference, Lancaster University: September.

Sudbury, Julia (1998) *'Other Kinds of Dreams': Black Women's Organisations and the Politics of Transformation*, London: Routledge.

Tomlinson, S. (1985) 'The "Black Education" movement' in M. Arnot (ed.) *Race and Gender*, Oxford: Pergamon Press.

Troyna, Barry (1993) *Racism and Education: Research Perspectives*, Buckingham: Open University Press.

Young, Iris, M. (1990) 'The ideal of community and the politics of difference' in Linda Nicolson (ed.) *Feminism/Postmodernism*, London: Routledge.

Part III

Reflections on social exclusion and inclusion

7 The exclusion of Black children: implications for a racialised perspective[1]

Richard Majors, David Gillborn and Tony Sewell

Letter to the *Times Educational Supplement*, 30 January 1998, p. 24

We welcome the Government's commitment to raising standards for all our school children.

The general issues of school exclusions and truancy have rightly been made a priority by the Government through its social exclusion unit. In order to focus our efforts, we strongly urge the unit and the Government to consult education partners to determine the reasons for ethnic minority over-representation among young people excluded from schools.

Having consulted, we would expect the Government to examine ways of putting in place the support that schools need to deal with it through local authority behaviour plans and other means.

This over-representation can not continue. A target date for its elimination agreed with education partners would help provide the stimulus needed to mobilise the system to end it. The same logic underlies the welcome literacy targets, and measures for dealing more generally with the underachievement of boys. With leadership and determination, targets such as these can be met.

Sir Herman Ouseley (Chairman, Commission for Racial Equality); Graham Lane (Chair, education committee, Local Government Association); Lee Jasper (Director, 1990 Trust); Sukvinder Stubbs (Chief Executive, Runnymede Trust); Peter Smith (General Secretary, Association of Teachers and Lecturers); Doug McAvoy (General Secretary, National Union of Teachers)

A letter to the *Times Educational Supplement*, signed by representatives of two of the largest teaching organisations and leading 'race relations' bodies, issues a powerful challenge to the educational system. We believe that the letter's goals, on reducing the exclusion and underachievement of Black students, are both practical and timely. Additionally, as active researchers in the field, we believe that many of the underlying causes have already been identified. We can no longer afford policies that fail to address the racialised and racially discriminatory practices and assumptions that currently permeate the education system. Our research continually reveals the importance of racism and culture as central issues in the processes that underlie exclusions from school. To address these issues constructively will take a radical shift in thinking, away from narrow punitive models (which place blame for exclusions on the students and their families) and towards a recognition that exclusions represent the tip of a much larger iceberg of differential treatment, lower expectations and discriminatory structures.

Teachers and other educationalists want support in addressing the existing inequalities. We believe that policy has a vital role to play in supporting and extending attempts to create a more inclusive education system.

While we value the potential contributions of Tony Blair's social exclusion unit and Estelle Morris's advisory group on Ethnic Minority achievement,[2] we believe that the issue of Black exclusions may not be addressed adequately or may get lost amidst the focus on achievement.

We therefore recommend that an independent commission be established which deals exclusively with exclusions. Thus we believe that the time is now ripe to identify the exclusion of Black children as an issue of national importance, as significant as the campaign concerned with literacy and numeracy, demanding concerted and sustained efforts across the system.

The recent report by the Social Exclusion Unit (1998) sets the first ever national target on exclusions: 'that by 2002 there will be a one third reduction in the numbers of both permanent and fixed-term exclusions'. In some respects this target is ambitious and welcome; unfortunately, it does not begin to address the issue that concerns us here, the exclusion of *Black children*. The problem with the target is that it is colour-blind; it sets a universal figure for reduction and makes no reference to the over-exclusion of Black children. This is out of keeping with other parts of the report which, for example, accept that African Caribbean children are much more likely to be excluded and that teacher stereotyping may be implicated in the process (Social Exclusion Unit, 1998; para 2.18). By failing to stipulate a specific target for a reduction in the exclusion of Black children the way is left clear for the situation to persist or even worsen. Previous research suggests that Black children are unlikely to share equally in any improvement, and that by 2002, therefore, we could be in a position where the relative over-representation of Black children has actually grown.

THE SIGNIFICANCE OF RACE AND CULTURE: A STATE OF EMERGENCY

The latest DfEE statistics show that boys account for the overwhelming majority of all exclusions (83 per cent of permanent exclusions in 1995–6). Within this total Ofsted and the DfEE have shown that African Caribbean boys are 4–6 times more likely to be excluded than their white counterparts. Therefore ethnic origin appears to play a significant role. Whenever data is broken down by ethnicity, Black young people are shown to be considerably more likely to be excluded than their white peers.

However it is known that the official statistics underestimate the true level of exclusions among black boys. For example, there are no national figures on the numbers of fixed term exclusions. Moreover, 'informal' or 'back door' exclusions complicate the problem. Parents are often persuaded to withdraw their child before formal exclusions occur. Additionally, teachers will often send a child home during the day, which goes unrecorded as an exclusion.

Taking into account the wealth of evidence, including the statistics above, it is vital that we racialise expulsions of Black boys, that is we address the role of 'race', culture and racism. Failure to do this will only exacerbate the current problem.

There is growing evidence that the exclusion of Black young people reflects the operation of deeply held, but complex, differential expectations and assumptions. Qualitative research, often involving detailed interview and observational work in schools, suggests that white teachers often expect Black children to present a more frequent and a more severe threat to their authority. This can lead to teachers acting against Black children more quickly and harshly than their white peers. Recent DfEE statistics (1995–96) highlight the racialised process of discipline and control towards Black boys. For example, the latest figures allow the calculation of how many individual young people are over-represented in the rate of exclusions: compared to the white and Asian exclusions each year, around 1000 extra Black young people are permanently excluded from school (Gillborn, 1998). Given such gross inequalities, it is reasonable to conclude that racism plays a major role in producing these extra exclusions. Therefore, race, ethnicity and the school you attend are often indicators of whether or not you will be excluded from school. Not only does the data show that exclusions have been racialised; many Black children feel personally that they have been victims of racism. For example, *The Black Child Report* (Amenta Marketing, 1997) found that 22 per cent of children they sampled felt they had been subjected to racism from the teacher over the previous four weeks. This is higher than the perceived racism from classmates.

This finding is not surprising, given the fact that research has found that Black boys often get excluded or disciplined for exhibiting culture specific behaviours (e.g. hair styles, eye behaviour, walking styles) in the classroom. Research has shown that the more Black children deny their Black culture and 'act white' in the classroom, the less likely they are to be over monitored, disregarded or harassed by teachers. This phenomenon has been referred to as 'racelessness' (see Fordham 1996; Sewell 1997).

To preserve culture and identity, Black boys can become involved in 'challenging' and/or protest behaviours with teachers to gain respect. Therefore, for many Black boys, school is not viewed as a place of learning but rather a battleground to gain recognition.

Exclusion is just the tip of the iceberg and is the last stage of a racialised process. Therefore many of the interactions between Black boys and teachers which precede exclusions are racialised. Areas of conflict between teachers and Black students that are frequently racialised are:

interpersonal relationships;
fear and stereotyping of Black boys;
the application of differential classroom management and discipline;
low expectations of Black boys;
harassment by teachers.

Recognising the role of 'race' in exclusions is not enough, what we need is a new model for understanding Black students in particular. The multicultural model (that focuses on dress, food, religion and festivals) is inappropriate for understanding deeper and profound aspects of one's culture. A more appropriate cultural model would be one that explores ones feelings, values, emotions and identity within a context of racialised and unequal power structures.

THE COST OF EXCLUSIONS

Social exclusion among Black boys threatens all our communities, challenges our school and criminal justice system and weakens our economy. The education for one permanently excluded pupil in 1994–5 cost the equivalent of £4,300, which is twice the cost of mainstream education. Taking into account the impact of exclusions on social services, health, criminal justice, the total cost of exclusions is about £84 million a year (Parsons 1996).

POLICY AND RECOMMENDATIONS

The school system is failing to engage Black boys. When Black boys have discipline or emotional problems, we have had a long history of separating them from institutions rather than claiming them or embracing them. We therefore believe exclusion will continue to grow, extracting an enormous cost on human potential and society until we racialise exclusions and underachievement.

In face of these issues, we need concerted and sustained policies to achieve justice and inclusion. Therefore, some of the areas we would like to address are:

- Competence in behaviour management across culture
- The development of an exclusion working group that focuses exclusively on exclusions and culture
- Short term and long term strategies to reduce exclusions
- Development of an implementation plan and target setting
- Ethnic monitoring
- Development of the curriculum to make it relevant to all pupils
- Development of a new pastoral system to meet the needs of children (some children who have been referred for help may not be seen by a specialist for up to a year).

A central tenet of Labour's policy proposals has been a concern with social justice, social inclusion and equality of opportunity. These are important aims and research suggests they can be achieved, even in difficult and complex fields such as this. We hope that by interrogating the best current research in this area, we *can* play a role in promoting future gains in this most vital of areas.

REFERENCES

Amenta Marketing (1997) *The Black Child Report*, London: Amenta Marketing.

Department for Education and Employment (1997) *Permanent Exclusions from School in England 1995/96*, London: DfEE.

Fordham, S. (1996) *Blacked Out: Dilemmas of Race, Identity and Success at Capital High*, Chicago: University of Chicago Press.

Gillborn, D. (1998) 'Exclusion from School: An Overview of the Issues', in N. Donovan (ed.) *Second Chances: Exclusion from School and Equality of Opportunity*, London: New Policy Institute.

Parsons, C. (1996) *Exclusions from School: A Public Cost*, London: CRE.

Sewell, T. (1997) *Black Masculinities and Schooling: How Black Boys Survive Modern Schooling*, Stoke-on-Trent: Trentham.

Social Exclusion Unit (1998) *Truancy and School Exclusion Report*, London: HMSO.

NOTE

1   This paper is based on a 1998 DfEE presentation by the authors. The paper originally appeared in *Multicultural Teaching* (Summer 1998) Vol. 16, No. 3. It appears here with kind permission of the publishers.

8 Educational psychologists and Black exclusion: towards a framework for effective intervention

Karl Brooks and Denny Grant

> Education is the only real way for Black people to have a chance of surviving in this country; exclusions rob our kids of that chance.
>
> (Black parent)

For the Black community in Britain exclusion from school has been a source of anger and dissatisfaction for several generations. It seems ironic to most Black parents that there is now such an outcry, when collectively the wider public have not taken any notice of the warning signs throughout the past decades. Perhaps it is as one parent suggested: 'It's only now that white kids are also getting excluded that you hear anything about it'.

Exclusions have risen dramatically, creating public interest, which has pushed the topic away from the margins of educational debate. Academics, legislators and the general public now seem to agree that it deserves more than just peripheral attention.

Despite the growing concern, educational psychologists as a professional group are still looking for coherence around their role in the exclusion process, or, even more positively, the part they can play helping to find solutions to the problem. In previous articles, the authors (Grant and Brooks 1996 and 1998) have argued for a framework of policies and good practice to address the needs of pupils at risk of exclusion. That should be seen as part and parcel of the service provided to all students with particular needs in the education process.

Others have joined in the call for a radical review of the role of educational psychologists, so that their 'expertise' can be used more productively in support of schools (DfEE Green Paper 1997), particularly in relation to pupils with emotional and behavioural difficulties. In his response to the Green Paper, Wood (1998) articulated a widely-felt need for a clear delineation of the psychological components of what educational psychologists can offer.

In this chapter an attempt is made to set out a framework of policies and procedures to enable psychologists to draw upon core professional knowledge and skills, working at all levels towards the prevention of exclusions. Examples are given of policies devised and implemented within a local education authority, as well as casework with individual pupils and their families.

HISTORICAL PERSPECTIVE: IMMIGRATION, EDUCATION IDEOLOGY AND COMMUNITY RESPONSE

Black people have been regarded as 'a problem' right from the early days of immigration to the present – though in the UK they still constitute less than 1 per cent of the population. This kind of prevailing attitude in the host community is still reflected in government legislation, which oscillates between immigration control and race relation guidelines.

Historically, educational policy development in Britain presents a patchwork approach to race issues. In effect there have been various attempts to ignore, remove or at least arrive at an accommodation of 'the problem'. This is illustrated by measures such as 'bussing' and Section 11 funding, and is further reflected in reports such as Plowden (DES 1967), Rampton (DES 1981) and Swann (DES 1985). The underlying fears of the host community have precipitated approaches attempting to accommodate Black pupils within the education system and to somehow dilute their perceived detrimental effect on schools – but without resolving the inherent conflicts.

TEACHER ATTITUDE AND WIDER SCHOOL EFFECTS

Factors such as those described above contribute to what Smith and Tomlinson (1990) call the 'school effect'. This can be further deconstructed into key elements, one of which is a 'teacher effect' that plays a significant part in deciding the success, or otherwise, of individual pupils.

Historical and ideological factors have all had an effect on the formative years of individuals who eventually become teachers. Furthermore, as researchers such as Tomlinson (1981) suggest, the influence of the media and the pervasive effect of various (racist) theories on Black–White differentials in intelligence (Jensen 1969 and Eysenck 1971) and language competence (DES 1967 and Bernstein 1971) have all had a negative influence on teachers' education and training.

The Elton Report (DES 1989) stated that the main reason for unruly pupils was bad management of the school as a whole, compounded by poor standards of teaching and management in the classroom. Further, the work being offered to pupils was seen as unsuitable and not well planned. It suggested also that many pupils, particularly adolescents, are disruptive because schools fail to recognise that they should be treated with respect. It is our contention and that of other writers (Callender 1997; Sewell 1997 and Gillborn 1990) that these issues are especially relevant when we consider the education, or mis-education, of Black children.

It is now more than a warranted assertion that a significant number of teachers will approach their task with deeply entrenched negative expectations of Black children. They will have had their attitudes, beliefs and behaviour conditioned by history, and then further shaped by popular myths (regarding child-rearing practices, Black–White differentials in IQ etc.) that are still prevalent in today's society. In a cumulative way they serve to perpetuate and legitimise the disadvantage that Black children suffer in school.

This helps to explain why Black pupils are regarded as a problem and how they become victims of discrimination in British schools through the 'host' community's systematic attempt to eradicate a perceived threat.

SPECIAL EDUCATION AND EXCLUSION LEGISLATION

The seemingly inextricable link between the educational experience of Black children and the development of special education is well documented (Coard 1971; Stone 1981). The Warnock Report (DES 1978) provides a historical reference point and the foundation for most of what exists for special educational needs. The notion of 20 percent of pupils at any given time having special needs has become a common yardstick among local authorities and schools. So too, the more stringent criterion that only the bottom 2 percent of children should require special school provision.

The 1981 Education Act was introduced to provide an objective and consistent framework for the identification and support of those children with greatest need. However, it soon became clear that there was a trend towards legislation and special needs procedures being used in such as way as to hasten the removal of Black students from mainstream education. Tomlinson (1981) found, for example, that the assessment process was twice as fast for Black children and four times more likely to end in an inappropriate placement in special school.

Similarly, in 1984 a survey within the Inner London Education Authority (ILEA 1984 Report 4627) showed that the over-representation of Black students in special schools and units tended to be within those categories of need that depended on the interpretative assessment of teachers and educational psychologists. Consequently, Black children were over-represented in schools for disruptive behaviour and language impairment.

More recently the Audit Commission (1992) observed that LEAs were still having difficulty implementing systems for managing the performance of schools in response to pupil needs. There was little evidence of the staged approach as outlined in the original Warnock Report. This reflected a national picture showing wide variation and lack of consistency that no doubt informed the highly prescriptive nature of subsequent legislation such as the 1993 Education Act and 1994 Code of Practice.

Those who are engaged in regular consultation to schools will have realised that there are often structural divisions in their internal organisation that impede the process of responding to and caring for pupils. This may be reflected in a lack of co-ordination between pastoral and curriculum responsibilities, such that some tutors and the students in their group spend little time together beyond a brief moment for daily registration. Yet teachers who are 'subject specialists' may be given neither the time nor any kind of brief for the special needs or social well being of students.

For many teachers special needs is well outside their own 'comfort zone'. Part of their defence mechanism is to regard those with special needs as somehow different from 'normal' children and justify shifting responsibility for their support to someone else. Added to that is another artificial dichotomy between special needs (seen as synonymous with learning difficulties) and behaviour problems. Therefore, in practice teachers have tended to refer children with learning difficulties (e.g. literacy problems) to educational psychologists but leave those with behaviour problems to go down the slippery slope towards exclusion.

EXCLUSION LEGISLATION: FURTHER CONFUSION AND ABUSE

The 1986 Education (No. 2) Act introduced three categories of exclusion – Fixed term, Indefinite and Permanent. The act provided a national framework for exclusions through which a coherent and consistent approach to its implementation ought to have been possible. Regrettably, this has not been so in practice as the number of exclusions across the country continued to rise at an alarming rate (*TES* 9 Dec. 1994). Furthermore, because of the differences in practice from school to school and the wide variations in the way LEAs collected the necessary data, the national picture remained extremely confused.

It is now clear that there was an increase of 30–50 per cent across all categories of exclusion. Initial estimates from a national survey suggested that between 1990 and 1992 there were over 6700 permanent exclusions (DES 1994). Figures for the academic year 1996–7 put the official total at 12,800 permanent exclusions. However, as before, there are indications that if all categories of exclusions were included, the figure would almost certainly be much higher.

In the past there was widespread abuse of indefinite exclusion, with children out of schools for years in some cases. Today there are still various permutations of unofficial exclusions. Apart from the better known types of exclusion, there is a significantly greater number of 'informal exclusions' and many forms of exclusions within schools that are virtually never recorded. 'Internal exclusions' occur in the form of the pupil being subjected to time-out both in and outside the classroom; placed in internal suspension or support units; on extended work-experience; or forced into alternative curricular options i.e. less academic subjects. There are also occasions when parents are encouraged to withdraw the child and find another school to avoid the formal processes and the stigma of permanent exclusion.

Thus, a legacy of confusing legislation has contributed to a morass of illegal and morally questionable professional practice (see *Childright*, Sept. 1994). The 1993 Education Act attempted to streamline and clarify regulations by allowing only two forms of exclusion – Fixed term and Permanent. Although this gave some hope that it would help improve matters, it seemed to have the opposite effect in giving rise to a 'dramatic increase in the exclusion rate' (*TES* December 1994).

RECENT DEVELOPMENTS IN EXCLUSION LEGISLATION

Exclusions from school have been the subject of much media attention, based on some high profile cases which, although few in number, have given rise to more open and public interrogation of the issues. There have been numerous national conferences to increase awareness and widen debate.

Resulting from this kind of attention some key factors have been identified (Grant and Brooks 1996; Gillborn and Gipps 1996) as contributing to the rise in exclusions:

economic factors;
local management of schools,
league tables;
Grant Maintained Status
increasing youth crime and delinquency, and
the National Curriculum.

While these factors apply to all pupils, there is no shortage of evidence showing a more severe impact on Black pupils – hence the disproportionately high rate of exclusion from that section of the school population.

Until the recent OFSTED publication (Gillborn and Gipps 1996) there had been no large-scale examination of the performance of Black pupils in British schools since the Swann Report (DES, 1985). It appeared therefore that issues of race and ethnicity had been slipping from the national policy agenda.

More recent publications (cited above) highlight a number of additional factors compounding the problem of exclusion for Black pupils. For example, despite the general increase in academic achievement in many LEAs, African Caribbean children continue to achieve below white children in schools. There is also evidence that the gap is widening. While Black children enter education on par with their counterparts, the evidence shows that white pupils are also making greater progress in primary school than ethnic minority children. It seems that Black children are at a disadvantage from the moment they enter school. There are unusually high levels of conflict between White teachers and African Caribbean pupils which Gillborn (1990) summed up by stating that for some Black pupils ability and hard work alone are not enough to achieve academic success. They must also develop strategies to handle White teachers' assumptions that they are a likely cause of disruption.

Other researchers (e.g. Mac an Ghaill 1988 and Callender 1997) suggest that in some cases this conflict is in evidence despite the best intentions of teachers. Sewell (1997) points to a combination of gender- and race-specific stereotypes that makes success particularly difficult for African Caribbean young men. This is especially true for those students who respond negatively to school as a means of resisting perceived injustices (see also Mac an Ghaill 1988). There are many complaints that racial harassment continues to be a widespread occurrence, yet many incidents go undetected or trivialised by teachers.

With this kind of complex inter play of factors, as part of the increase in the number of exclusions from school, African Caribbean students are estimated to be between three and six times more likely to be excluded than whites. This rather gloomy picture is exacerbated by the fact that two out of three pupils permanently excluded from school never return to mainstream education.

NEW GOVERNMENT PROPOSALS

The government's latest proposals relating to exclusion have been set out in the Education Act 1997. In a previous article the authors provided a more detailed critique of this Act in relation to exclusions (Grant and Brooks 1998). Since that time the long awaited DfEE guidance, following the 1997 Act, was issued only in late autumn 1998. It does however include some definite steps to address the problem of rising exclusion:

- targets to reduce the level of exclusions by a third between 1998 and year 2002;
- money to be taken from the school's budget and follow the student if they are permanently excluded;
- LEAs to ensure that permanently excluded pupils get full-time education.

While the proposed legislation attempts to present financial disincentives to schools, it does not provide any radical changes in exclusion procedures and is therefore unlikely to impact on the rate of exclusions from school in the way anticipated by the government. Indeed, this is made less likely while, at the same time, there are new regulations to give more powers to schools and reduce the role of the LEA in the exclusion process. Parents could be left even more at the mercy of headteachers, without the possibility of any effective support from the LEA.

Black students are still most likely to continue to suffer because of the absence of any radical government proposals to eliminate exclusions by attacking the problem at the root cause. What is still lacking is an acknowledgement of the underlying racism giving rise to the large number of Black children excluded from school. There are reservations regarding how effective target setting is likely to be in bringing about a net reduction in the rate of exclusions. However, Majors *et al.* (1998) argue that by failing to set a specific target for a reduction in the exclusion rate for Black pupils it is likely that the present over-representation is set to continue or get worse.

Little has changed therefore, since it is still left to Black parents, concerned professionals and members of the community to develop strategies to combat exclusions. Effective initiatives are even more urgent as the latest estimates suggest that in parts of Britain, the over-representation of Black children among those who have been permanently excluded could be as high as fifteen times the rate of their White peers (*TES* 11 December 1998).

EXCLUSION AND THE ROLE OF EDUCATIONAL PSYCHOLOGISTS

Educational Psychologists (EPs) have traditionally considered themselves some-how removed from the exclusion process. The *Core Principles for the Training of Educational Psychologists* (BPS, 1998) does not mention this important area in a list of items put forward to form the core curriculum for training. For most educational psychologists in training, exclusion forms part of a one-off input on behaviour or discipline. Only more recently has this begun to change and courses are including a focus on exclusion. For some courses there may even be a more thorough analysis of the issues, with particular reference to race and gender.

The traditional approach for educational psychologists when asked to comment on issues regarding exclusion has been to offer some general advice about behaviour but make it clear that they have no role in the exclusion process. This has been regarded as within the sole domain of the headteacher who has the absolute right to exclude a pupil. There is little to indicate how headteachers arrive at such a critical decision, in terms of the life chances of a pupil; nor what support structures they can call upon when doing so. To what extent are educational psychologists regarded in schools as a possible source of support around this issue?

The work of educational psychologists is largely governed by the regulations of the 1981 Education (Special Educational Needs) Act, which have been updated but not radically altered by subsequent legislation. The 1981 Act, founded on the egalitarian principles of the Warnock Report, gave educational psychologists a clear and pivotal role in assessing and meeting the needs of children who did not fit neatly into the educational process. These children were considered in need of extra support to have the benefit of a worthwhile education. However, the legislation gave no consideration to the fact that Warnock principles could also encompass the needs of children who might be under consideration for exclusion. And exclusion has scarcely been mentioned in successive special education legislation until the aforementioned 1997 Education Act.

Kay Kinder (1997) provides some pointers to the role of EPs in combating exlusions in her review of a study by the National Foundation for Educational Research. This research looked at the way in which exclusions are used by schools and identified a range of strategies that seemed to be effective in 'allowing for recovery and reintegration' with pupils who had been excluded.

> Small group settings, therapeutic intervention, alternative learning experiences, positive and sustained relationships with key adults who offer respect and regard, and training pupils in managing emotions and behaviour seemed to be recurring features.
>
> (Kinder 1997: 10)

Kinder arrives at the following conclusion:

> All this suggests the need for schools and parents to be skilled in **understanding** behaviour and not just **managing** it.
>
> (op. cit.: 10)

Kinder also alludes to a function for educational psychologists in the exclusion process when she argues that the right to remove 'socially dysfunctional' pupils should be matched by a clear statutory requirement to teach the skills and thinking that underpin responsible behaviour. Educational psychologists are uniquely placed to provide training and support to parents, teachers and pupils in both understanding and managing behaviour. There are well documented accounts of educational psychologists using a functional analysis approach in helping to understand and modify even the most severe and challenging behaviour, see for example Pitchford (1994) and Roderick *et al.* (1997).

Similarly Guishard (1998) provides an account of a proactive approach using a multi-disciplinary model to prevent problems developing in a school context, working closely with the pupil and her/his parent. Bearing in mind the observations of Majors and colleagues (1998) it is important that educational psychologists are especially vigilant in addressing the needs of Black pupils, including the manner in which they are identified, assessed and supported within school. In doing so, educational psychologists should heed the warning of Phoenix (1996) and others to ensure that they do not contribute to the process by which the performance of White children is used as the norm against which Black pupils are judged. Cultural sensitivity and the adoption of a reflective perspective would help to promote an anti-racist approach within the profession and in the wider society.

LOOKING TO THE FUTURE: TOWARDS A FRAMEWORK FOR EFFECTIVE INTERVENTION

Crucial to any framework or basis for intervention are the underlying principles that inform practice. As well as those that are non-controversial, such as the aim to improve communication and achieve greater consistency, others are more problematic and therefore often neglected. Early intervention seems a particularly important principle when considering the negative experiences of Black students and their prevalence in exclusion statistics. So too are principles of partnership, parental involvement and equal opportunity. These will be considered in more detail, particularly in terms of their implication for Black parents.

PARENTAL INVOLVEMENT AND EQUAL OPPORTUNITY

Commentators such as Acland (1971), Lunt and Sheppard (1986) and Gross (1996) attest to the benefits of involving parents closely in their children's education. Acland (1971) suggested that the essence of parent participation is that parents come to school, learn about the way the school operates and through doing this become more effective so far as their child's education is concerned.

Calliste (1993) highlights some prerequisites for effective parental involvement:

> . . . this is possible only with a considerable change in professional attitude and awareness on several counts: a) one's own manner of operating as a professional; b) the needs of the parents; and c) factors in the wider society.

> (Calliste 1993: 77)

Parental involvement is however not a simple, straightforward matter and gives rise to a number of attendant issues. There is for example an equal opportunities issue, with Black and minority ethnic groups particularly feeling dissatisfied with state education, the lack of consultation and mistrust of education professionals (Rehal 1988; Calliste 1993). Black parents have tended to stay clear of bureaucratic structures and procedures. Hornby (1994) suggests that we need to consider the 'special needs of parents' and look at the circumstances of the whole family during the process of assessment and support. It is important that at this point we begin to recognise a raft of fundamental principles, such as those mentioned above, which are all closely interwoven. It is important that a framework for intervention should involve a commitment to early action and sustained involvement.

EARLY INTERVENTION THROUGH LIAISON MEETINGS

Some of the best examples of Warnock principles put into practice were established before the 1994 Code of Practice. There seems little doubt that the national framework was based on examples of good practice observed by government officials up and down the country. Among those 'leading lights' was the London Borough of Hackney Special Needs Profiling system which was informed by the core principles mentioned above, such as parental partnership and equal opportunity (Grant, awaiting publication). An important element also was that Hackney's Profiling system was established on a sound foundation of multi-professional service delivery. Long before the construction of the profiling system, the educational psychology service had established a model of service delivery based on regular liaison meetings. These were meetings convened by the head with help from the school's educational psychologist and attended by key professionals working in support of the school. Essentially these were half-termly meetings with the following main functions:

(a)   to provide an opportunity for teachers to consult specialist and support professionals at an early stage (i.e. Warnock Stage 2) either directly or through the school's special needs co-ordinator or headteacher;

(b)   to facilitate joint work in support of pupils and to review progress;

(c)   to share information pertaining to work with individual pupils or the school in general, in order to ensure a co-ordinated approach;

(d)   to consider parental views and involvement in work with teachers and/or other professionals;

(e)   to decide, jointly, on the most appropriate form of support or action to be taken, including any referral to outside agencies e.g. Educational Psychologist Service (EPS), Education Welfare Service, Child Guidance, off-site support etc.;

(f)   to ensure that there is feedback on actions agreed at an earlier meeting, through a process of review and evaluation; and

(g)   to provide regular updates on support agencies and to develop a common understanding of their respective roles.

There is a growing emphasis on the need for professionals working with special needs children to increase their effectiveness by developing collaborative relationship with parents (Hornby 1994), and by helping to establish a supportive network of professional contacts for their clients (Holland 1997).

While the models of Liaison Meetings in schools and the more recent Profiling system have been established in the London Borough of Hackney for many years, there are reports of a very similar approach in the form of School Liaison Groups operating in the West Lothian region of Scotland. In both areas the model has been found to be highly effective in preventing exclusions from school.

Procedures like Liaison Meetings and the Profiling system help to achieve key objectives in terms of intervention at an early stage, before teachers begin to feel 'at the end of their tether', and also in avoiding some of the artificial dichotomies in school e.g. between special needs (or learning difficulties) and behaviour problems. Teachers can be helped to refine their thinking or 'construing' of the problem (Kelly 1955) and supported in finding solutions or making appropriate referrals to outside support agencies.

As well as their direct input through a range of strategies, educational psychologists can act as a catalyst in bringing together the energies of others before either the student fails or the system fails them.

DEVELOPMENTS AT SERVICE LEVEL

Evidence of the need for EPs to focus attention on exclusion is provided by our own studies but also those of others such as Hartnell (1998). She investigated cases of permanent exclusion of students in Years 9 and 10 (i.e. ages 13–14 years) between January 1996 and May 1997. Not only did the pupils and parents describe their experiences as very traumatic, with parents reporting feelings of anger, frustration and abandonment, most mentioned explicitly a lack of support or communication from the excluding school. Hartnell also found that approximately half of her sample of permanently excluded pupils was previously unknown to the educational psychology service. Another of her findings was that some of students had significant reading difficulties, with a reading age 3 or more years below their chronological age. She goes on to make a number of recommendations to try and improve the support available to students and their parents. These include:

- a clear assessment of the pupil's needs;
- good communication between school and support agencies;
- support agencies must be proactive and reflective in addressing the needs of pupils at risk of exclusion;
- schools must follow guidelines (e.g. Code of Practice) when dealing with pupils at risk of exclusion;
- pupils need a key worker to offer advice, monitoring and advocacy; to ensure long-term planning; and to ensure good inter-agency communication;
- high targets should be set for re-entry to school;

- schools should be encouraged to feel ownership of the problem of exclusion and placement; and
- different models for supporting re-entry to education should be piloted and assessed.

A MODEL FOR SERVICE DELIVERY

To give some idea of the process of development and expectations of educational psychologists in their practice within the new framework, parts of the service policy in a London borough are presented below.

Enfield Educational Psychology Service Policy: Educational psychologists and exclusions from school

Exclusion is generally regarded as a disciplinary sanction. The role of the educational psychologist is not in the exclusion process itself but in helping schools to take action at the whole-school, group or individual level in order to prevent exclusion occurring. At the whole-school level, such an involvement may include:

helping draw up a whole-school behaviour policy;
giving INSET/advice on behaviour management to staff.

At the individual level, educational psychologists may be involved in helping schools with early identification and interventions for pupils who have emotional and behavioural difficulties, and thereby prevent initial or further exclusion of such pupils.

DfEE Circular 10/94 'Exclusions from School' states:

> Pupils who show signs of emotional and behavioural difficulties which are not resolved by the general arrangements embodied in the school's behaviour policy should move to the school-based stages of assessment . . . The prompt recognition of children's difficulties may alleviate the child's difficulties and avoid the need for a later exclusion.
>
> (DfEE 1994b: p. 6)

The Association of Educational Psychologists (AEP 1993) also suggests that the emphasis is best placed on prevention:

> The involvement of an Educational Psychologist is most effective when it is initiated well before an exclusion is planned or even contemplated. This will help to ensure that parental consent can be given freely, that the referral is not seen by the pupil and parents as part of the exclusion process and that there is time to implement preventative strategies.
>
> (AEP 1993: 3)

Table 8.1 EPS involvement at different stages of exclusion process

Incidents/developments	Response
a) Any instance of inappropriate behaviour where school feels fixed term exclusion is warranted	School contact with parents to consider possible explanation, developments at home, possible pattern emerging.

Meeting of teacher with pupil and parent(s) to consider what support is necessary. |
| b) Where pattern of inappropriate behaviour continues and could lead to a second exclusion | Code of Practice (COP) Stage 1: strategies agreed before pupil returns to school

COP Stage 2: with input from EP (and/or others, e.g. Child and Family Service, Education Welfare Service, Behaviour Support Service, Secondary Tuition Centre Outreach) through Liaison Meeting |
| c) Where problems remain unresolved | COP Stage 3: Direct EP involvement Possible meeting with EP, parents, teacher and pupil.

Also other outside agencies as appropriate. |
| d) Where problems remain unresolved | Request for Section 323 assessment to Special Educ. Needs Panel |

The service policy outlined in Table 8.1 shows the possible stages of developments for pupils in schools under threat of exclusion and the appropriate Educational Psychology Service (EPS) response, making reference to Code of Practice stages.

The EPS policy statement gives guidelines for the allocation of educational psychologist support for pupils in the 'exclusion zone' and then details the role of the educational psychologist. This should include interviewing the child and his/her family. Assessment would consider their ability to cope in mainstream and whether the pupil has any special educational needs. The EP is expected to make recommendations on the most appropriate strategies or options to meet the pupil's educational needs. These include the student being supported in school with the use of strategies such as refocusing pastoral support, mediation, mentoring and, where indicated, direct work with the family. Along the support continuum, it is possible that a recommendation could be made for an alternative mainstream placement, with the Educational Psychology Service (either the present case-EP or the new school-EP or both) supporting the receiving school in devising a programme for a fresh start.

The need for screening is clearly identified in the model in order to determine whether alternative mainstream school would be appropriate or whether the statutory assessment (Stage 4d) process should begin in order to identify any acute special educational needs the child may have. Depending on the age and special educational needs of the student, a range of options are considered in the policy statement.

DEVELOPMENTS AT LEA LEVEL: ENFIELD'S EXCLUSION PROTOCOL

At the local government level, education authorities have also begun to acknowledge the need for policy and practice statements on exclusions. An example of this is provided by Enfield Education Authority. In a document entitled 'Permanent Exclusions in Primary Schools' (Enfield Education Directorate 1998) the LEA declares its wish to reduce the incidence of permanent exclusions in primary school and to ensure that schools are able to support their most challenging pupils. This policy states that primary aged children should only be considered for permanent exclusion from school in very exceptional circumstances. If the child is wrongly placed in a mainstream school, exclusion should not be the route to alternative provision.

Headteachers are expected to make use of all relevant agencies and appropriate strategies prior to any exclusion. Therefore, permanent exclusion will, in the main, be the exception and the LEA is unlikely to confirm the decisions of governors of county schools if there is strong evidence that the pupil was not guilty of the alleged offence; the nature of the offence did not warrant exclusion; or there is overwhelming evidence of policy and procedures not being adhered to, e.g. the school had not made use of appropriate agencies. The LEA will also reverse the decision of the headteacher and governing body if there is a likelihood that the pupil will succeed if reinstated, given appropriate support.

The LEA lays clear expectations on the school prior to any move to exclude permanently a primary age pupil. It expects there to be documented consultation about the pupil's difficulties with relevant school staff; parents and the pupil; and a range of support agencies. Support from a multi-professional team such as the Child and Family Service is also included as an option. There is also an expectation that the school will offer increased support to the vulnerable pupil from their own resources through a range of options:

- drawing up a Record of Pupil Progress and Concern;
- drawing up or revising the Individual Education Plan (IEP) including use of appropriate behaviour strategies;
- getting advice from the SENCO re teaching and learning strategies;
- arranging access to counselling, monitoring or mediation;
- change of teaching set;
- change of tutor group;
- modification of classroom arrangements and management;
- structured playtime arrangements and activities;
- use of incentive, e.g. letter home, reward system;
- alerting parents of the possibility of permanent exclusion; and
- home school contract to strengthen links.

The document suggests that disciplinary systems within school should be based on the premise that conflict resolution can be part of the learning process for pupils and teachers. It concludes by urging schools to involve outside agencies when they are unable to resolve the pupil's difficulties from their own resources. Reference is made to the agencies listed above as well as Refugee Support Team, LEA Mediation Service, Parents' Centre, mentoring scheme and SEN services for pupils with statements. Schools are also advised to hold a case conference on the pupil and include appropriate external agencies. In the case of statemented pupils schools are expected to hold a review meeting.

As a final recommendation to headteachers, the document urges that before contemplating permanent exclusion they should seek further advice from a senior LEA officer, from a short-list that includes the Principal Educational Psychologist.

Case examples

Case One: Gary, secondary (Year 8)

The head of Learning Support rang the Principal Educational Psychologist (DG) to seek advice about Gary (age 14). He had been excluded before and was considered close to another, possibly even permanent, exclusion. Gary had brought a lighter into school, which was against their behaviour policy, but concerns were also raised because he was reported to be setting fire to things.

In line with the LEA's new protocol, the headteacher suggested that they should enlist outside support. (Although the new protocol as yet only applies to primary schools, the head had been party to discussions around rising exclusion rates.) The school's own educational psychologist was not available so the head of Learning Support asked to speak to a senior educational psychologist.

In seeking clarification of the facts, it became clear that Gary had set light to a tree and there was no evidence that he had done anything like that before. However, there was a suggestion of earlier emotional and behavioural difficulties and an indication that he had been referred to the local Child and Family Service within the past few years. The head of Learning Support had put his name on the list of those students to be discussed at the next Liaison Meeting which was only a week away. The telephone discussion gave an opportunity to clarify:

- what stage in the special needs procedure they had reached in supporting Gary;
- who needed to be present at the Liaison Meeting – in particular who was Gary's main support person in school;
- what was expected to be the focus of discussion for the meeting.

Following consultation and negotiation the school felt they could cope at least until the Liaison Meeting; that the head of Learning Support would convene the meeting and ensure appropriate representation from within the school; and also that the Principal Educational Psychologist would brief the school's EP and a representative from the Child and Family Service in preparation for the meeting.

At the meting Gary was moved to stage 3 for individual educational psychologist and assessment and intervention. At the time of writing he was also under consideration for further outside support.

Case Two: Delroy, primary (Year 3)

Delroy was brought to the attention of the school's educational psychologist at the end of Year 2 (age eight), due to his behaviour difficulties. From classroom observation and discussion with the classteacher, it became clear that Delroy was quite bright. The teacher's main concerns were that he would not listen, would not comply with instructions and 'liked to do his own thing'.

During his time at the infant school, Delroy's needs were assessed by an EP and recommendations made, but it was not clear to what extent these had been implemented, especially since his move to the juniors. On this occasion, it seemed that a major part of the problem was a mismatch of expectations between home and school.

As an only child living with a single mother, he was expected to be independent and self-reliant. Yet in class, he was told to be compliant, wait for instructions and not do anything without the teacher's permission. A meeting was set up to discuss with the classteacher and Delroy's mother ways for both of them to adjust their levels of expectation so that there could be more consistency in the messages he was given. Suggestions were made for the teacher to be able to control the options open to Delroy in the classroom, so that he could show his ability and continue his imaginative work, but with close supervision and support to set clear boundaries. A series of four sessions was agreed with Delroy and his mother to work on difficulties around peer relationship, listening skills and appropriate levels of responsibility.

CONCLUDING REMARKS

In the present climate, with league tables and notions of value added, schools are expected to make a difference in the lives of the children they educate. Unfortunately, for many Black children the net result of their experience in school is all too often a minus.

Although there are new government initiatives to reduce the levels of exclusion nationally, as others have remarked elsewhere in this book (see in particular the chapters by Majors *et al.*), there is still little recognition of the race issue underlying the over-representation of Black children in exclusion statistics. Based on the arguments outlined in this paper we would argue that along with a clear initiative to address the issues underlying exclusions, specific targets should be set to achieve a reduction in the proportion of Black pupils excluded from school.

This chapter has given examples of approaches using existing legislation to make a positive contribution in the fight to combat not only exclusion but other forms of disadvantage faced by Black children in the education process. Educational psychologists have a key role in statutory procedures. Through their work with schools they should be providing a clear lead in the struggle to reduce the high rate of exclusion of Black pupils.

In summary, we echo the words of a leading Black activist:

> Education is an important element in the struggle for human rights. It is the means to help our children and people rediscover their identity and increase self-respect. It is our passport to the future, for tomorrow belongs to the people who prepare for it today.
>
> (Minister El Hajj Malik El Shabazz (Malcolm X))

REFERENCES

Acland, H. (1971) 'Parental participation', *New Society*, **51**, 16.

AEP (1993) 'Circular 17/93: Exclusions', Durham: Association of Educational Psychologists.

Audit Commission (1992) *Getting in on the Act*, London: HMSO.

Bernstein, B. (1971) *Class, Codes and Control, Volume 1: Theoretical Studies Towards a Sociology of Language*, London: Routledge and Kegan Paul.

BPS (1998) *Core Principles for the Training of Educational Psychologists*, Leicester: British Psychological Society.

Callender, C. (1997) *Education for Empowerment*, London: Trentham Books.

Calliste, J. (1993) 'Partnership with parents: A model for practice', *Educational Psychology in Practice*, **9**, 2, pp. 73–81.

Childright (1994) 'How schools exclude black children', Issue No. 109, London: The Children's Legal Centre.

Coard, B. (1971) *How the West Indian Child is Made Educationally Subnormal in the British School System*, London: New Beacon.

Cohen, R., Hughes, M., Ashworth, L. and Blair, M. (1994) *School's Out: The Family Perspective on School Exclusion*, London: Barnados Family Service Units.

Commission for Racial Equality (1985) *Swann: A Response from the CRE*.

Department for Education (1994b) *Exclusions from School. Circular No. 10/94*, London: HMSO.

Department for Education and Employment (1997) *Education Act*, London: HMSO.

Department for Education and Employment (1997) *Excellence for All Children: Meeting Special Educational Needs*, London: HMSO.

Department for Education and Science (1967) Plowden Report: *Children and Their Primary Schools*, a report of the Central Advisory Council for Education, London: HMSO.

Department for Education and Science (1978) *Special Needs in Education (Warnock Report)*, London: HMSO.

Department for Education and Science (1981a) *Education Act*, London: HMSO.

Department for Education and Science (1981b) Rampton Report: *West Indian Children in our Schools: Interim Report of the Committee of Enquiry into the Education of Children from Ethnic Minority Groups*, London: HMSO.

Department for Education and Science (1982) *Education Act*, London: HMSO.

Department for Education and Science (1985) *Swann Report. Education for All*, London: HMSO.

Department for Education and Science (1989) *Discipline in Schools: Report of the Committee of Enquiry chaired by Lord Elton*, London: HMSO.

Enfield Educational Psychology Service (1989) 'Educational Psychologists and Exclusion from School', policy document, Enfield EPS, 8 Dryden Road, Enfield EN1 2PP.

Enfield Education Directorate (1989) 'Permanent Exclusions in Primary Schools – LEA Policy Statement', Enfield Education Directorate, Civic Centre, Silver Street, Enfield ENI.

Eysenck, H. (1971) *Race, Intelligence and Education*, London: Temple Smith.

Gillborn, D. (1990) *'Race', Ethnicity and Education: Teaching and Learning in Multi-ethnic Schools*, London: Unwin-Hyman/Routledge.

Gillborn, D. and Gipps, C. (1996) *Recent Research on the Achievements of Ethnic Minority Pupils*, London, HMSO.

Grant, D. (Awaiting publication) *Special Needs Profiling: Before and After the Acts*.

Grant, D. and Brooks, K. (1996) 'Exclusions from school: responses from the Black community', *Pastoral Care in Education*, **14**, 3, pp. 20–27.

Grant, D. and Brooks, K. (1998) 'Exclusions from school: the way ahead', *Educational Psychology in Practice*, **14**, 1, pp. 26–31.

Gross, J. (1996) 'The weight of evidence: Parental advocacy and resource allocation to children with statements of special educational needs', *Support for Learning*, 11, 3–9.

Guishard, J. (1998) 'The Parents' Support Service – brief family work in a school context', *Educational Psychology in Practice*, **14**, 2, pp. 135–139.

Hartnell, N. (1998) *Avoiding Exclusion*, Research carried out by Naomi Hartnell, Educational Psychologist. Hertfordshire Educational Psychology Service, Civic Close, Herts AL1 3JZ, unpublished.

Holland, S. (1997) 'The special needs of parents', *Educational Psychology in Practice*, **12**, 1, pp. 24–30.

Hornby, G. (1994) *Counselling in Child Disability*, London: Chapman and Hall.

Inner London Education Authority (1984) *Committee Report 4627: Survey of characteristics of pupils in schools and units*.

Jensen, S. (1969) 'How much can we boost IQ and scholastic achievement?', *Harvard Educational Review*, **39**, 1: 1–123.

Kelly, G. (1955) *The Psychology of Personal Constructs*, New York: W. W. Norton.

Kinder, K. (1997) 'Exclusion – where do parents come in?' *Parent Forum Newsletter*, No. 8.

Lunt, I. and Sheppard, J. (1986) 'Introduction', *Educational and Child Psychology*, **3**, 3.

Mac an Ghaill, M. (1988) *Young Gifted and Black*, Milton Keynes: Open University Press.

Majors, R., Gillborn, D. and Sewell, T. (1998) 'The exclusion of Black children: implications for a racialised perspective', *Multicultural Teaching*, Spring 1998, pp. 35–7.

NFER (1997) *School Attendance, Truancy and Exclusions*, Windsor: National Foundation for Educational Research.

Parsons, C. (1995) 'Policies and procedures for the identification of, and provision for, children out of school by reason of exclusion or otherwise', *DfEE: National Survey of Local Education Authorities*, London: HMSO.

Phoenix, A. (1996) 'Constructing identities, obscuring racisms: issues for the study of identities', unpublished paper delivered at the *British Psychological Society Annual Conference*, April 1996.

Pitchford, M. (1994) 'Activity analysis as a means of clarifying teachers' expectations of pupils', in Gray, P. , Miller, A. and Noakes, J. *Challenging Behaviour in Schools. Teacher Support, Practical Techniques and Policy Development*, London: Routledge.

Rehal, A. (1988) 'Involving Asian parents in the statementing procedure – the way forward', *Educational Psychology in Practice*, **4**, 4, 189–197.

Roderick, C., Pitchford, M., and Miller, A. (1997) 'Reducing aggressive playground behaviour by means of a school-wide "raffle"', *Educational Psychology in Practice*, **13**, 1, pp. 57–63.

Sallis, J. (1997) 'Partnerships not contracts', *Times Educational Supplement*, 29 August 1997.

Smith, D. J. and Tomlinson, S. (1989) *The School Effect: A Study of Multi-racial Comprehensiveness*, London: Policy Studies Institute.

Sewell, T. (1997) *Black Masculinities*, London: Trentham Books.

Social Exclusion Unit (1998) *Truancy and School Exclusion Report*, London: HMSO.

Stone, M. (1981) *The Education of the Black Child in Britain*, Glasgow: Fontana.

TES (1994) '"Dramatic" increase in exclusions rate', *Times Educational Supplement*, 9 December 1994.

TES (1998) 'Blacks 15 times more likely to be excluded', *Times Educational Supplement*, 11 December 1998.

Tomlinson, S. (1981) *Education Subnormality: A Study in Decision-making*, London: Routledge and Kegan Paul.

Thornton, K. (1998) *Times Educational Supplement*, 11 December 1998.

Wood, A. (1998) 'Okay, then: what do EPs do?', *Special Children*, May 1998.

9 Black exclusions in a moral vacuum

Richard Harris and Carl Parsons

INTRODUCTION

A change in the British government in May 1997 brought policy changes in education, health and welfare but no distinct reversal of Conservative party policies. The Labour government's *Third Way* (Blair 1998) is a compromised mix of humanitarian endeavour and cost consciousness. Though the notion of 'joined up problems' and the need for 'joined up solutions' (Social Exclusion Unit 1998) has taken the discussion beyond the simplistic position which has long existed with regard to school exclusions, the problem is not yet viewed in a way which is joined up enough. Some groups are particularly vulnerable to a range of educational misfortunes such as low attainment and exclusion. Looked-after, traveller and African Caribbean children are disproportionately represented in these categories. This represents a worrying, enduring inequality which is not addressed in national policy.

The numbers of permanent exclusions from schools have risen over the 1990s in England, though there are differences in the recorded numbers from different sources as in Figure 9.1. Earlier figures are known to be an under-recording, while the difference between results estimated from sample surveys of LEAs (the larger print numbers in Figure 9.1) and the returns directly from schools (the smaller italicised numbers in Figure 9.1) persist, with DfEE figures recording around 1,000 fewer permanent exclusions. Knowledge of the permanently excluded population is poor both at national and LEA level. DfEE figures can indicate National Curriculum year, gender, ethnicity, looked after status and special needs registration but do not reveal what happens to differently defined groups in terms of either return to school or longer term outcomes from their education.

It is suggested that if an education system is designed for a known population with known variation then it must aim to serve all sections of that population. The designed system is at fault if some sections of the target population are poorly served. The over representation of black and African Caribbean pupils in exclusion statistics is a system fault, not a deficiency in children that is linked to ethnicity.

This chapter has three goals:

1   to report the costs to the full range of services of permanent exclusions from schools in England;

Number of permanent exclusions

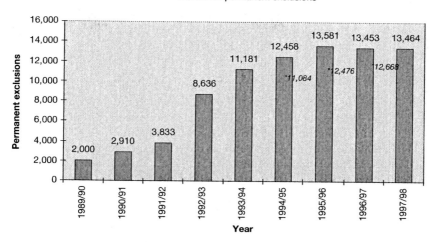

Figure 9.1 Permanent exclusions from schools in England – 1990–98

2   to consider the ethical environment in which resource allocation decisions are made with respect to children excluded from school; and
3   to judge the impact of school exclusion legislation and policy on defined subgroups of the population.

THE COST OF EXCLUSION

Studies agree (CRE 1996; Knapp 1986; Shapland *et al.* 1995) that costing information is important since policy decisions are, in part, decided by cost and effect. There are too few structured, experimental, comparative studies to allow a rigorous comparison of different policy options with the costs which they entail. We have to make the best of natural variations which occur which inevitably involve uncontrolled and non-calculable variations.

The average annual cost for mainstream schooling in 1994/95 was approximately £2,300 for secondary pupils and £1,700 for primary pupils. The costings for permanently excluded pupils in six LEAs reveal that they cost, on average, over £4,300 in full year equivalent replacement education and other education costs. The amount of education received during the first year of permanent exclusion was under 10 per cent of a full-time education, a consequence of the delayed start and the part-time nature of the replacement education. This is inevitably damaging to the individual pupil and makes return to mainstream school more difficult.

Thirty per cent of the excluded pupils finished their compulsory schooling at the end of the school year, while forty-six per cent of the 1994/95 permanent exclusions were continuing exclusions into the following year. These cost on average £5,134, a more substantial charge on the education budget in 1995/96 than new exclusions.

Generalising from this sample to England as a whole gives figures which must be treated with great caution. Most significantly it would mean that LEAs in England would be dealing with nearly 20,000 excluded pupils – 13,500 for the 1995/96 year and 46 per cent of the 12,500 from the previous year (see Figure 9.1).

Approximately 20 per cent of permanently excluded pupils are social services cases costing on average £1,100; and about 10 per cent call upon health services resources, but incurring small expenditure, amounting to an average of less than £100. Average police costs of over £2,000 arise with a little over a quarter of permanently excluded pupils. Police and criminal justice costs vary from the caution (around £35) to a prosecution which runs to something approaching £3,000; where remand or multiple court appearances are involved the expense is obviously greater. Based on these calculations, the total cost, to education and other services, of permanently excluded pupils from school in England reaches £76 million.

The rise in numbers and in expenditure is such as to make this group of pupils a significant cost to the public services. They are no longer a rare anomaly but a fixed part of the picture for which routine provision will need to be made – in mainstream school or elsewhere. Treating them as an aberration which may go away is a mistake in terms of the quality of provision for them, in terms of the likely outcomes for the individuals themselves and for their prospects of becoming contributing citizens. The costs to the state in the short and longer term, let alone the less quantifiable costs to an excluded child and family, demonstrate that it is considerably cheaper to continue to educate than to pursue the route towards incarceration.

Aside from the financial costs to the statutory services there are the human costs of disrupted family lives, diminished life chances, stress and despair, sometimes with very young children (Parsons 1994).

THE DIFFERENTIALS OF HARM AND INSTITUTIONAL RACISM

Policy and social morality find expression in budgetary allocations. What for? how much? and on whom? are indicators of social commitment to inclusiveness. Groups of young people with particular characteristics suffer disproportionately from school exclusion. Funding was not for prevention and not enough to compensate for the loss of full-time education. Until recently, it was not expended in a targeted way on schools to promote inclusion.

Education remains a service that is relatively non-adjustable, non-negotiable in the UK; it cannot be changed to suit particular groups. Blame for exclusion rests with the individuals or their families, not the schooling which misses their needs. Here one can see the disdain of officialdom for groups which are 'other' and, thus, branded difficult: black exclusions, traveller exclusions and the exclusions of children in care.

Majors and Mancini Billson (1992) in the USA and Sewell (1997), Mac an Ghaill (1994) and Gillborn (1990) in Britain have examined race and education and have considered particularly the style of masculinity played out in marginalised ethnic youth cultures. Sewell describes the pressures towards 'racelessness' in his case study school and gives instances of a lack of acceptance and flexibility in the face of cultural differences. Furthermore, some marginalised and socially relegated groups will react in challenging ways to what are experienced as an alienating and exclusionary school regime. Majors and Mancini Billson take this further and relate resistance and 'cool pose' to psychological self-preservation; 'the cool, black male epitomises control, strength and pride' (p. 2) in a context where he has learned that 'the classic American virtues of thrift, perseverance and hard work did not give them the same tangible rewards that accrue to whites' (p. 1).

WHO IS SCHOOL FOR, ANYWAY? THE ETHICAL ISSUES

The intellectual emphasis of the school system emerges from the traditional understanding of education as rational development. Aristotle described a number of key virtues that a good, i.e. a rounded and successful person, needed to have. These include the moral virtues, developed through early training so that they become a matter of habit. They are shaped by the emotions and attitudes. The history of schooling in the West was strongly influenced by Aristotle's account of moral development and the moral virtues.

A child is good if parental and school authority is obeyed. Authorities are concerned with fundamental social values, order and justice. They want the child to internalise these values as part of his or her character. They act towards the child as if obeying their rules is fully a matter of choice. A rule infringement is not just a wrong, but morally bad (Wilson 1990). At school and home, moral training or character development is frequently mixed or confused with straightforward socialisation. For example, children who are excluded from school for failing to conform to uniform rules can hardly be said to have acted immorally. The school wants obedience for reasons of power and control and might, as part of its strategy to achieve this, portray obedience to its rules of conduct as a moral duty. However, the school requirement that children conform to a whole mass of regulations has more to do with the scale of school operations than with a desire to develop the moral life of its pupils.

Schools are classic bureaucracies in which calculable, predictable actions are highly valued (Cuff, Sharrock and Francis 1990; Hartley 1987). Bureaucracy fosters an externalised and conformist understanding of moral life and action. It is here that the locus of difficulty for the excluded child is to be found. The exclusion response of schools to the behaviour of children relies on the notion that the responsibility is the child's. The child can be good (i.e. conform to teacher expected behaviour – be like us) if he or she tries. The child is made analogous to a criminal in breach of a rule, with the school seeing rule obedience as being the key to morality and orderly public life. The school, acting as a bureaucracy, operates a consequentialist morality. The right thing to do is to let punishment follow a disapproved act. Although the consequence of exclusion might be very harsh for the child, on a calculus of benefits to the many and harm to the one, the better result is obtained if the one is excluded from school.

This account of how schools might justify exclusion decisions does not sit easily with the classical role of schools in the whole personal development of children, including their emotional and moral development. Schools are radically different social worlds from the home (Sluckin 1981; Dunn 1988). Children meet new peers and in such numbers that pupil culture in school typically has a complex, dynamic but predictable social and value pattern (Pollard 1984). The evidence is not sanguine that schools have an awareness of their own pupil cultures or their willingness to take responsibility for them. School bullying research demonstrates this (Smith 1994). They are blind to the strong racial prejudice some young white children have towards blacks and others viewed as outsiders (Aboud 1988; Barrett and Short 1992). As a bureaucracy, the school is interested in overt behaviour towards its post holders and compliance with its rules. The private world of thought and feeling has practically no place. This is very different from a well adjusted family in which the parents are interested in the moral, emotional and dispositional development of the children (Persaud 1998). That is, there is for the parents no barrier of interest or of intervention between what the child thinks and feels and what the child does. Vital steps in emotional and moral development are taken in the early years at school. For instance, the insight that a person's outward display of emotion can be deliberately changed to mislead onlookers is typically reached at 6; older primary children also develop strategies that are vital for healthy childhood and adulthood, such as indulging in distracting activities to block out painful and disturbing thoughts and feelings (Harris 1989). In England, schools hardly begin to play the role of educator and moral mentor for children in these key aspects of their lives. This is a particular failing for black Afro-Caribbean children for whom the school itself will usually present to the young child as demanding that they should become like us (assimilationist model: Sewell 1997). The very process of academic schooling confronts the child with a morally fractured world, a world in which black children are sharply aware of their powerlessness (Durkin 1995). Public and unthinking conformity is required to rules which mix and confuse managerial routines with moral matters of substance (hanging coats on pegs neatly magnified into a marker of respect for others; looking directly at the teacher a marker of respect for teacher authority). Yet children are left to the privacy of their own thoughts about despair, happiness, success and self-valuation. A high level of responsibility is placed on the child to master emotion and to behave just like the white, confident middle class and to give unreflective conventional conformity to their rules. Pupils who cannot or will not follow the rules are labelled as morally bad, therefore exclusion is seen as a consequence that 'naturally' follows misdemeanour.

It is the paradigm of blame and total individual moral responsibility that precipitates a punishment response. A model that saw the child as a person with intellectual, affective and social dimensions, all of which need educating (leading out – start where the child is coming from) in order to enable full flourishing and readiness for adult society, would organise around the need to target educational and social resources upon the child in school rather than out of it. The blame paradigm is, perhaps, one reason why black pupils suffer a high rate of exclusion (Majors, Gillborn and Sewell 1998). And in a society with a racist history and substratum,

African-Caribbean boys are labelled as outsiders who are potentially boisterous and not academic (Phillips 1998). They are seen as a threat. Schools ought to be concerned with the whole development of their pupils. The very act of bringing them to school has cast children into a new and morally challenging environment. Moral growth and judgement involve the rational engagement of mental and emotional faculties. How one should feel about the death of a grandparent, how one should react when a friend is spiteful, why some people are racist and how to respond to racism, how to recognise and control one's own anger – these are all issues that ought to be systematically addressed in school and that involve facts about the world, reasoning as well as emotion. Schools need to adjust to the needs and attributes of the children they take.

Because school authorities hold power, schools act as though the child's moral failure is the issue rather than their own failure to welcome and accommodate black children's cultural styles. How can the school system not take responsibility for this failure? It amounts to a failure to take responsibility for building the character of these children, to educate them not just in the academic curriculum but in the social skills needed for life at the very schools they have been compelled to attend, a responsibility to educate them in emotional self awareness and control, in short, to morally educate them.

RULE UTILITARIANISM AND EXCLUSION

Schools are hierarchical and bureaucratic, even when they are small. The psychological outlook found in school management is remarkably close to that found amongst managers elsewhere (Miller 1973). The uniformity and historical rigidity of the internal structure of maintained schools (e.g. Mortimore 1988) is a testimony to the inertia and lack of imagination of much school management, despite sterling exceptions. There has been little re-engineering to meet new goals with new pupil populations (Stoll, Reynolds, Creemers and Hopkins 1996; Morgan 1986). Consequentialist, utilitarian ethics dominate bureaucratic systems. This is the idea that the best way to produce good states of affairs is to calculate the benefits to individuals caused by a particular action, less the harm done to other individuals. The best action to take is the action that maximises benefit (the greatest utility). This theory is often adopted in the variant form called rule utilitarianism. A rule utilitarian works with a set of rules designed to promote the greatest benefit for the greatest number of people. The central point is that one should stick with the rules even though in a particular instance the best result would be achieved by breaking them. Ignoring the rules does greater harm and school rules can be thought of as being like this.

When a problem arises with, for example, a young male Afro-Caribbean, the school authorities are going to ignore the subjective in the boy's mind and cultural background and treat him as though he were a colourless, classless actor without a history (the actor has no more or no less intrinsic worth than the persons who suffer the consequences of the action and it is irrelevant whether actor is male or female, black or white, etc.). It is easy to see how the school manager becomes the instrument of, at best, an assimilationist set of values that gets smuggled into the utilitarian's perspective. Everything that is distinctive about young black male culture is discounted; with action based on this theory it is easy to see why a child is excluded from school. The calculation: the work environment would improve a little for 30 children if one is excluded, less a lot of harm to the one excluded; contrast this with continuing educational benefit to the one if there is no exclusion, less a little harm to 30 children if the child is not excluded. It is perhaps not fanciful to imagine headteachers and governors reasoning in this manner and deciding that exclusion of a child who doesn't fit in is right. It is odd that a school can, by itself, add costs to other social agencies. If the calculation is done without real measuring instruments, exclusion will take place. Subjective preferences, including the possibility of prejudice, come into play (Majors, Gillborn and Sewell 1998). Exclusion will be the right thing to do as the majority will benefit.

There are a number of problems with this reasoning. Most relevant is that utilitarian doctrine does not respect minorities. It is clearly not in the interest of the excluded child that others should benefit at his or her exclusion. Utilitarian reasoning is blind to minorities. Here lies another objection to utilitarianism: it makes no sense to an individual for that individual to sacrifice a benefit so that another person can receive one (Davies and Holdcroft 1991). Utilitarianism tries to stand on the ground that everyone is equal. Given there are acts which impact differentially on people in contact with the actor, the way to recognise the equal standing of individuals is to be blind to personal interests of the actor and to focus on the consequences upon those individuals (are they made happy?). There are other, non-utilitarian, ways of thinking about the distribution of social good.

Rawls' theory of justice

Rawls argues that resources should be distributed to make the worst off as well off as it is possible for them to be, then the next worse off group, and so on (1972: 83). This idea shares with classical utilitarianism the notion that ethical value is an impartial function of individual well-being and of nothing else. Rawls' interest is in the distribution of benefits, thus his is a theory of justice in contradistinction to classical utilitarianism's theory of happiness. Rawls starts by suggesting that we draw a 'veil of ignorance' over our true social situations. Suppose you were asked to construct the rules of your society.

> First of all, no one knows his place in society, his class position or his social status; nor does he know his fortune in the distribution of natural assets and abilities, his intelligence and strength, and the like.
>
> (Rawls 1972: 138)

We might be the black primary school child who experiences occasional abuse from peers and whose teachers know little about the food, culture and music of the world in which we live. What would we like the rules of our various social groups, the wider world and the school, to be like? Rawls argues that rational rule makers would operate a preference for the most disadvantaged consistent with liberty for all. A result of Rawls' reasoning must be that any child who is poorly coping in school would command the skilled multi-disciplinary resources we would wish were we that child. Rawls uses decision theory and game theory to facilitate costing; but he does not use his ideas at the micro-social level as has been done here. Rawls's position has difficulties that it is not possible to discuss here, but his argument would be that inaction is nothing but 'culture bound prejudice' (Pettit 1980: 169).

The key difference between Rawlsian and utilitarian arguments is that Rawls attempts to strengthen the position of minorities and the weak. Rights theories do this more trenchantly, a modern rights theorist such as Dworkin arguing that rights are 'trumps' which can defy a collective goal (1977: ix). The idea of rights is rooted in an intuition about the requirements of justice that arises from the experience of the law courts. In them a judge often has to determine what the rights of the litigants might be and whether any of them have been violated. Legal rights are distinct from ethical rights, but are an appealing image upon which to construct a moral claim. Dworkin states that:

> the ultimate justification for rights is that they are necessary to protect equal concern and respect. . . . They are justified . . . in order to make more perfect the only justification upon which . . . other institutions may themselves rely.
> (Dworkin 1978: 135–6)

And the 'other institutions' in a liberal society include schools. For Dworkin, rights are generated in the tension between the questions 'how do I want to be?' and 'how do I want other people to be' (Dworkin 1977). It is this tension that he claims creates the need for individual rights to protect minorities and unpopular groups against prejudice and oppression from the majority.

But what kind of a thing are rights? They are obviously not natural objects in the world and unless they can be armoured with some kind of Kantian style imperative that requires rational people to accept them, they will fall to the criticism that Pettit makes of Rawls (which is a modern version of Bentham's dictum 'nonsense upon stilts'). For excluded children, a significant aspect of this problem is the difficulty in seeing how general statements of rights bite on real life problems such as child behaviour in school. This can be seen in the ineffectiveness of laudable general declarations of rights in the lives of children. An example is the European Convention of Human Rights and Fundamental Freedoms article 28–31 on the right to education and cultural freedoms (Cretney and Masson 1996). This has hardly changed the daily lives of children as it is unclear how the practical connections should be made. Critics of rights theories argue that rights just fail to deliver the benefits that are claimed for them. They do not give a 'relatively objective and . . . uncontroversial way of determining entitlements' (Campbell 1988).

The point for Campbell and for many critics is that rights promise more than they can deliver. What minorities really want are remedies: the ability to turn a school into a learning community based upon mutual respect and dialogue, rather than continue with what exists and allocate 'rights'; the need for resource and management changes that touch political priorities that the claim to rights does not. For Campbell and others, Dworkin is seen to have produced a rights thesis that is a shadow image of Dworkin's liberal and humanitarian moral preferences. But the point is to ground them.

DO SCHOOLS HAVE A MORAL DUTY NOT TO EXCLUDE CHILDREN?

If schools and teachers take seriously the demand of the Education Reform Act 1988 s.1(2) and 1(3)[1] to cater for pupils' moral, mental and social education, then it has been argued that schools have a vital role in the development of intellect, emotion and autonomy and ought to keep children within the school community. If there are problems with individuals, then targeting them for specific educational intervention is called for. If there are problems with an ethnic group, then retooling the school so that it meets these very goals with the full range of its pupils would be another goal. All this would certainly involve teachers being trained to understand, respect and build on the cultural diversity found amongst their pupils (Davies 1997; Argyle 1986). The fact that many schools do not succeed with their Afro-Caribbean boys ought to cause them to examine the breadth and quality of the total educational experience they are offering. This would involve reconsidering the rules being enforced so that well known areas of difficulty, social class and cultural clashes of expectation, are avoided. This is excellently discussed in Sewell (1997: 187ff.).

How to provide a full education to all pupils, including Afro-Caribbean boys, is a question wider than the school. It involves the LEA and multi-agency inputs. Indeed, the utilitarian perspective that appears to justify schools in excluding pupils might well give a different result if the calculation of benefits and harm were made in the context of the wider community. This is pointed to in the allocation of financial costs caused by exclusion and the poor outcome for the children and society generally of the exclusion process.

A claim that children have a right to full time education initially seems a promising route to protecting the interests of minority children, especially those who are resistant to school. But the reality is that these children require preferential resource allocation to keep them in school, to help them overcome their difficulties with the school and the school to examine whether it has a need to change. Campbell is correct in noting that what is needed is a remedy to the problems these children and their schools face. This remedy consists of more resources and better trained staff who recognise that it is their task to socially and morally educate all their children, not just school them in the overt curriculum. Resourcing is a political issue, and we need the politicians to understand the precise need. The evidence is that schools vary widely, too widely, in their effectiveness (Mortimore 1988). This result is probably reflected in the variation of exclusion rates between schools. These results point to the importance of school factors rather than child factors in the successful avoidance of difficulties, let alone happy and successful education. It has been argued that schools have an educational and moral duty to work with all their pupils. The government must help and require them meet that challenge.

The experience of permanent exclusion from school is deeply damaging to the pupils and distressing for the parents and carers. In some cases, these are families already beset with a range of problems and exclusion from school is a further difficulty. The financial costs which follow from exclusion are considerable. Compared to school, the monies expended buy a vastly inferior educational experience which poses risks for the development of a small section of the future citizenry. The justice of exclusions is rarely questioned because the blame reasoning which underpins it is superficially attractive. It is flawed and must be rejected, especially in its impact on minorities.

NOTE

1   'a balanced and broadly based curriculum which –
    (a) promotes the spiritual, moral, cultural, mental and physical development of the pupils at the school and of society; and
    (b) prepares such pupils for the opportunities, responsibilities and experiences of adult life'

REFERENCES

Aboud, F.E. (1988) *Children and Prejudice*, Oxford: Blackwell.

Argyle, M. (1986) *The Psychology of Happiness*, London: Methuen.

Audit Commission (1996) *Misspent Youth . . . Young People and Crime*, London: Audit Commission.

Barrett, M and Short, J. (1992) 'Images of European people in a group of 5–10 year old English schoolchildren', *British Journal of Developmental Psychology*, **10**, pp. 339–63.

Blair, T. (1998) *The Third Way: New Politics for the New Century*, London: Fabian Society

Campbell, T. (1988) *Justice*, London: Macmillan.

CRE (1996) *Exclusion from School: The Public Cost*, London: Commission for Racial Equality.

Cretney, S. and Masson, J. (1996) *Principles of Family Law*, London: Sweet and Maxwell.

Cuff, E.C., Sharrock, W.W. and Francis, D.W. (1990) (3rd edition) *Perspectives in Sociology*, Routledge: London.

Davies, H. and Holdcroft, H. (1991) *Jurisprudence: Texts and Commentary*, London: Butterworth.

Davies, T. (1997) 'ABC of mental health', *British Medical Journal*, pp. 1536–39.

Dunn, J. (1988) *The Beginnings of Social Understanding*, Oxford: Blackwell.

Durkin, K. (1995) *Developmental Social Psychology*, Oxford: Blackwell.

Dworkin, R. (1977) *Taking Rights Seriously*, London: Duckworth.

Dworkin, R. (1978) 'Liberalism' in Hampshire, S. *Public and Private Morality*, Cambridge: Cambridge University Press.

Gillborn, D. (1990) *Race, Ethnicity and Education: Teaching and Learning in Multi-Ethnic Schools*, London: Unwin Hyman.

Harris, P. (1989) *Children and Emotion*, Oxford: Blackwell.

Hartley, D. (1987) 'The time of their lives: Bureaucracy and the nursery school' in Pollard, A. (ed.) *Children and Their Primary Schools*, London: Falmer Press.

Knapp, M. (1986) 'The relative cost-effectiveness of public, voluntary and private providers of residential child care' in Culyer, A.J. and Johnson, B. *Public and Private Health Services*, Oxford: Blackwell.

Levin, M.L. (1991) 'Cost-benefit and cost-effectiveness analyses of interventions for children in poverty', in Huston, A.C. *Children in Poverty: Child Development and Public Policy*, Cambridge: Cambridge University Press.

Mac an Ghaill, M. (1994) *Young, Gifted and Black: Student-teachers Relations in the Schooling of Black Youth*, Buckingham: Open University.

Majors, R. and Mancini Billson, J. (1992) *Cool Pose*, New York: Touchstone.

Majors, R., Gillborn, D. and Sewell, T. (1998) 'The exclusion of Black children: Implications for a racialised perspective', *Multicultural Teaching*, Spring, pp. 35–7.

Miller, P.J. (1973) 'Factories, monitorial schools and Jeremy Bentham: the origins of the "management syndrome" in popular education', *Journal of Educational Administration and History*, **5**, pp. 10–20.

Morgan, G. (1986) *Images of Organization*, London: Sage.

Mortimore, P. (1988) *School Matters*, London: Open Books.

Parsons, C. (1994) *Excluding Primary School Children*, London: Family Policy Studies Centre.

Parsons, C. (1999) *Education, Exclusion and Citizenship*, London: Routledge.

Persaud, R. (1998) *Staying Sane*, London: Metro.

Pettit, P. (1980) *Judging Justice: An Introduction to Contemporary Political Philosophy*, London: Routledge and Kegan Paul.

Phillips, T. (1998) 'Why is the face of exclusion so often black?', *Times Educational Supplement*, October 23, 15.

Pollard, A. (1984) 'Goodies, jokers and gangs' in Hammersley, M. and Woods, P. *Life in Schools*, Milton Keynes: Open University Press.

Rawls, J. (1972) *A Theory of Justice*, Oxford: Oxford University Press.

Sewell, T. (1997) *Black Masculinities and Schooling*, Stoke-on-Trent: Trentham Books.

Shapland, J., Hibbert, J.I. Anson, J., Sorsby, A. and Wild, R. (1995) *Milton Keynes Criminal Justice Audit*, Sheffield: Institute for the Study of the Legal Profession, University of Sheffield.

Sluckin, A. (1981) *Growing Up in the Playground*, London: Routledge and Kegan Paul.

Smith, P.K. (1994) *School Bullying: Insights and Perspectives*, London: Routledge.

Social Exclusion Unit (1998) *Truancy and Exclusions from School*, London: Social Exclusion Unit.

Stoll, L., Reynolds, D., Creemers, B. and Hopkins, D. (1996) 'Merging school effectiveness and school improvement: practical examples' in Reynolds, D., Bollen, R., Creemers, B., Hopkins, D., Stoll, L. and Lagerweij, N. *Making Good Schools*, London: Routledge.

Wilson, J. (1990) *Practical Methods of Moral Education*, London: Heinemann.

Part IV
Rites of passage, manhood training and masculinity perspectives

10 Enhancing achievement in adolescent black males: the Rites of Passage link

Keith Alford, Patrick McKenry and Stephen Gavazzi

INTRODUCTION

The following maxims are repeatedly used to convey the importance of education in society: 'Education is the key to success,' 'You need an education in order to survive,' and 'Book sense makes good sense.' Yet, some might question if these allegorical statements have fallen on the deaf ears of adolescent Black males. To answer this query, one needs to understand the crippling societal structures that many adolescent or young Black males face in both the United States and Britain. Are Black males truly an 'endangered species,' as noted some years ago by Jewelle Taylor Gibbs (1988), or is educational success theirs for the taking? This population is being studied more closely in recent years due to the many social indicators that suggest this group to be at high risk for numerous health, social, educational, and economic problems (Majors & Billson, 1992; King, 1994; Rasheed & Johnson, 1995; Taylor, 1995; Gavazzi et al., 1996; Miller, 1997; Harvey & Rauch, 1997). This chapter will concentrate on the role educational systems in the United States and Britain play in the lives of young Black males. The challenges of living or surviving, as some have termed it, faced by Black males will be discussed. Moreover, Africentricity's role, a worldview that illuminates the values of people from African descent, will be explored in relation to accentuating the strengths of Black youth and their culture. African American Rites of Passage (AA-RITES), an initiative that is being implemented in communities across the United States, is one such program that has been designed to provide and instill the fundamentals of African and African American culture, history, life skills, and character development training to maturing Black males. From an educational standpoint, AA-RITES have served to increase the self-esteem and ethnic pride of adolescent Black males, hence, helping them to be better fit, both mentally and socially, to receive the academic regimen placed before them. Details about the implementation of the AA-RITES initiative in the state of Ohio for Black adolescent males will be discussed in relation to its salience for teachers, administrators, and other school personnel in the United States and Britain.

Throughout the chapter, voices of young Black males who have participated in Ohio's AA-RITES will be heard in an effort to present the program's essence and curative value. For confidentiality purposes, these voices will be identified through the use of fictitious names. Observations of the researchers will also be noted.

Building on the AA-RITES framework, the authors will highlight points of interest that educational environments need to understand, appreciate, and hopefully integrate into their academic curricula. While the focus of this chapter is on young Black males who are deemed high risk, there are numerous Black male youth who have succeeded, educationally and economically, in spite of a malingering, racially oppressive, social climate. These individuals deserve to be commended for their perseverance and determination and their life trajectories should be carefully examined to identify those factors that seem to account for their success, sometimes against overwhelming odds.

THE STATUS OF BLACK MALES IN THE UNITED STATES AND BRITAIN

It would be careless in any discussion of Black males in the United States and Britain if attention specifically were not given to the debilitating effects of racism. Understanding the need to address pragmatically racial inequities and polarization, Martin Luther King, Jr., made the following statements on August 28, 1963, during his historic March on Washington speech:

> There will be neither rest nor tranquility in America until the Negro is granted his citizenship rights. The whirlwinds of revolt will continue to shake the foundations of our nation until the bright day of justice emerges...So I say to you, my friends that even though we must face the difficulties of today and tomorrow, I still have a dream. It is a dream deeply rooted in the American dream that one day this nation will rise up and live out the true meaning of its creed—we hold these truths to be self-evident, that all men are created equal.

Today, as the world embarks upon a new millennium, the dream that Dr. King spoke of is still only a dream for many young Black males. Racism, be it overt or covert, continues to permeate Western society. A recent horrendous incident gives glaring testimony to the societal context that exists for many Black males in the United States. In Jasper, Texas, during June of 1998, James Byrd, Jr., was savagely beaten by three White men and then chained to a truck and dragged down a road for several miles. This murder is reminiscent of the brutality endured by Black men and women during America's slave era and the subsequent lynchings of Blacks during the period leading up to the Civil Rights Movement. Astonished that such an incident could still occur in 1998, Black Americans and many European Americans vehemently denounced this heinous act.

Today, Black male youth in many western societies live in an atmosphere where racism is pervasive. Countless Black males are socially stifled by their experiences of racism. Hardy and Laszloffy (1995) state that vestiges of racism ignite a cultural rage in many young Black males. They trace this phenomenon back to the injustice of slavery. 'The limited opportunities for Black people as a collective to vent the intense emotions that accumulated during generations of injustice, along with recurring experiences with racism and discrimination, have sustained rage' (Hardy & Laszloffy, 1995, p. 59). Coping with racism's unsettling touch has not been easy for Black Americans, particularly young Black males. Pierce (1975) and Peters and Massey (1983) assert that there is a certain level of mundane extreme environmental stress that exists for African Americans due to the ubiquitous presence of racism. This stress level becomes more evident when such racially motivated acts, as unfair housing practices, police brutality, unresponsive educational systems, and discriminatory employment practices, occur on a regular basis, giving rise to mundane extreme environmental stress. While problems of teen parenthood, delinquency, substance abuse, homicide, suicide, poor school performance, and a variety of other high-risk social behaviors have dramatically increased among the general population, they have been disproportionately found among young Black males because of higher rates of economic distress and greater barriers to social mobility (Gibbs, 1988; Lerner et al., 1994; McAdoo, 1994; Taylor, 1995; Weddle & McKenry, 1995). Majors & Billson (1992) maintain that these social problems should be referred to as social symptoms of a history of oppression. They also assert that for many Black males, the expression of 'cool behavior,' for instance, is a coping strategy that helps manage feelings of rage and stress in the face of prejudice and discrimination (Majors & Billson, 1992, p. 5). This aloofness or front, for many is a way of masking damaged pride and shattered confidence.

While most attention focusing on young Black males in the United States has been linked to the residual effects of slavery and widely acknowledged patterns of institutional racism, the United Kingdom has also suffered from the debilitating impact of racial disdain. It is important to clarify the term 'Black' with respect to its usage in British society. Blacks in today's Britain are people of non-White origin. They come from the Caribbean, India, Pakistan, Bangladesh, and East Africa (Saggar, 1992). According to Jackson (1996), even if a person has mixed race parentage, it is the skin color that is the deciding factor. Most people who are not White European are considered Black in a derogatory sense. This monolithic ordering of different groups is unfair, given the intrinsic strengths each group has to offer, and its unique cultural background. It also sends a message of racial hierarchy, a structural positioning that portends the possibilities of a myriad of racial injustices. The use of the term, 'Black,' for the purposes of this chapter is offered in respect to those individuals in both the United States and Britain who are of African and/or Caribbean descent. The authors anticipate that other groups viewing the information contained in this chapter will find it useful and applicable to them.

Historically, Black presence in Britain dates back to the days of the Roman Empire. As time progressed, African slaves were used to help shape the emergence of industrialization in Britain (Saggar, 1992). Unfortunately, racial superiority on the part of the dominant culture has perpetuated itself in various degrees throughout history. Solomos (1988) reports that despite macro attempts in the late 1960s and early 1970s by such organizations as the Commission for Racial Equality (CRE), the Manpower Services Commission (MSC) and other central government departments to address race-related issues in British society, young Blacks continued to feel alienated from the mainstream. Evidence of high levels of unemployment, low levels of attainment in schools, and homelessness among young Blacks continued to accumulate during the 1970s. Also, during this period, a number of reports in the press surfaced denoting the growing tension between police and Black communities. Complaints by Black youth that they were being cast as a 'problem group' by police accentuated the growing and divisive racial climate (Solomos, 1988). These issues were more pervasive for young Black males who were the brunt of harsh criticism by the general public. They were often perceived as troublemakers, as opposed to individuals trying to gain a respectful place in society. The image of rioters at the Notting Hill Carnival of 1976 continues to epitomize society's view of Black youth. Alexander (1996) contends that this is symbolic of society's failure to meet the needs of its most vulnerable members.

Since the 1970s, the combination of unemployment with criminality, urban decay, and social disorder has led to a culturalist definition of disadvantage, exemplified acutely through the political jargon of 'special needs' (Solomos, 1998; Wrench, 1992; Alexander, 1996). An emphasis has been placed staunchly on the cultural 'handicap' as it relates to Blacks in Britain, rather than structural or institutional exclusion (Alexander, 1996). Young Black males, in particular, have difficulty cultivating a sense of nationhood in British society. In fact, for many, calling themselves British is a controversial issue. It is difficult for an adolescent Black male to accept the designation of 'British' when racial disparities remain omnipresent. The Black male peer group, in some British circles, has become a buffer to an otherwise oppressive society. Aside from familial influences, identity formation for adolescent Black males is developed through their inclusion and association with 'the boys,' the Black male peer group. However, the absence of what some would call a full national blessing, obstructs the development of a national consciousness for young Black males living in Britain. They want their cultural heritage as people of African decent or Caribbean descent to be respected and appreciated.

James (1988) recalls when schools in Britain were not necessarily courteous in their deportment toward Black children. Teachers dismissed Black students as irritants or people to be pitied because they lacked a full understanding of the mainstream cultural backlash Black students routinely received. Such attitudes did not go unnoticed by the Black population. Consequently, schisms formed between teachers and students. There was a general sense of outrage that permeated this period. In the wake of racist attitudes about Black students, vocal Black opposition by African Caribbean parent groups ensued. Currently, the issue of teacher-student relations remains a central concern for many individuals associated with Britain's educational system.

RITES OF PASSAGE PROGRAMS IN THE UNITED STATES

Now let us focus attention on rites programming in the United States as a precursor to our discussion of implications for educational systems in addressing the needs and issues faced by young Black males. The 1960s saw the inauguration of a wide range of federal initiatives in the United States to combat the problems of poverty, dependency, family breakdown, and delinquency among the nation's underclass;

many of these initiatives focused on Black families and specifically Black youth (e.g., Moynihan report of 1965). These policies represented a great departure from historical practice wherein government took much less responsibility for social problems (Murray, 1984; Taylor, 1995). Such programs have not proven to be very successful as the focus has been on employment and training interventions. Remedial programming to help Black youth function and thrive within a racially oppressive society has been lacking (Sklar, 1987; Taylor, 1995). In recent years, rites of passage programs have been adapted and developed for young Black males to serve the purpose of providing Black youth many of the strengths that have been denied them as an oppressed group; such strengths include ethnic pride, self-esteem, self-respect, respect for others, and a variety of other 'healthy' behaviors (Warfield-Coppock, 1992). Equally crucial is the need to expose young Black males to the strength of understanding and appreciating the role of Black men in history and culture (Lee, 1996). This strength ranks high in terms of lessons to be learned by rites of passage participants.

Many of the difficulties being witnessed in contemporary society, including the increase in substance abuse and violent behaviors among adolescents – both considered antecedents of poor school performance – have been linked to society's underutilization of rites of passage (Lantz & Pegram, 1989; Blumenkrantz & Gavazzi, 1993; Campbell & Moyers, 1988). The void created in the absence of socially prescribed transitional markers, in turn, is thought to be filled by adolescents through destructive and excessive engagement in drinking, sexual activity, and gang activities (Quinn et al., 1985; Hill, 1992). These self-defeating behaviors seemingly represent pseudo rites of passage that have claimed too many Black males, halting any promise of realizing the extent of their human capacity.

BUILDING ON THE STRENGTHS OF ADOLESCENT BLACK MALES THROUGH AFRICENTRIC IMMERSION

The Africentric theoretical perspective undergirds the African American Rites of Passage Program. This theoretical framework places Africa as the historical point of generation. The holistic premise of Africentricity is thought to be functional, because it gives direction and purpose to the thoughts and actions of African American people (Hill, 1992). Hill (1992) explicitly defines the Africentric theoretical perspective as:

> . . . enabling one to approach feelings, knowledge, and actions as a comprehensive whole rather than as disparate segments. It enables one to move from a position characterized by a neo-colonial mentality to one of relative autonomy . . . Paramount in the Africentric perspective is that the struggle of African Americans has historically had the central goal of gaining some measure of human dignity in a society which too often disregards the culture of non-Western peoples.

(pp. 34-35)

Furthering the knowledge base of participants about their African and African American heritage is a central component of rites programming. Jamal, a two-year participant in the AA-RITES program, says:

> I think it is important for everyone to know your roots—understanding of your people. You need to know yourself. It is real important to know your roots whether you are White, Black, Asian, or Hispanic. Stop by the library and look things up.

Learning about African culture and the contributions of their African ancestors permits rites of passage program participants to gain greater appreciation of their ethnic and racial identity and learn about the prominence of people who look like themselves (Harvey, 1994).

Ideas of interconnectedness, collective consciousness, and oneness with nature are considered primary concepts of the Africentric theoretical perspective. Interconnectedness promotes the idea that all things are interdependent. It also provides the foundation for all human interactions because harmony and positive relations are necessary parts of social activity (Warfield-Coppock, 1992; Lee, 1996). Collective consciousness refers to the sense of being related to all members of one's ethnic group with the group being more important than the individual. Oneness with nature asserts the premise that spiritual forces, human beings, and nature are invaluable, interconnected, and deserving of universal respect (Warfield-Coppock, 1990).

Hill (1992) purports that the successful execution of an African American Rites of Passage Program for adolescent males should include objectives that emphasize youth's achievements in the following areas: (a) a sense of true identity and feeling of connectedness to the Black community and diaspora; (b) a degree of social knowledge and understanding that will equip him to overcome racism and other debilitating circumstances; (c) a reverence for the natural worth and dignity of one's parents, extended family, and community; (d) a masculine ideal that conforms to profamily and prosocial values; and (e) a philosophy that honors and facilitates continued growth and development. In essence, under the tutelage and direction of program leaders and elders, young Black male participants in rites of passage learn about their ancestral background and how to govern themselves in a difficult world as they prepare to enter manhood. 'It takes a village to raise a child,' is an African proverb (Hill, 1992, p. 55) lauded by AA-RITES program leaders as representative of its basic educational approach.

For AA-RITES participants, Nguzo Saba serves as a value system worthy of daily implementation. Serving the same function as the Nguzo Saba, the principles of Ma'at (path of righteousness), are also emphasized in the AA-RITES program. These principles draw from the teachings of Egyptian men and women who believed that they had to practice the principles of righteousness, truth, and justice in daily living if they hoped to be divinely judged at death and to successfully enter the afterlife (Gavazzi et al., 1996). Other principles of Ma'at include reciprocity, balance, harmony, order, sense of excellence, and sense of appropriateness (Kelsey,

---

Application of the Nguzo Saba and Ma'at

The AA-RITES program closely follows the Nguzo Saba (Seven Principles) which closely parallels the Africentric perspective. The Swahili terms that define the Nguzo Saba, designed by Dr. Malana Karenga (1988) in the mid 1960s, include the following:

Umoja (**Unity**) – striving and maintaining unity in the family, community, nation, and race.

Kujichagulia (**Self-Determination**) – defining and molding ourselves from a strengths-oriented perspective as opposed to being incorrectly defined or spoken for by others.

Ujima (**Collective Work and Responsibility**) – working collectively toward resolving problems and maintaining our community.

Ujamaa (**Cooperative Economics**) – building and preserving our stores, shops, and businesses in an effort to jointly enjoy the profits.

Nia (**Purpose**) – making a concerted attempt to build, develop, and cultivate our community in order to reclaim the inherent greatness of our people.

Kuumba (**Creativity**) – thinking of and executing ways to improve our community both intrinsically and aesthetically.

Imani (**Faith**) – having steadfast determination and belief in ourselves, parents, teachers, and leaders, all of whom have struggled for racial justice and equality.

1991). Both the Nguzo Saba and the principles of Ma'at supply AA-RITES participants with a constructive outlook and serve as cultural bulwarks in the context of an unpredictable societal milieu.

While Ohio's AA-RITES program has achieved great success in reaching adolescent Black males, the proliferation of other rites of passage programs across America continues to soar. The Young Lions and Black Manhood training programs for pre-teen and adolescent Black males, respectively, both developed by Courtland Lee, have received critical acclaim for their collective emphasis on educational and social empowerment. Dr. Lee, a former teacher and school counselor, presently serves as professor of counselor education at the University of Virginia. He is of the opinion that young people learn best through experiential means (Lee, 1996). Various art forms are used in these programs to help facilitate group discussion around pressing cultural and social themes. Such art forms include inspirational poems about Black people, rap music that sends a message of survival and triumph, and testimonies of Black men who have overcome adversity. For instance, a goal for one session is to have participants critically examine the dynamics of academic and social problems confronting them as students. Lee (1996) affirms that an enterprising method of facilitation associated with this topic area is to play the recording, 'Bad Times,' by the vocal group Tavares. A series of role-plays are developed around the lyrics of this song, which involve confrontations with teachers. Lee (1996) says that through the use of these role-plays, the leader helps participants develop strategies for dealing with disagreements and utilizing self-control. Similarly speaking, to explore the role of Black men as fathers, the recording, 'Pappa Was a Rolling Stone,' by the Temptations, is shared with group participants. Two of several questions that emanate from this exercise for group discussion include: 'Does making babies make you a man?' and 'Does fatherhood bring responsibilities with it?' In other sessions, the leader may want to help the youth engage in a self-introspective process. To facilitate this endeavor, literary works by Langston Hughes and other prominent Black writers are recited and processed.

INTERWEAVING RITES OF PASSAGE CONCEPTS AND IDEAS IN THE EDUCATIONAL SYSTEM

Several implications for schools come out of the rites of passage movement. The concepts and ideas of a rites of passage initiative have much to offer educational systems if schools are to become more successful in preparing young Black males to assume positive roles in adulthood. First, schools must adopt a proactive cultural posture. This would include being consciously aware of the 'Black experience.' In the United States and Britain, the Black experience entails the survival of Black individuals and families in the midst of racial struggle. The emphasis on 'struggle' involves the fight for equality and social justice (Chestang, 1972). Because Blacks in the United States and Britain have had to endure the debilitating effects of oppression and second-class citizenship, many parents, caretakers, and mentors teach their children to be mindful of the social environment's benefits and hazards. This warning is ensconced with the notion that society will judge them more harshly than their White counterparts. There remains a stigmatizing perception that people of color are not to be trusted and do not deserve to be treated fairly and with respect. This stereotype is more pervasive, depending on one's given region or locality. Nonetheless, it exists and the conduct of people in positions of authority and power is often governed by this belief.

Lee (1996) reminds us that low achievement, and damaged pride occur in young Black males when teachers and other school personnel manifest such racist notions as evaluating Black males differently than other students and not believing that they can master certain academic tasks. Black males are more likely to be profiled for failure through disproportionate placement in special education classes, suspended from school more frequently, and complete high school at profoundly lower rates than any other ethnic/gender group. Given this dubious profile, it is no wonder that Black males develop a guarded disposition. 'Cool pose,' referenced earlier in this chapter, is literally an invisible coat of arms that is used by men of color to combat the injustices they routinely endure by virtue of their skin color (Majors & Billson, 1992, p. 5). However, when faced with such defense mechanisms by Black male students, teachers become daunted and uncertain about how to begin or even maintain communication.

Professionals from all helping disciplines should be aware that the walking style, talking style, handshakes, and nonverbal aloofness of Black males are often expressions of their masculinity. These expressions receive sanction from the peer group because society has not legitimately sanctioned the social existence of Black males. In support of this position, Majors (1991) asserts that expressive behaviors of Black males are sometimes used to keep Whites off guard. How, then, is the teacher to handle certain behavioral expressions of this kind? Consistent with the Africentric perspective, it will be imperative for teachers to seek understanding of the exhibited expressions and reflect on their personal attitudes and behaviors that may, in some way, be associated with the prevailing racial climate. These caveats serve as psychological markers for AA-RITES leaders and elders as they begin manhood training with AA-RITES participants. Moreover, these markers assist in forming a framework for addressing with participants' concerns around racism.

The etiology of racism against people of color is explored as a part of the AA-RITES experience. It is usually discussed in conjunction with African and African American history. Skill building exercises on how to combat racism in an effort to maintain one's honorable deportment and self-confidence are strongholds of the AA-RITES experience. An AA-RITES researcher had the opportunity to observe a rites session in progress. Racism was one of the topics discussed at this session. The following are his observations:

> Today I was fortunate enough to witness an AA-RITES session in progress. One of the elders was conducting a session on African American history. The lesson involved a chronology of the struggles African Americans have had to endure since their arrival in this country. This session was complete with a film, lecture, and discussion. Racism was also discussed. It was integrated into the discussion of African American history. Truthfully and constructively done, the elder broached the subject matter in a sedate tone. Every participant was keenly attentive while the elder spoke. It was obvious that he commanded respect and rightly so. I was spellbound as I sat in amazement at the group dynamics as well as the poignant delivery of the speaker.

Racism's destructive quality has been a prime cause for the self-hate that many Blacks endure; therefore, AA-RITES leaders and elders must equip young Black males with positive aspects about their history as a race of people. History lessons are not offered for the sake of memorization, but for empowerment and cultural elevation. Kwame, an AA-RITES participant, voices the following:

> You gotta know where you come from – your heritage. If you were to tell somebody that you're Black and they ask you where you came from – what part of Africa? If you were to say you were from Africa, you gotta know everything about it. You gotta know yourself. You can't let anyone tell you that nothing's wrong or lead you down the wrong path.

Another young man offers these words, '. . . we survived all the pain and suffering of enslavement. We are still striving. We are very important.' This youth understands the historical significance of what people of African descent suffered while they were enslaved. He also reflects a strong belief in the fortitude of his people in modern existence. Educational systems can enhance the well being of all students, regardless of their race, by incorporating progressive dialogue about race relations. Ignoring racial disparities that exist is an insult to adolescents who often are hit the hardest with negative race-based attitudes from the general public.

Hale-Benson (1986) affirms that educational environments should respond to the desires of Black parents in broadening traditional curricula to include the study and legitimizing of African and African American culture. She also notes that Black parents want to see the Black experience integrated into songs, arithmetic problems, science experiments, arts and crafts activities, social studies, and dance forms. Such efforts toward cultural integration into the programmatic schema of an educational system would benefit the self-esteem levels of Black students, enhance the quality of basic education, and expose other students to enriching new experiences (e.g., Lee, 1996). British schools would need to expand modern curricula to include the study of all individuals that fall under the socially constructed definition of 'Black.' An unsung benefit of broadening traditional curricula is that it affords students and teachers the opportunity to explore cross-cultural commonalties. Often, in our quest to respect and celebrate cultural differences, we pay little attention to cross-cultural commonalties. These commonalties can help cultivate bonds between people and open paths of communication that might not otherwise occur (Alford, 1996).

The African proverb, 'I am because we are, and because we are, therefore I am,' espoused by the AA-RITES program, envelopes the worthiness of total community involvement. The AA- RITES program touts the mentoring experience as a fundamental part of adolescent development. When possible, mentors should be incorporated in daily classroom activities. They could easily serve as speakers, tutors, and confidants in matters that require a listening ear. Mentors also serve a correctional role from the standpoint of helping adolescent males process behavioral issues and make life choices. Although mentors for young Black males can be male or female, with respect to helping young Black males, it is important that the mentor be a productive and responsible male. Mentors invariably serve as role models and because of their potential impact on young lives, it is pivotal that these men govern themselves in a respectful manner. Matching young Black males with responsible Black mentors is a wonderful example of 'giving back' to the community one's talents, knowledge, and common sense (e.g., Denby, 1996). Lee (1996) adamantly states that responsible adult Black males who truly know about the dynamics associated with Black male development should be utilized as resources.

Holland (1989) cites the need for American schools to recruit more Black males to teach at primary grade levels. Schools in Britain would also benefit by following this practice. He states that most boys do not have male teachers until the later elementary grades or junior high school, and, for inner-city boys, this is too late. The role modeling that Black male teachers and mentors can provide is invaluable. According to Holland (1989), ' . . . students – especially boys – who fail to complete high school dropout psychologically and emotionally by the 3rd or 4th grade. Inner-city, Black male children drop out or leave at truly alarming rates' (p. 88). Thus, the mentor's job is both serious and rewarding. Given this, it would behoove educational systems to provide orientation training for all men who volunteer to fulfill this role. Orientation training should include the provision of general demographics about the population being served without breaking confidentiality. It should also provide information with respect to expectations of the mentor regarding time, travel, money, emotional support, and interaction with the student's family of origin. No assumptions should be made regarding the mentor's understanding of expectations. All mentors should be educated on racial socialization of young Black males. They also must support the notion of the inculcation of Nguzo Saba and principles of Ma'at in the lives of Black males. Mentors are charged with the task of helping youngsters develop good problem-solving and decision-making skills. Relying on established frameworks like Nguzo Saba and Ma'at, notwithstanding the wisdom acquired through daily living, is crucial for providing effective guidance and counsel. Strengthening the young Black male's internal locus of control leads to greater self-worth (Alexander, 2000). Overall, understanding the impact and ramifications of the Black experience will help mentors improve their relational skills. Like the Africentric training required for all AA-RITES leaders and elders, mentor orientation training helps solidify certain relational competencies that are needed to effectively engage the service population.

AA-RITES program leaders and elders work diligently to be expressive and open in their concern for young males under their tutelage. The communication of warmth and empathy is a strong component of the AA-RITES experience. Likewise, creating a caring, humanistic educational environment deserves close attention. Kunjufu (1990) cites the stark words of American Jeff Fort, a major gang leader of the Chicago Blackstone Rangers, 'We will always have the youth because we make them feel important.' This powerful statement by a gang leader is quite revealing. He clearly understands that to maintain the interest and loyalty of young male gang members it is vital that they feel appreciated and respected. White & Johnson (1991) note that youngsters place great emphasis on the necessity of having partners or comrades. They further note that in the Black community, the peer group, as part of the extended family, helps the Black child fulfill the need for belongingness. Educational systems would do well to encourage affirmative peer group interaction. Kunjufu (1990) states that it is the responsibility of the adult community, including educational systems, to spend time with Black youth and make them feel good about themselves so that they will not need to turn to gangs for comfort or security. Kunjufu is articulating the mandate that educators and community leaders must exert the human factor when interacting with adolescent Black males.

Teachers not only teach in didactic ways, but they also teach through their actions. The human factor in education should be cultivated as it relates to ensuring the success of students. This is particularly so for adolescent Black males. Their awareness of racial oppression makes them a vulnerable group. As a result, educators should make every effort to provide positive reinforcement when success is achieved.

Quite simply, adolescent Black males need social support, and social support is an action-oriented activity. The human factor and social support are synonymous. Richman et al. (1998) suggest that social support in the form of being a good listener, offering emotional comfort and encouragement, and providing academic assistance is strongly needed as a preventive measure vis-à-vis school failure. The inherent combative quality of social support against school failure and other concerns is worthy of exploration and implementation. Understanding this need and the overall concern of urban educational reform, the Portland, Oregon, Public School System, in the late 1980s, identified its own challenges as they relate to young Black males within the context of larger national problems (i.e., homicide, suicide, crime, delinquency, and school truancy) and initiated actions to prevent their escalation (Green et al, 1989).

The Portland, Oregon, Project saw correlations between national problems and student discontent in school, low reading scores, student expulsions, and dropouts (Green, 1987; Green et al., 1989). Like the AA-RITES program, the project sought to address these areas strategically through developing multiple opportunities for student success; ensuring that teachers conveyed high educational expectations to students; emphasizing a multiethnic curriculum through which pride in self-defined reference groups is supported; intense focusing on basic skills of reading, writing, communication, computation, and critical thinking; accessing major participation by community agencies and groups in program design and empowerment; ongoing assessment and monitoring of progress related to content elements; and acknowledging and countering the effects of institutionalized racism and rules of domination (Green et al., 1989). Since the inception of the Portland, Oregon, Project, many school districts across the United States have adopted its strategies in conjunction with components of the AA-RITES program.

Lee (1996), in his discussion of empowerment strategies for young Black males, believes that parental endorsement and support are necessary components of any youth-related helping process. Just as we affirm the peer group, we should do the same for parents. He encourages parents' workshops that are designed to help promote academic and social development of male children. Believing that this effort should be sponsored and supported by educational systems, Lee (1996) cites the following issues as relevant for workshop topics:

1   parenting in a racially-conscious society;
2   the history and legacy of the Black family,
3   school success, and
4   the developmental stages of childhood

Single parents, particularly those in female-headed households, benefit the most from workshop participation because of its informative and holistic value. Educational systems stand a greater chance of maintaining and ensuring cognitive and social growth of students when they build upon the collectivity of the group. Orchestrating activities that are inclusive of the family and community promotes solidarity.

Like the circle of a family, interconnectedness and a sense of belonging should be extolled at the macro level by individual schools. Bringing students together through school-wide assembly programs when they have individually and collectively mastered certain skills or attained a special achievement is a public way of condoning that which is positive. Adding a degree of pageantry to school assembly programs denotes its seriousness. Some would argue that Britain, more than the United States, is replete with pageantry, rituals, and festivities. Utilizing this collective strength in a culturally specific way is a proactive measure toward addressing the needs of Black male students. Conscious steps should be taken to seek out young Black males and honor their accomplishments (i.e., grade level promotions, good citizenship, commitment to family and community, respect shown to women, maintaining productive behavior, and perfect attendance). Paying homage to all of the aforementioned achievements validates the inherent importance of each in the minds of students, school personnel, parents, caretakers, and community members.

Hare and Hare (1985) note that, as a society, we give enormous attention to such celebratory activities as graduations and birthdays. Parties are often held in recognition of these events. Ironically, little attention, other than verbal praise, is given to behavioral and social accomplishments. During many AA-RITES ceremonies, younger African American males (pre-adolescents) watch their older counterparts (adolescents) receive the proper acknowledgment that signals transition from one stage of life to another. Symbols, such as certificates and gifts, are often given as gestures of recognition. In addition, the public acknowledgment of achievements by the community often adds greater meaning to the event. Educational systems that openly embrace the concept of 'ceremonial' school assemblies position themselves well, as in the case of AA-RITES, to advance student achievement and set examples for younger students to follow.

CONCLUSION

If education is truly the key to success, educational systems must be creative in pinpointing new ways to effectively reach all students. The unique circumstances, presented above, of young Black males in the United States and Britain should not be ignored. Holland (1991) contends that, after the family, the school stands as the most important cultural institution contributing to the education and socialization of children. Given this, initiatives like AA-RITES, should be meticulously examined for their applicability toward enhancing the educational resilience, self-esteem, and ethnic pride of adolescent Black males. Black male students should not be denounced or berated, but embraced as contributing members of society. This is why it is especially critical that educational advocacy exist for Black male students in an effort to counter the systemic barriers that continue to mount. Seminars, workshops, and ongoing trainings should be customary as these relate to instructing school personnel on the dynamics of Black male development (Lee, 1996). Educational systems that actively and wholeheartedly address students' needs are unquestionably answering the global charge of investing in the well being of humankind.

Keith Alford et al.

REFERENCES

Alexander, C. (1996). *The art of being Black.* Oxford: Clarendon Press.

Alexander, R. (2000). Counseling, treatment, and intervention methods with juvenile and adult offenders. Canada: Brooks/Cole.

Alford, K.A. (1996). Multicultural realities: A prescription for positive coexistence. *Open Eyes Minds, Shades of Us: University of Minnesota Community Guide for Students of Color, 2,* 171–181.

Blumenkrantz, D. & Gavazzi, S.M. (1993). Guiding transitional events for children and adolescents through a modern day rite of passage. *Journal of Primary Prevention, 13,* 199–212.

Campbell, J., & Moyers, B. (1988). *The power of myth.* New York: Doubleday.

Chestang. L. (1972). *Character Development in a Hostile Environment.* (Occasional Paper No. 3). Chicago, Illinois: University of Chicago, School of Social Service Administration.

Denby, R. (1996). Resiliency and the African American family: A model of family preservation. In S. Logan (Ed.), *The Black family: Strengths, self-help, and positive change* (pp. 144–163). Boulder, Colorado: Westview Press.

Gavazzi, S.M., Alford, K.A, & McKenry, P.C. (1996). Culturally specific programs for foster care youth: The sample case of an African American rites of passage program. *Family Relations, 45* (2), 166–174.

Gibbs, J.T. (1988). *Young, Black, and male in America: an endangered species.* Dover, MA: Auburn House.

Green, R.L. (1987). *Expectations: Research implications on a major dimension of effective schooling.* (Report) Cleveland, Ohio: Cuyahoga Community College.

Green, R.L., Franklin, C. & Hammond, N.J. (1989). *Increasing the achievement of Black male students: The Portland, Oregon public schools approach.* (Report) Cleveland, Ohio: Case Western Reserve University & Cuyahoga Community College.

Hale-Benson, J.E. (1986). *Black Children: Their roots, culture, and learning styles.* Baltimore: The John Hopkins University Press.

Hardy, K. & Laszloffy, T. (1995). Therapy with African Americans and the phenomenon of rage. *In Session: Psychotherapy in Practice, 1* (4), 57–70.

Harvey, A. (1994). Afro-centric model of prevention with African American adolescent males: The MAAT rites of passage program. In J.B. Rauch (Ed.), Community-based, family-centered services in a changing health care environment (pp. 115–130). University of Maryland.

Harvey, A., & Rauch J. B. (1997). A comprehensive Afrocentric rites of passage program for Black male adolescents. *Health & Social Work,* 22(l), 30–37.

Hare, N. & Hare, J. (1985). *Bringing the Black boy to manhood.* San Francisco: The Black Think Tank.

Hill, P. (1992). *Coming of Age: African American male rites-of-passage.* Chicago: African American Images.

Holland, S. (1989, September/October). Fighting the epidemic of failure. *Teacher Magazine.*

Holland, S. (1991). Positive role models for primary-grade Black inner-city males. *Equity & Excellence,* 25(l), 40–44.

Jackson, V. (1996). *Racism and child protection.* London: Cassell.

James, W. (1988). A long way from home: On Black Identity in Britain. *Western European Education,* 20(4), 60–94.

Karenga, M. (1988). *African American holiday of Kwanzaa.* Los Angeles: Sankore Press.

Kelsey, M. (1991). *Rites of passage: Road to adulthood.* Columbus, Ohio: Africentric Personal Development Shop.

King, A. (1994). An Afrocentric cultural awareness program for incarcerated African American males. *Journal of Multicultural Social Work*, 3(4), 17–28.

King, M. L. (1963). I have a dream. (Speech).

Kunjufu, J. (1990). *Countering the conspiracy to destroy Black boys. Volume Three.* Chicago: African American Images.

Lantz, J., & Pegram, M. (1989). Cross cultural curative factors and clinical social work. *Journal of Independent Social Work.* 4(I), 55–69.

Lee, C.C. (1996). *Saving the native son: Empowerment strategies for young Black males.* Greensboro, North Carolina: ERIC Counseling and Student Services Clearinghouse.

Lemer, R. M., Entwisle, D. R., & Hauser, S. (1994). The crisis among contemporary American adolescents: A call for the integration of research, policies, and programs. *Journal of Research on Adolescence*, 4, 1–4.

Majors, R. (1991). Nonverbal behaviors and communication styles among African Americans. In R. Jones (Ed.), *Black psychology.* (pp. 269–294). Berkeley, CA: Cobb & Henry.

Majors, R. & Billson, J. (1992). *Cool pose: The dilemmas of Black manhood in America.* New York: Simon & Schuster.

McAdoo, J. L. (1994). Health risks of African American adolescents. In P. C. McKenry, & S. M. Gavazzi (Eds.), *Visions 2010: Families and adolescence* (pp. 34–35). Minneapolis, MN: National Council on Family Relations.

Miller, D. B. (1997). Adolescent fathers: What we know and what we need to know. *Child and Adolescent Social Work Journal*, 14 (1), 55–69.

Moynihan, D. P. (1965). *The Negro family: The case for national action.* Washington, DC: Department of Labor.

Murray, C. (1984). *Losing ground: American social policy, 1950–1980.* New York: Basic Books.

Peters, M., & Massey, G. (1983). Mundane extreme environmental stress in family stress theories: The case of Black families in White America. *Marriage and Family Review.6(1/2)*, 193–225.

Pierce, C. (1975). The mundane extreme environment and its effect on learning. In S. Brainard (Ed.), *Learning, disabilities: issues and recommendations for research.* Washington, DC: National Institute of Education.

Quinn, W., Newfield, N., & Protinsky, H. (1985). Rites of passage in families with adolescents. *Family Process*, 24, 101–111.

Rasheed, J. & Johnson, W. (1995). Non-custodial African American fatherhood: A case study research approach. *Journal of Community Practice*, 2 (2), 99–116.

Richman, J. M., Rosenfield, L. B., & Bowen, G. L. (1998). Social support for adolescents at risk of school failure. *Social Work.*43(4), 309–323.

Saggar, S. (1992). *Race and politics in Britain.* New York: Harvester Wheatsheaf.

Sklar, M. (1987). *The federal response to Black youth unemployment:* An analysis of the effectiveness of the job training partnership act in four metropolitan areas. Washington, DC: Joint Center for Political Studies.

Solomos, J. (1988). *Black youth, racism and the state.* Cambridge: Cambridge University Press.

Taylor, R. L. (1995). *African American youth: Their social and economic status in the United States.* Westport, CT: Praeger.

Warfield-Coppock, N. (1990). *Afrocentric theory and applications, Vol. I: Adolescent Rites of passage.* Washington, DC: Baobab Associates.

Warfield-Coppock, N. (1992). *Afrocentric theory and applications, Vol. II: Advances in the adolescent rites of passage.* Washington, DC: Baobab Associates.

Weddle, K. D., & McKenry, P. C. (1995). Self-destructive behaviors among Black youth: suicide and homicide. In R. L. Taylor (Ed.), *African American youth: Their social and economic status in the United States* (pp. 203–224). Westport, CT: Praeger.

White, J. L., & Johnson, J. A. (1991). Awareness, pride and identity: A positive educational strategy for Black youth. In R.L. Jones (Ed.), *Black psychology* (pp. 409–418). Berkeley, CA: Cobb & Henry.

Wrench, J. (1992). New Vocationalism, Old Racism and the careers service. In P. Braham, A. Rattansi, and R. Skellington (Eds.), *Racism and antiracism*. London: Sage.

11 An after-school manhood development program

Aminifu R. Harvey

Children are the reward of life.

(African proverb)

INTRODUCTION

According to Dryfoos (1990), one in four young people in America 'do it all' and are in jeopardy of not growing into responsible adults unless immediate interventions occur. This is more likely to happen among those with low self-esteem, low educational aspiration, low social skills, and low social approval (Botvin and McAlister 1981; Millman and Botvin 1983).

This chapter presents a range of social and psychological services to high-risk African American adolescent males based on an Afrocentric approach that incorporates the principles of spirituality and collectivity. For the purpose of this article *spirituality* is defined as living a life grounded in individual moral principles. The principle of *collectivity* refers to exhibiting behaviors that enhance one's group of origin (Harvey and Coleman 1997).

It is recognized that high-risk behaviors are significantly interrelated, especially among youths (Penkower, Dew, Kingsley, Becker, Satz, Schaerf and Sheridan 1991). For this reason it is suggested that prevention programmes be developed that target the underlying determinants of several theoretically and empirically related problem behaviors (Botvin 1982; Swisher 1979). These observations suggest that generic interventions addressing more than one behavior or predisposing factors are preferable to approaches that target only one risk factor, or that employ only one intervention method (Harvey 1997).

Kunjufu (1985) identified the following factors that enable African American youths to overcome the negative influences of inner-city life: strong family background, positive peer pressure, social survival skills, participation on athletic teams, high teacher expectations, high student–teacher ratio and religious participation. Similarly, Lewis and Lewis (1984) identified effective mental health prevention programs for African American families and children as those that helped them in developing satisfying relationships, acquiring effective cognitive problem solving skills, managing personal stress and maintaining positive self-concepts. It is widely assumed that an effective prevention program should aim at promoting youths' general personal and social competence, vocational aspirations, and self-esteem, thereby affecting the factors that underlie many types of delinquent behaviors (Harvey 1997).

EMPOWERMENT

Solomon (1976) affirmed empowerment as a process and goal for oppressed peoples. She defined *empowerment* as 'a process whereby the (social) worker engages in a set of activities with the client or client system that aim to reduce the powerlessness that has been created by negative evaluations based on membership in a stigmatized group' (p. 19). She defined *powerlessness* as 'the inability to manage emotions, skills, knowledge, and/or material resources in a way that effective performance of valued social roles will lead to personal gratification' (p. 16).

Solomon hypothesized that powerlessness is derived from direct and indirect power blocks. Institutional agents apply direct power blocks. For example, the health care system may fail to provide adequate community-based health services. Consequently, individuals' health and functioning is diminished. Indirect power blocks are incorporated into individuals' developmental experience. For example, a parent may foster low self-esteem by denigrating a dark-skinned child's color (Harvey 1995). A lack of self-confidence is created, thus the child may give up when school work is difficult and may not develop basic reading, writing and arithmetic skills. The concept of indirect power blocks is akin to internalized racism, but broader. As in internalized racism, indirect power blocks connote rejection of self and others like oneself because of race. Indirect power blocks, in addition, connote inability to function in important roles because of psychological factors, lack of interpersonal skills, lack of knowledge of systems and resource management deficits (Solomon 1976).

Solomon (1976) posited that direct and indirect power blocks interact to generate powerlessness. In the aforementioned scenario, for example, the child might continue to fail because the school does not provide adequate instruction (direct power block). Behavioral and emotional problems may emerge (indirect power blocks), further impeding his learning. Solomon's model (1976) implies that intervention needs to address psychological factors, interpersonal skills, knowledge deficits, technical skills, and resource management. The goal is to enable oppressed people to transcend indirect power blocks to create satisfying lives and become part of an empowered community to effectively address direct power blocks. The approach is congruent with research findings which suggest that adolescent risk behaviors tend to cluster in the same individual and require multifaceted, rather than categorical, interventions (Carnegie Corporation 1995; Irwin and Ingra 1994; Jessor 1992).

CULTURAL COMPETENCE

Perkins (1986) states that an Afrocentric cultural approach is needed to effectively deal with the antisocial behavior of high-risk African American youth and outlines a youth rites of passage program as such a mechanism. According to Warfield-Coppock and Harvey (1989), the rites of passage approach is based on African and African American cultures that seek to restore traditional social constraints on the behaviors of African American youths, help them to develop emotional and cognitive abilities in a constructive fashion, and prepare them to become responsible members of society.

A culturally competent system of care 'acknowledges and incorporates' – at all levels – the importance of culture, the assessment of cross-cultural relations, vigilance towards the dynamics that result from cultural differences, the expansion of cultural knowledge, and the adaptation of services to meet culturally unique needs. Cultural competence can be envisioned as a continuum with negative and positive poles (Cross, Bazron, Dennis and Isaacs 1989). The negative pole is cultural destructiveness, or attitudes, policies and practices that harm a particular culture and, consequently, individuals within the culture. At the point of cultural incapability, the system is biased, believes that the dominant group is superior, and is paternalistic towards populations perceived as inferior. Culturally blind practitioners and agencies believe that all people are the same and that dominant helping approaches are universally applicable. Culturally precompetent agencies and practitioners recognize weaknesses in serving diverse populations, desire to improve and act to do so (i.e. hiring community residents) (Harvey and Rauch 1997). Basic cultural competence occurs when organizations and practitioners respect difference, engage in on-going cultural self-assessment, expand their cultural knowledge and skills, and adapt services to fit the community's culture, situation and perceived needs. With cultural proficiency, the group's culture is esteemed and new approaches are developed based on deep cultural knowledge. All health organizations and practitioners are at different points along the continuum (ibid.).

Program practice principles

The orientation of the youth workers is critical. Workers must recognize that failure to engage African American youths may be a manifestation of practitioner and organizational racism, classism and/or cultural ignorance. It is important for the workers to change ways of thinking and speaking about youths of African descent, from individual modes that label the person to ecological modes that comprehend youths as coping with high-risk, oppressive situations. Staff training in Afrocentric principles, programs and techniques is crucial, in addition to using pictures, fabrics, accessories, music, food, and so forth to create a culturally welcoming environment (Harvey and Rauch 1997). These programs should be formulated from a group work perspective since African American youths move through adolescence in peer groups. With African American youths, it is necessary to place the group within the context of a program rather than label it a 'group'. Many of the youths have been involved in psychotherapeutic groups in institutions and believe that being involved in a group implies that something is innately wrong with them or that they are 'crazy'. Structure is important, and each session needs to be planned. Nevertheless, the worker/teacher must be flexible enough to focus on the concerns the youths might have during each session (Harvey 1997).

In working with African American youths it is critical for the workers to respect their opinions and their right to voice their opinion, even when these differ from that of the workers. This does not mean agreeing with their opinions but rather giving them the opportunity to fully develop and express their ideas. It also means that it is the workers' responsibility to challenge their opinion but not use their authority to impose views (ibid.).

The transformational process is greatly enhanced if the group leaders are African American, as they act as positive same-race role models. The lack of positive African American role models is one factor in African American youths being at risk. This lack of same-race role models has been a critical factor in fostering a sense of hopelessness in African American boys (Harvey 1997). This deficit can be overcome by hiring staff who live in the community and, if that is not possible, hiring staff who esteem African and African American culture and desire to learn about the community (Harvey and Rauch 1997).

AN AFROCENTRIC APPROACH

Afrocentricism provides a culturally specific paradigm for serving African Americans. An Afrocentric approach contends that aspects of European American practice are inappropriate for people of African descent. It is viewed that the African ethos, as transmuted into African American culture, has been, and is, central to African Americans' ability to survive racist oppression.

African Americans experience the 'Paradox of Blackness'. They are penalized when their behaviors are congruent with African and African American culture. When their behaviors are congruent with European American culture, they are rewarded. The paradox of blackness fosters self-hatred and self-destructiveness. Consequently, consciousness raising regarding racism and its effects is an important component of the Afrocentric approach to prevention and treatment. In Afrocentric practice, treatment – conceived of as healing – takes place within and through positive, rewarding connections with African and African American culture and with other people of African descent (Harvey and Rauch 1997).

It is within the African culture – a holistic and naturalistic orientation to the world – that the value system and behavioral patterns of people of African descent has its roots. The philosophical concepts are ones which work in conjunction with the natural order, working toward such principles as balance in one's environment; family/personal life and a multifunctional, discretionary, harmonic approach to life rather than a one-dimensional, predetermined, conflictual approach. The Afrocentric approach incorporates the individual, family and community as an interconnected unit, so that any intervention must include interactions with all three entities (Harvey 1997). This approach recognizes the presence of spirituality (Pinkett 1993) and interconnectedness (Richards 1989) in the African American community and that these characteristics are key in understanding the psychosocial dynamics of the African American community, family and individual in order to develop and implement appropriate and effective interventions. The goal is to facilitate the development of the kind of person who is aware and can operationalize their sense of unity or collective extended self (Nobles 1976).

MAAT center program – a model

The MAAT Center for Human and Organizational Enhancement, Inc., a non-profit African American operated agency, served the Washington, DC community from 1986 to 1997. *Ma'at*, an ancient Egyptian word, means an ethical way of life (Karenga 1990). The MAAT Center served African American children, youth and families using an Afrocentric orientation to prevention and treatment. This orientation views humanity collectively through shared *concern* for the well-being of others (Daly, Jennings, Becket and Leashore 1995); and promotes an understanding of one's spiritual self (Pinkett 1993; Mbiti 1969) rather than an orientation which relies on individualism and material gain. This is accomplished by providing youths with higher values to employ as life guidelines and a support group of peers who can assist each other in self-evaluation and provide emotional and physical support to 'do the right thing' (Harvey 1997).

MAATian youth group model

The small group model employed is a manhood development model, a group model many African American practitioners advocate (Perkins 1986; Hare and Hare 1985; Warfield-Coppock and Harvey 1989; Warfield-Coppock 1990; Long 1993). The manhood development after-school program helps youths to develop interpersonal skills while fostering new relationships and building a positive self-concept and cultural group renewal. The emphasis is on youths interacting with youths to develop constructive lifestyles and positive solutions to life problems, as well as to recognize their personal and cultural strengths and abilities (Harvey 1997).

The purpose of these groups, from an Afrocentric perspective, is the capacity of the group to help adolescent African American males develop the skills they need to make a positive transition from adolescence to manhood (Hill 1992), and to help each youth develop a network of peers and other individuals with similar values to socialize with as he incorporates new and constructive attitudes and behaviors into his lifestyle (Oliver 1989). Primary attention during group sessions is given to enabling these youths to gain knowledge and positive behaviors that help them eliminate involvement in gangs, the effects of negative peer pressure, and the misperceptions regarding the African American race and culture; discard distorted images of manhood, fatherhood, and male–female relationships; avoid escalating acts of violence and crime; ignore substance abuse; and give up delinquent behaviors and low educational and occupational aspirations that create disruptive life crises for them and the community (Isaacs 1992).

Nguzo Saba values clarification system

The Nguzo Saba (the African name for what has been called the Seven Principles (Fraser 1994; Karenga 1965, 1987, 1990)) is used to teach youths the principles of spirituality, culture, family, education, economics, community, and youth activities to help them understand themselves, others, and the world in which they live. Many youths develop a greater sense of unity, identity, and purpose as they understand and begin to incorporate the principles of Nguzo Saba into their world view (Fraser 1994; Assante 1988; Bennett 1993; Billingsley 1992).

In the area of values clarification, the adolescent is confronted with making choices about the individuals (peers and adults) with whom he will associate. Adolescent African American males learn to rely on the Nguzo Saba principles of self-determination (Kujichagulia) and creativity (Kuumba) as their world view in making such decisions. Specifically, the principle of self-determination teaches the adolescent to be committed to defining and developing himself, instead of being defined and developed by others. The principle of creativity teaches the adolescent to be committed to building rather than destroying, to engaging in positive action, and to pursuing a continual search for new and fresh ideas that can improve his life and the lives of others (Fraser 1994; Assante 1988; Bennett 1993; Billingsley 1992).

African American adolescent males are encouraged to rely on the principles of collective work and responsibilities (Ujima), and cooperative economics (Ujamaa) to avoid negative economic lifestyles. The principle of collective work and responsibilities provides the adolescent with a sense that people must work together for the common good, even though each person accepts responsibility for both the successes and failures of the group (Fraser 1994; Assante, 1988; Bennett 1993; Billingsley 1992). The adolescent learns from these principles that high economic rewards obtained illegally often lead to failures that the youth must sustain alone.

The youths experience a series of sessions where they are taught in a collective experience the skills of painting, plumbing and electrical repairs. The principle of cooperative economics helps the adolescent to understand that wealth, talents, and resources can be shared for the common good (Fraser 1994; Assante 1988; Bennett 1993; Billingsley 1992). The youths learn that cooperative economic efforts between individuals provide a reciprocal relationship for building a better economic foundation and occupational alternatives. From both principles the adolescent is encouraged to appreciate the importance of being a part of the mainstream job market and the youths need to incorporate a sense of spirituality as part of their life skills. The principles of unity (Umoja) provide the adolescent with a concept for developing his spiritual self. The principle of unity provides the youths with a sense of togetherness and collective action among family, community, nation, and one's ethnic group (Fraser 1994; Assante 1988; Bennett 1993; Billingsley 1992).

Finally, the principle of faith (Imani) has the potential to provide the adolescent with a sense of self and group pride. The principle of faith provides the adolescent with a means for believing in African Americans as individuals, as a people with abilities, and the right to control their own destinies as a race of people (Fraser 1994; Assante 1988; Bennett 1993; Billingsley 1992).

Principles of Afrocentrism

Underlying the Nguzo Saba, which are principles to develop a sense of the collective self, are the Principles of Afrocentrism, which assist in developing a sense of the moral personal self. The principles of Afrocentrism (called RIPSO) are the 7 Rs: Responsibility, Reciprocity, Respect, Realness, Restraint, Reason and Reconciliation; 3 Is: Interconnectedness, Interdependence and Inclusivity; 3 Ps: Participation, Patience and Perseverance; 3 Ss: Sharing, Sacrifice and Spirituality; 3 Others: Cooperation, Discipline and Unconditional love. The following is a cultural activity that enhances the development of the moral self. Program participants are provided with the biographies of famous people of African descent. Various problem solving and decision making scenarios are created in which the youth are required to think, feel, and behave as one of these historical figures would. As African American adolescent males experience these exercises they can begin to eliminate the negative misperceptions about themselves and their race, and develop a sense of self pride and a belief that their own personal life has the potential to improve (Harvey and Coleman 1997).

Manhood development program

Each group is composed of ten to fifteen adolescents and is led by a trained staff person. The youths participate in an orientation entitled 'Brotherhood Training', which lasts for eight weeks. This is to prepare them for the sacredness of the transformation of the manhood development program. During this period the youths are oriented to the group process and principles of life, and the group is accepting new members during this period. Upon completing this eight-week period the youths, *Pre-initiates*, participate in a weekend retreat focusing on cultural appreciation and personal development and enhancement of the community. At the end of the weekend the youths are selected to become *Initiates* based on an evaluation conducted by the co-leaders and a group of older male adults called 'Elders'. *Initiates* are then required to take an Initiates' Code of Conduct Oath. At this time they also participate in an initiation ritual where they pledge to uphold the Nguzo Saba, receive an African name based on the day of the week on which they were born (Assem and Dodson 1994), and are given a special identifying symbol to be worn at all group sessions. At this point in the group process, membership is closed. The group develops a sense of we-ness; its members are integrated into the group, trust each other and are ready to work.

The group meets after school three times a week for two hours. Each participant is expected to take part in a unity circle that is the opening ritual. All members hold each other's hands and one member reads a spiritually oriented text. Water, a symbol of life, is poured into the a group-owned plant, a symbol of growth and transformation, as names of historical and personal ancestors are called out loud by the members. Each group is co-led. The leaders have included social workers, teachers, historians, artists, actors, and musicians. Group meetings are supplemented by follow-up visits or telephone contact with the family, focusing on the impact of the program on the youths' overall development. African American guest presenters are invited to conduct meetings on specific subjects. All aspects of the group are structured to develop an appreciation for African and African American culture (Harvey 1997). The group sessions are defined by modules that support a high level of knowledge enhancement through interactive techniques, such as role-playing and ceremonial rituals. The youths participate in each module as they progress through the program. Some topics included in group module sessions are:

- African American Culture and Heritage
- Principles and Guides for Living
- African American Lifestyles: The Influence on Person Life
- Oppression and Racism
- Learning the Adolescent Stages of Development
- Male Physical Development
- Female Physical Development
- Birth Control
- Fatherhood – Marriage
- Physical Health Issues
- Diet and Exercise
- HIV/AIDS and Sexually Transmitted Diseases
- Drugs and Other Harmful Substances
- Entrepreneurial Development
- Win-Win Relationships
- Mediation as a Means to Self-Development and Self-Control (Harvey and Coleman 1997).

Each module consists of four to six sessions. The first session includes a presentation by a person of African descent who is knowledgeable concerning the topic area. The second session consists of a discussion of the information contained in the topic presentation and how it relates to the youths' lives. In the remaining sessions, the youths develop a project related to the topic to demonstrate transformation on the cognitive, emotional, spiritual, and behavioral planes.

The adolescents receive a certificate for the completion of each module. Upon completion of all modules, each youth will conduct a self-evaluation and is evaluated by his peers, the group leaders and the Council of Elders in order to pass into the final phase: a transformational weekend. The Council of Elders employs the Seven Principles of African Life (Nguzo Saba) Assessment Scale in evaluating the development of the youths. Each youth must score at least 3 out of 5 points on each dimension of the Likert-type scale in order to graduate from the program (Harvey 1997). During this experience the *Initiates* are expected to demonstrate all they have learned and prepare for their manhood community presentation ceremony (Harvey 1997).

On successfully completing the transformational weekend, *Initiates* participate in a final manhood presentation ceremony witnessed by family, friends, and the general community in which they demonstrate specific knowledge, attitudes and skills indicative of maturation. They announce their sacred names and receive a symbol and certificate of sacred transformation. Each family who participates in the program will also receive a certificate of transformation. The *Initiates*, in conjunction with the group leaders, plan and implement the ceremony (Harvey 1997).

In summary, the manhood development program provides individual and collective interventions from an Afrocentric world-view to high-risk adolescent African American males to reduce and/or eliminate negative lifestyle behaviors (Harvey and Coleman 1997).

Results

Results indicate that over 80 per cent of the youths completing the orientation phase of the program complete the entire program. Family members report an increase in school attendance and better grades, in obeying curfew, in performing household chores, assisting siblings with and providing proper guidance and demonstrating respect. In an oral survey conducted with one cohort of manhood development program youths when asked what they learned from the program, all of the partic31pants reported that they learned to respect themselves and others and appreciate their heritage (Harvey 1997). They also stated they would recommend the programs to their peers. This is a giant step toward collective racial self-determination, which has the potential to be a significant resiliency factor against what Akbar (see Kambon 1992) describes as a self-destructive disorder. These preliminary results are important because these are the inoculations to the critical factors that place African American male youths at risk (Kunjufu 1985).

CONCLUSION

This article has detailed an Afrocentric After-School Manhood Development Program for African American adolescent males that has been implemented successfully in an urban community. The social problems that these youths experience are the same for all youth of African descent who are educated in European dominant systems that directly or indirectly contribute to the absence of group cultural knowledge, understanding, appreciation and expression needed to develop a strong sense of rootedness and belonging. When no culturally competent intervention is provided, youths perceive themselves as misfits, as abnormal and deviant in relation to the dominant society. It is, thus, imperative that Afrocentric programs be developed for school-age males of African descent where intervention/treatment takes place within and through the original cultural orientation of the disempowered group. It is the author's belief that this program can be successfully implemented in rural areas and other countries where youths of African descent face similar problems and concerns.

REFERENCES

Assante, K.A. (1988) *Afrocentricity*, Trenton, NJ: African World Press.
Assem, K. and Dodson, J. (1994) 'Strengthening the African-American family: the birth to re-birth life cycle' in Preudhomme, G. R. and Assem, K. (eds) *National Public Policy Document*, Detroit, MI: The National Association of Black Social Workers pp. 6–15.
Bennett, W.J. (1993) *The Book of Virtues*, New York: Simon and Schuster.
Billingsley, A. (1992) *Climbing Jacob's Ladder: The Enduring Legacy of African American Families*, New York: Simon and Schuster.
Botvin, G.J. (1982) 'Broadening the focus of smoking prevention strategies' in Cotes, T., Petersen, A.C. and Perry, C. (eds), *Promoting Adolescent Health: A Dialog on Research and Practice*, New York: Academic Press pp. 137–148.
Botvin, G.J. and McAlister, A. (1981) 'Cigarette smoking among children and adolescents: causes and prevention' in Arnold, C.B. (ed.) *Annual Review of Disease Prevention*, New York: Springer pp. 222–49.
Carnegie Corporation of New York (1995) 'Great transitions: preparing adolescents for a new century', *Concluding Report: Carnegie Council on Adolescent Development*. New York: Carnegie Corporation.
Cross, T.L., Bazron, B.J., Dennis, K.W. and Isaacs, M.R. (1989) *Towards a Culturally Competent System of Care: A Monograph on Effective Services for Minority Children who are Severely Emotionally Disturbed*, Washington, DC: CASSP Technical Assistance Center, Georgetown University Child Development Center.
Daly, A., Jennings, J., Beckett, J.O. and Leashore, B.R. (1995) 'Effective coping strategies of African Americans', *Social Work*, **40**, 2, pp. 240–8.
Dryfoos, J. (1990) *Adolescents-at-risk: Prevalence and Prevention*, New York: Oxford Press.
Fraser, B. (1994) *Success Runs in Our Race*, New York: Avon Books.
Hare, N. and Hare, J. (1985) *Bringing the Black Boy to Manhood: The Passage*, San Francisco, CA: The Black Think Tank.
Harvey, A.R. (1995) 'Afro-centric model of prevention with African American adolescent males: the MAAT rites of passage program', in Rauch, J. (ed.) *Community-based Family Centered Services in a Changing Health Care Environment: Selected Papers from a Conference held June 6–7, 1994, Baltimore, Maryland*, Baltimore, MD: School of Social Work, University of Maryland, Baltimore pp. 115–30.
Harvey, A.R. (1997) 'Group work with African-American youth in the criminal justice system: A culturally competent model' in Grief, G.L. and Ephross, P.H. (eds) *Group Work with Populations at Risk*, New York: Oxford Press pp. 160–73.
Harvey A.R. and Coleman, A.A. (1997) 'An Afrocentric program for African American males in the juvenile justice system', *Child Welfare*, LXXVI, 1, pp. 197–211.
Harvey A.R. and Rauch J.B. (1997) 'A comprehensive afrocentric rites of passage program for Black male adolescents', *Health and Social Work*, **22**, 1, pp. 30–7.
Hill, P. (1992) *Coming of Age: African American Male Rites of Passage*, Chicago, IL: African American Images.

Irwin, C.E., Jr and Ingra, V. (1994) 'Adolescent risk-taking behavior', in Wallace, H.M., Nelson, R.P. and Sweeney, P.J. (eds), *Maternal and Child Health Practice*, 4th edn, Oakland, CA: Third Party Publishing Company pp. 585–601.

Isaacs, M.R. (1992) *Violence: The Impact of Community Violence on African American Children and Families*, Arlington, VA: National Center for Education in Maternal and Child Health.

Jessor, R. (1992) 'Risk behavior in adolescence: a psychosocial framework for understanding and action', in Rogers, D.E. and Ginsberg, E. (eds) *Adolescents at Risk*, Boulder, CO: Westview Publishers pp. 19–33.

Kambon, K.K.K. (1992) '*The African Personality in America: An African-centered Framework*', Tallahassee, FL: Nubian Nation Publications.

Karenga, M. (1987) *Kwanzaa Origin, Concepts and Practice*, Los Angeles, CA: Kawaida Publications.

Karenga, M. (1990) 'Towards a sociology of maatian ethics: literature and context', in Karenga, M. (ed.) *Reconstructing Kemetic Culture: Papers, Perspectives, Projects*, Los Angeles, CA: University of Sankore Press pp. 66–96.

Kunjufu, J. (1985) *Countering the Conspiracy to Destroy Black Boys*, Chicago, IL: African American Images, Vol. II.

Lewis, J. and Lewis, F. (1984) 'Prevention programs in action', *Personnel and Guidance Journal*, **62**, 9, pp. 550–53.

Long, L.C. (1993) 'An Afrocentric intervention strategy', in Goddard, L.L. (ed.) *An African-centered Model of Prevention for African-American Youth at High Risk*, CSAP Technical Report No. 6. Rockville, MD: US Department of Health and Human Services pp. 87–92.

Mbiti, J. (1969) *African Religions and Philosophy*, New York: Praeger.

Millman, R.B. and Botvin, G.J. (1983) 'Substance use, abuse, and dependence' in Levine, M.D., Carey, W.B. and Crocker, A.C. (eds) *Developmental-behavioral Pediatrics*, Philadelphia, PA: W.B. Saunders Co. pp. 683–708.

Nobles, W.W. (1976) 'African consciousness and Black research: the consciousness of self' in King, L.M., Dixon, V. and Nobles, W. (eds) *African Philosophy: Assumption and Paradigms: Research on Black Persons*, Los Angeles, CA: Fanon Center Publication pp. 163–174.

Oliver, W. (1989) 'Black males and social problems: prevention through Afrocentric socialization', *Journal of Black Studies* **20**, 1, pp. 15–39.

Penkower, L., Dew, M.A., Kingsley, L., Becker, J.T., Satz, P., Scherf, F.W., and Sheridan, K. (1991) 'Behavioral, health, and psychosocial factors and risk for HIV infection among sexually active homosexual men: the multi-center AIDS cohort study', *American Journal of Public Health*, **81**, pp. 194–6.

Perkins, U.E. (1986) *Harvesting New Generations: The Positive Development of Black Youth*, Chicago, IL: Third World Press.

Pinkett, J. (1993) 'Spirituality in the African-American community', in Goddard, L.L. (ed.) *An African-American Model of Prevention for African-American Youth at High Risk*, CSSAP Technical Report No. 6. Rockville, MD: US Department of Health and Human Services pp. 79–86.

Richards, D.M. (1989) *Let the Circle be Unbroken: The Implications of African Spirituality in the Diaspora*, Trenton, NJ: Red Sea Press.

Solomon, D. (1976) *Black Empowerment: Social Work in Oppressed Communities*, New York: Columbia University Press.

Swisher, J.D. (1979) 'Prevention issues', in Dupont, R.L., Goldstein, A. and O'Donnell, J.A. (eds) *Handbook on Drug Abuse*, Washington, DC: National Institute on Drug Abuse pp. 423–35.

Warfield-Coppock, N. (1990) *Afrocentric Theory and Applications: Adolescence Rites of Passage (Vol. I)*. Washington, DC: Baobob Associates.

Warfield-Coppock, N. and Harvey, A.R. (1989) *Teenage Pregnancy Prevention: A Rites of Passage Resources Manual*, Washington, DC: MAAT Institute for Human and Organizational Enhancement, Inc.

12 Black boys at school: negotiating masculinities and race

James Earl Davis

INTRODUCTION

Black boys are loved and loathed at school. They are heroes and standard bearers of hip-hop culture and athleticism in schools, while simultaneously experiencing disproportionate levels of punishment and academic marginality. This positionality, as Tony Sewell (1997) suggests, between being 'the darling of popular youth sub-culture' and 'the sinner in the classroom' has lead to a range of behaviors, strategies, and constructions within and beyond school that frames the overall educational experience of Black boys. How do these boys respond to a context that defines them as both 'sexy and as sexually threatening' and purchase a space in schools that is self-maintained and reproductive? Because schools are important sites for gendered learning and development, they are also useful contexts to explore how students adapt to and make sense of their masculine position within these academic settings (Gilbert and Gilbert 1998).

Schools are important sites for study because they represent a generated masculine space where Black boys make meaning of who they are, what they do, and how they are perceived by other students and teachers. Black boys often engage in gender-specific stylistic behavior such as 'cool pose' that further problematizes their school experience and results in increased conflict with teachers and peers (Majors and Mancini Billson 1992). However, little research attention has been given to how Black males construct personal meaning for their lives in and out of school. Through the voices and experiences of Black boys, this chapter attempts to frame a critical discussion of how race, gender and masculinity intersect in school settings. Based on observations, interviews, and focus groups with Black boys in a middle school, I try to articulate and link social constructions of the masculine 'self' and the masculine 'other'. Black males' narratives about parameters of accepted and unaccepted behaviour and self-presentation in school are presented and unraveled. The chapter concludes with implications and suggestions for school policy and practice (e.g. male mentoring programs) directed toward improving learning environments for Black boys.

During the past decade, a corpus of journal articles, reports, scholarly and popular books have detailed the precarious nature of Black males in school and society (Garibaldi 1988; Gibbs 1988; Kunjufu 1983; Mincy 1994; Majors and Gordon

1994; McCall 1994; Polite and Davis 1994). While the current plight of young Black males in school is the focus of much of this work, very little is known about how school context affects their educational and social experiences. The interaction of school context and masculine identities and socialization is also important to consider. Related to this work, an array of strategies have captured the attention of school administrators, local communities and parents as possible solutions to the problems associated with Black males in public schools. These programs are of two primary genres: assistive/supportive and reconstructive. The assistive programs aim to augment and support current school structures by providing the positive presence of adult Black men in school settings. Mentoring programs that assign professional Black men as role models for young boys, typically in elementary and middle schools, have been established in many school districts, both urban and suburban. Likewise, Black men serve as teacher's aides, tutors, and reading partners for Black boys needing academic support and guidance. The justification for these initiatives points to the need for consistent and positive Black men in educational settings who provide models for young Black males to emulate (Holland 1987). These programs try to counter negative gender role socialization of Black males that is peer driven and leads to maladaptive masculine identity (Cunningham 1993). The development of conceptions and expressions of masculinity that are not antithetical to expected behaviors, roles and attitudes in school settings is the primary objective of these interventions.

Reconstructive strategies, on the other hand, such as those promoted by all-male schools and classrooms take a more radical approach to current schooling conditions. Given the severity of problems associated with Black males in schools, advocates for race/gender exclusive schooling defend these strategies that reconstruct the gendered nature of schools and classrooms as the most appropriate recourse (Watson and Smitherman 1991). Both of these intervention strategies highlight the potential role schooling plays in a broader social narrative about the 'crisis of Black males'. As a way of countering the crisis in public school education, assistive/supportive and reconstructive approaches are grounded in the assumption that public schooling disproportionately victimizes Black boys. The feminizing culture of schools is believed, in part, to be responsible for this victimization. Therefore, both intervention genres serve as compensatory devices aimed at restoring a normative masculinity to the center of Black boys' schooling experiences. This narrative sees teachers in particular (mostly White women) imposing feminine standards of behavioral expectations on Black boys that induce oppositional behaviors in academic attitude and engagement (Holland 1992). Similarly, alternative Afrocentric models of masculinity are being proposed as alternatives to European conceptions of masculinity (Akbar 1991; Kunjufu 1983; Langley 1994; Madhubuti 1990). These models call for an overthrow of western ideas of male socialization and a regrounding of the Black male experience in a new cultural awareness. While the ideas of these models are transformative in many ways, images of a normative masculinity being either unfulfilled or misdirected still dominate the discourse.

RESEARCH ON BLACK BOYS AND SCHOOLING

Although Black boys as well as Black girls are negatively affected by schooling, some research suggests that the problems facing Black boys are more chronic and extreme, thus deserving special policy and programmatic attention (Polite 1993; Garibaldi 1992; Watson and Smitherman 1991). Others cite cultural messages about Black males and how they are negatively constructed and perceived in the media and in everyday life (Blount and Cunningham 1996; Belton 1995; Harper 1996). These images portray the young Black male as violent, disrespectful, unintelligent, hyper-sexualized, and threatening. These cultural messages, without a doubt, carry over into schools and negatively influence the ways Black male students are treated, positioned, and distributed opportunities to learn. In almost every category of academic failure in schools, Black boys are disproportionately represented. One study documents that only 2 per cent of African American males enrolled in the public school system of a large Midwestern US city achieved a cumulative grade point average of at least a three on a four-point scale. At the same time, three-fourths of Black males in that system were performing below average (Leake and Leake 1992). Additionally, a report on academic performance comparing Black males in a large urban and suburban school district found that less than 3 per cent of Black males were enrolled in honours classes (Wright 1996). Clearly, by all measures of school attainment and achievement, Black males consistently lag behind other students.

Studies on Black males in school is relatively recent and lean, and centers typically on discussions of factors that characterize or place these students 'at risk' as learners and for other social outcomes. Little attention is given to how Black males construct personal meaning for their lives in and out of school. Particularly, discussion about how Black boys make sense of their own masculinity and others around them has been noticeably absent. The connection between Black boys' meanings of masculinity and the processes of schooling are often in contrast with each other (Holland 1989).

Although the body of research on Black boys in school is limited, it provides some useful insights. Much of this work, comparative in nature, examines the academic experiences and outcomes of black boys relative to other students. Slaughter-Defoe and Richards (1994) suggest that as early as kindergarten, Black males are treated differently than other male and female students. Throughout elementary and middle school, Black boys are consistently rated lower by teachers for social behavior and academic expectations (Irvine 1990; Rong 1996). In their study of factors related to school outcomes for Black males, Davis and Jordan (1994) suggest that student school engagement reflected in study habits and attendance were positively related to achievement and grades. Simply and unsurprisingly, Black boys who spend more time on homework and attend school regularly also perform better academically and are more engaged in their schooling. They also found that remediation, grade retention, and suspensions are linked to academic failure among Black boys in school. The following explanation is offered by these researchers:

... extra help delivery mechanisms and disciplinary sanctions are both symptoms and causes of failure. The reason that students are placed in remedial classes or held over is because performance is below the expectations of teachers or because their skills lag behind their cohort. But remediating students the old-fashioned way with repetitive, boring material, or requiring to repeat the same grade seldom helps them back on track.

(Davis and Jordan 1994 p. 586)

Recent studies on the effectiveness of culturally centered and Afrocentric school experiences for Black boys have been mixed. Fifth-grade Black boys enrolled in a cultural immersion school were found to take more personal responsibility for their intellectual and academic achievement than their peers in a traditional school. The immersion school, however appears to account for no other achievement or esteem differences (Sanders and Reed 1995). Conversely, Hudley (1995, 1997) has identified potential benefits, although minor, for Black males, enrollment in separate Afrocentric classrooms on academic self-concept. One reason commonly mentioned for the poor academic performance and alienation of some Black males is that they perceive most schooling activities as feminine and irrelevant to their masculine sense-of-self and development (Holland 1989). Another explanation of the negative consequences of Black boys in school is associated the 'cool pose'. In short, the cool pose hypothesis suggests that young Black males adopt and display behaviors and attitudes that they think convey a sense of their coolness, esteem, and cultural attachment. Majors *et al.* (1994) argue that these demeanors of students are misunderstood by White middle-class teachers and school administrators as defiant, aggressive, and intimidating. In essence, the consequences of cool pose position Black boys in school as both victims and participants in their educational marginalisation. Others contend that the increased presence of committed and successful black male adults in educational environments is essential for enhancing black boys' academic and social development. This positive male presence could possibly diffuse 'cool pose' and its negative consequences. Until successful interventions such as theses are developed, other socializing agents are at play – ones that are operated and enforced by Black males for Black males.

Although research on the schooling experiences of Black boys is developing and often relevant for policy and pedagogy, it appears ironic that scant attention has been given to the perspectives that young Black males have concerning the social experiences of their own schooling situation. In particular, little is known about how Black boys construct their own gendered meanings. This research frames a critical discussion of how race, gender, and masculinity intersect in a middle school setting and is informed by the expectations and experience of this context. Based on observations, interviews, and small group discussions with middle-grade students, this study presents and links constructions of masculinities to an interactive process of being Black and male. In doing so, I try to unravel student narratives about parameters of masculine identity and Black male self-presentation.

Setting and methods

The project site for this research is a medium-sized middle school located in a large suburban county in a northeastern state. Since 1978, the school was part of a larger countywide desegregation effort. The post-desegregation era of school choice began at the start of the 1996 school year. Our research team has collected data at this school during the past three academic years. We have organized our data collection to document discourses of race and gender, specifically how students construct, talk about and make sense of these issues in a middle school environment. Research team members also attended various school activities, during and after school and observed and talked to students during class, between class and at lunch. These frequent and prolonged observations of middle school students in a natural school setting provided rich information about the everyday lives of students. These observations of authentic student lives – encompassing social interactions and behaviors – are supplemented by small group and in-depth individual interviews in various informal and more formal settings.

The school is located in a very affluent upper middle class neighborhood. The middle school is very similar in structure to many of those constructed in the early 1970s with its rather sterile hallways, a large cafeteria/auditorium at the east wing of the building and the gym at the other end. The students are mostly white, clean cut and neatly dressed with a sampling of retro-attire including plat-form shoes, wide-legged bell-bottomed pants and other fashion staples including Tommy Hilfiger, FUBU, beltless baggy jeans and Nikes. The middle school enrolls students from a range of socioeconomic and racial backgrounds, including a significant number of Black students from a nearby urban center. During the 1997–98 academic year, 798 students were enrolled at the middle school. Twenty-six percent of the study body participates in the free lunch program and almost all of these students are Black. There are very few low income White students at the school and those who are from low-income families are not likely to partic-ipate in the free lunch program because of the program's racial stigma. Black students make up 29 percent of the enrollment and White students comprise 63 percent, followed by Asian Americans 5 per cent and Hispanics/Latinos 3.5 per cent. Each of the grade levels at the school has appropriately 30 Black boys (Data Service Center 1998). Like Black students generally attending the school, Black boys (ages 10–13) represent a diversity of social and economic backgrounds. While most reside in the city, some also live in suburban neighborhoods near the school.

Working closely with the school principal, we designed a series of small group interviews to address questions about a racialized and gendered schooling context. All of the group meetings were both video and audiotape recorded. We were particularly interested to facilitate conversations between students about their experiences, interactions, and ideas, around race and gender. In the small groups we encouraged students to talk as members of their racial and gender group about their experience at school. For instance, we asked questions such as 'What is it like to be Black and male in this school?' The small group sessions were structured to capture informal peer conversations with free flowing discussion about their lives in school. In addition to small group interviews, we observed in classrooms, the lunchroom, hallways, the main office, detention periods, special assemblies, study halls and before and after school activities. We also had conversations with and observed teachers and school administrators.

All the members of the research team tried to establish a neutral and non-threatening identity and presence in the school. We made contact with all students before group or individual interviews and stressed our openness to hearing their voices in a confidential and supportive way. In order to gain trust from students, it was important for our multiracial team members to present themselves as different and distinct from school authority figures such as teachers and school administrators. By presenting ourselves as neutral and caring, we built rapport with students and gained access to their personal feelings and experiences. In my thematic analysis of the student data, I have searched for patterns and topics that characterize typical thinking of Black boys at the school. My intent here is not to offer findings that generalize to all Black boys in all school settings. Rather, my purpose is to understand the parameters of masculinities in one school and how the constructions of masculinities play themselves out socially for these Black boys.

Theoretically, this study in grounded in symbolic interaction in which understanding of the social relations of school life emerges through interaction and interpretation. Gendered social interaction at the school is informed by and informs the broader context in which meanings of masculinity are constructed (Mac an Ghaill 1994). By far, what goes on at school concerning Black boys is not the full responsibility of boys. Rather, school culture not only reflects the dominant gender ideology and conceptions of the broader culture, but in some ways is directed by boys in the creation and reproduction of gendered meaning and experience. The following section represents some overarching themes from the database that delineate how Black boys make meaning of their selves and experiences in school. I will provide examples of how Black boys think and talk about what it mean to be male, particularly their constructions of masculinity and social positioning at school.

BLACK MASCULINITIES AT SCHOOL: CONVERGENCE AND CONFLICT

A distinct black male-centered cultural space is organized at school around a set of competing and complementary social forces. Specifically, gender, racial and sexual identities help frame a masculine middle school orthodoxy that is dominated by the needs and demands of boys themselves. Black boys at the school clearly understand and embrace an accepted code of masculinized conduct. This code is more than a masculine coping strategy, or racialized identity formation (Majors and Mancini Billson 1992; Fordham 1996). Rather, it crosses and connects boundaries of race, gender, class and sexuality, while maintaining its solid normative masculine core. Drawing on my reading of a particularly alienating schooling environment for Black boys, I contend that a social responsive subculture around masculine expectations and acceptability has emerged. This subculture is distinct from traditional school cultural behaviors and norms of boys in middle school. In short, a 'Black boy-centered' cultural space is fashioned by the confluence of a distinct racialized experience, framed by racial stereotypes, and a gendered schooling experience with its own notions.

There is much evidence from this study to support the idea of a well defined code of conduct and behavior that prescribes a conformity of Black males' social, academic, and masculine identities. Through this masculinized code, Black boys are engaged in producing and reproducing an authentic Black masculine identity. Since they are well aware of their marginalized academic and social status at the middle school, the masculine code creates their own space for resistance to a school culture and climate that excludes and labels them as at-risk city boys with very few academic strengths. The code in turn functions as a vehicle where their masculinity serves as a form of protest and defiance that wrestles against negative expectations of teachers and peers.

Interview data from small groups and from individuals inform our understanding of a vulnerable school social experience for Black males. These young men carry a heavier weight of expectations from fellow students and teachers. These expectations encompass both social and academic behaviors and dispositions. For instance, they bear the burden of cultural stereotypes surrounding issues of sexuality. Along with the constructed baggage of troublemakers in and outside of class, Black boys also hold a special sexualized place at the school. According to Michael, a very thoughtful and articulate Black male who is well liked by teachers and consistently appears on the honor roll, this special status is supported by general acceptance of sexually charged stereotypes:

> Right now Black guys are very popular. It seems like White guys have lost their status, they are more invisible. I think a lot of White girls buy into the myth of Black guys.

By all indications, interracial dating is socially unacceptable at this middle school. In the rare times when these relationships occur – only among Black boys and White girls – they are very secretive for fear of peer criticism. Recently, however, several Black boys at the school, mostly eighth graders, have become the objects of affection for some White girls. Juan, a Black eighth grader, acknowledges that he finds White girls attractive and enjoys interacting with them at this racially diverse school:

> Before coming to school here, I went to school with all Black people. I lived in an all Black neighborhood and only associated with other Blacks. Now I live in the suburbs, mostly White neighborhood. Since being in a school that's mixed, I've gotten to know all different kinds of people. Before, I really didn't have contact with White girls. But being at this school you get to know them and I like that.

Juan also feels that a few Black boys have become 'specialized' and very popular at school, primarily because of the 'sex thing'. He reflects on his personal experience and the precarious nature of this social status at school. He laments, 'Last year I was in the most popular in-group at the school, but I was kicked out this year, I don't know why.' Unlike Juan, Michael who has been criticized by other Black students at the school for acting like a 'geek' and not 'knowing how to dress', feels the social pressure to date or at least talk about the desire to date White girls. By doing so, he would present himself in a more conforming masculinized way at school.

These masculine expectations of behavior related to White girls also create a rigidity in the kinds of non-sexualized relationship Black boys are allowed to have with Black girls. The masculine proscriptions for boy–girl interactions provide some insights to the state of gender relationships among Black students at the school. For the most part, strong platonic friendships between Black boys and girls are nonexistent, unless the friendship can be socially recognized as the precursor for a sexualized relationship. It should be noted that by all accounts, there appears to be little actual sexual activity among boys and girls at this middle school. Therefore, sexualized relationships are usually constructed around the talk of sex, not actual sexual relations. For instance, the masculine code dictates appropriate social relationships and interaction style between males and females and it imposes meaning on those interactions. The non-sexual content of opposite sex friendships provides opposition and problems for the masculine code. Unfortunately, because of limited relationships centering on academic work, these potentially beneficial contacts generally fall victim to the code. One exception, however are honor classes where very few Black students, boys or girls, are enrolled. For example, Rob is the only Black boy in his seventh-grade math honors class. He comments on how he interacts with Black girls in his class:

> I can talk to these girls about school and stuff. Since we are the only Blacks in the class, we have to stick together. Usually, guys and girls don't hang, unless they are trying to hook-up. They do their own thing, we do ours.

While the social climate among Black boys and girls is supportive, friendly and mutually protective, their relationship is generally based on their racialized status and struggles at the school. Black boys tend to only deal with Black girls from their mutual position of racial status and oppression. In effect, their gendered relationship has no common ground and continues to be controlled by a masculine hegemony that limits the possibilities of these relationships, both socially and academically.

Teachers also play a very significant role in the school lives of Black boys. Since most of the school day is spent in classrooms under the supervision and guidance of teachers, perceptions of teachers and their influence on boys are important to consider. When asked about his experiences with teachers and what teachers think of Black males at the school, Malik responded:

> Black males at this school have a bad reputation. Some of the teachers have had trouble with them. But if she doesn't know you and what you are like, there

usually is a problem. But once she gets to know you, then you have a better reputation with her.

Malik, a seventh grader who lives in the city, considers himself a good student. He made the honor roll during the last marking period and is very conscious about doing good schoolwork. He doesn't have a definite peer group that he 'hangs with', but he floats between various friendship circles at the school. He continues his thoughts on teachers' responsibilities:

> I think they should take the time to talk to us and let us know what's going on and how we are doing in our life and everything. I think they would feel better about Black males if they knew something about us and what's behind our background. The problem is they don't know what's going on in our life.

Malik's desire for more personal connection with teachers at the school is shared by other Black males. They feel they are often misunderstood and wrongly judged because of they way they talk, dress, and carry themselves. Additionally, teachers and school administrators bear a disproportionate role in monitoring social relationships, not only in their classrooms, but also in other social spaces in the school.

To get a sense of how Black boys thought of their peers, we asked who they considered to be the most popular Black boys at the school. There were two young males that were consistently mentioned. Reasons given for the popularity included their physical build, the clothes they wore, their reputations of being popular with girls, and in the case of one of these boys, his strong academic record. This guarded admiration for popular Black boys usually revolves around physical prowess and personal ties. As an eighth grader, who identified one peer he considers popular, explained:

> He's really cool and he dresses nice. And he helps you when you are in need. One time, he really helped me out. One time I was about to get banked near the corner store where I live by a bunch of other guys (cause I had fought one of the guy's brothers) and he came up there and help me out. He's a good guy.

The restrictive masculine culture of Black boys at this school also serves as a policing agent for normative masculinity enforcement. Boys who do not adhere to the prescribed rigid masculine orthodoxy are victimized due to their masculine transgressions. One prominent area of transgression is self-presentation style. The school's masculine code makes very clear what's accepted masculine presentational behavior including hallway walk, how one talks, school attire – particularly sneakers and over-sized shirts and pants, lunchroom seating patterns, and how boys carry their books and book bags. Unsurprisingly, these boys are ostracized and socially sanctioned by their Black male peers. Also, Black boys who dare to verbalize alternative views on masculinity and any aspect of the code in effect violate the masculine code. These actions conflict with the notions of what's appropriately male, and thus he is usually expelled from the confines and benefits of boy networks at the school. Interestingly, social punishment seems to be more relationally aggressive, commonly practiced by adolescent girls and viewed as a less masculine peer enforcement tactic (Rys and Bear 1997; Crick and Grotpeter 1995).

REFLECTIONS AND DIRECTIONS

As I have tried to illustrate in this chapter, middle school is a place where Black boys make meaning about their gendered identities. In the process, a cultural milieu is created that forces and feeds upon a masculine hegemony of behavior, attitude and presentation. This middle school culture only endorses a monolithic masculinity that's framed by sexualized relationships with girls and self-presentational style. How boys position themselves relative to girls and how they present themselves and behave publicly are important in maintaining a normative masculine school code.

Certainly a broader definition of acceptable masculinity is being called for in middle schools. But, from this reading of middle school culture, only a narrow conception of masculinity is really available to Black boys. The restrictive nature of the code creates a very rigid masculine dichotomy for Black boys. Any thought, action or response counter to the masculinity norms at the school is considered inappropriate masculinity. This regulation of masculinity requires a level of gender negotiation that must be understood in order to survive socially at school. To be sure, the dynamic nature of negotiating identity categories is difficult for all Black middle school boys. The difficulties experienced by Black boys at school are not distributed equally, however. A group of boys, due to their non-traditional masculinities, bear a disproportionate level of criticism and social estrangement. Ultimately all boys are disadvantaged by this strict gender code. Conformity to expected behavioral roles not only increases the level of anxiety about being socially ostracized, but also circumscribes boys' range of social, emotional and academic experiences in school. Also, the inability to engage other ideas of gender identity limits the kinds of friendships boys have with girls and have with each other. In turn, the development of a school culture that acknowledges diversity in the ways of doing gender is disabled and rendered silent.

During the past two decades, the idea that schools are dominated by women and therefore impose a feminine culture on boys, took hold in policy and programmatic discourse. Simply, the over-representation of female teachers not only leads to male underachievement, but to improper masculine development of boys (Parry 1997). In essence, boy culture is marginalized and suppressed at best – and destroyed at worst – and males develop to manhood with difficulty in establishing true manliness. To continue the narrative, teachers impose a feminine standard of behavioral expectations that Black boys are least likely to meet. Because of particular racial and gender experiences of these teachers, there is an implicit understanding that they are ill-prepared to teach Black boys about being Black and male and becoming men

(Holland 1987, 1992). Hence, educational policy and programs attempt to redress the masculine imbalance that boys experience in school. Although at earlier historical points, it may be argued that an anxiety about the feminization of boys was reflected in the development of boy/man oriented programmes like the Boy Scouts; the importance of proper masculine identity development is more urgently expressed in fears and anxiety about the lack of male role models in schools for Black boys. Specifically, recent development of manhood training and rites of passages programs aimed at bringing Black boys into manhood reflects this general anxiety around masculinity.

The notion of Black boys' victimization in schools continues to create a ground swell of activity directed toward improving their educational chances. In almost every school where there are significant numbers of Black males, programs are in place to turn the tide. Hundreds of rite of passage, mentoring, male tutoring, and manhood training programs are operating. Although these programmes emerge out of concern for Black boys' relative lack of educational success, too many of them are unfortunately framed narrowly by a traditional masculinity. Black boys are recast exclusively as victims, at the hands of female teachers, administrators, and girls in school (Parry 1997). Although teachers are blamed, both assistive and reconstructive program efforts ironically ignore teachers as potential sources for enhancing the school experience of Black males. Clearly the message to teachers in elementary and middle school is that race and gender are crucial in educating Black boys. Therefore, it is no surprise that Black male organizations such as Concerned Black Men, Inc., The Brotherhood, Black Fraternities, and Million Man March Chapters are at the forefront of many of these school-based programs.

Given that economic success is closely linked to school success and failure in school contributes to limited economic opportunities for Black boys as adults, schooling remains one of the few vehicles for upward mobility. However, schools do not always offer a level playing field for young Black males. Rather than fostering positive social environments for them, schools far too often reduce or minimize their spirit and potential. Much evidence exists that schools not only neglect the social, emotive and developmental needs of Black boys, but also socially abuse them. Indeed, Black people traditionally have placed much faith in public schools, only to be disappointed time and time again. The current schooling experience of many Black boys is yet another disappointing moment. For many young Black males, schools ignore their aspirations, disrespect their ability to learn, fail to access and cultivate their many talents, and impose a restrictive range of masculine options. Unfortunately, within this overwhelming oppressive schooling context, many Black boys simple give up, academically and socially – beaten by a system which places little value on who they are and what they offer. In response, our thinking needs to be refocussed and centered on the lives created and lived by Black boys in schools, in connections with teachers and other students. Understanding how Black boys make sense of who they are in school and their relation to a code of masculine orthodoxy, offers practice and policy implications.

While it's true that school is an important site of critical social and cultural intervention (Connell 1993; Browne and Fletcher 1995), policy and practice need to be informed by where Black boys are positioned in school. These multifaceted and complicated school lives of Black males regrettably are too often ignored, misunderstood and rendered invisible. In order to target intervention strategies that broaden the range of masculine behaviors, talents and other social resources available to boys, important work must be done. This work must include non-traditional gender projects that make visible and take into account relationships between Black boys and their constructions of masculinity.

REFERENCES

Akbar, N. (1991) *Visions of Black Men*, Nashville, TN: Winston-Derek Publications.

Belton, D. (1995) *Speak My Name: Black Men on Masculinity and the American Dream*, Boston, MA: Beacon Press.

Blount, M. and Cunningham, G. P. (eds) (1996) *Representing Black Men*, New York: Routledge.

Browne, R. and Fletcher, R. (1995) *Boys in Schools: Addressing the Real Issues – Behavior, Values and Relationships*, Sydney: Finch Publishing.

Connell, R. W. (1993) 'Disruptions: Improper masculinities and schooling' in Weis, L. and Fine, M. (eds) *Beyond Silenced Voices: Class, Race and Gender in United States Schools*, Albany, NY: SUNY Press pp. 191–207.

Crick, N. R. and Grotpeter, J. K. (1995) 'Relational aggression, gender, and social–psychological adjustment', *Child Development*, **66**, pp. 710–22.

Cunningham, M. (1993) 'Sex role influence on African American males', *Journal of African American Male Studies*, **1**, pp. 30–7.

Data Service Center (1998) *School Planning Data Summary*, Wilmington, DE.

Davis, J. E. and Jordan, W. J. (1994) 'The effects of school context, structure, and experience on African American males in middle and high school', *Journal of Negro Education*, **63**, pp. 570–87.

Fordham, S. (1996) *Blacked Out: Dilemmas of Race, Identity and Success at Capital High*, Chicago, IL: University of Chicago Press.

Garibaldi, A. M. (1988) *Educating Black Male Youth: A Moral and Civic Imperative*, New Orleans, LA: Committee to Study the Status of Black Males in the New Orleans Public Schools.

Garibaldi, A. M. (1992) 'Educating and motivating African American males to succeed', *Journal of Negro Education*, **61**, pp. 12–18.

Gibbs, J. (1988) *Young, Black and Male in America: An Endangered Species*, Dover, MA: Auburn House.

Gilbert, R. and Gilbert, P. (1998) *Masculinity Goes to School*, Sydney: Allen and Unwin.

Harper, P. M. (1996) *Are We Not Men?: Masculine Anxiety and the Problem of African-American Identity*, New York: Oxford University Press.

Holland, S. (1987) 'Positive primary education for young black males: Inner-city boys need male role models', *Education Digest*, **53**, pp. 6–7.

Holland, S. (1989) 'Fighting the epidemic of failure: A radical strategy for education inner-city boys', *Teacher Magazine*, **1**, pp. 88–9.

Holland, S. (1992) 'Same-gender classes in Baltimore: How to avoid the problems faced in Detroit/Milwaukee', *Equity and Excellence*, **25**, pp. 2–4.

Hudley, C. A. (1995) 'Assessing the impact of separate schooling for African American male adolescents', *Journal of Early Adolescence*, **15**, pp. 38–57.

Hudley, C. A. (1997) 'Teacher practices and student motivation in middle school program for African American males', *Urban Education*, **32**, pp. 304–19.

Irvine, J. J. (1990) *Black Students and School Failure: Policies, Practices, and Prescriptions*, Westport, CT: Greenwood.

Kunjufu, J. (1983) *Countering the Conspiracy to Destroy Black Boys*, Chicago, IL: African-American Images.

Langley, M. R. (1994) 'The cool pose: An Africentric analysis' in Majors, R. G. and Gordan, J. U. (eds) *The American Black Male: His Present Status and His Future*, Chicago: Nelson-Hall pp. 231–44.

Leake, D. O. and Leake, B. L. (1992) 'Islands of hope: Milwaukee's African-American immersion schools', *Journal of Negro Education*, **61** pp. 4–11.

Mac an Ghaill, M. (1994) '(In)visibility: Sexuality, race and masculinity in the school context' in Epstein, D. (ed.) *Challenging Lesbian and Gay Inequalities in Education*, Buckingham: Open University Press.

McCall, N. (1994) *Makes Me Want To Holler: A Young Black Man in America*, New York: Vintage Books.

Madhubuti, H. (1990) *Black Men: Obsolete, Single and Dangerous*, Chicago, IL: Third World Press.

Majors, R. G. and Gordon, J. U. (1994) *The American Black Male: His Present Status and His Future*, Chicago, IL: Nelson-Hall Publishers.

Majors, R. G. and Mancini Billson, J. (1992) *Cool Pose: The Dilemmas of Black Manhood in America*, New York: Lexington.

Majors, R. G., Tyler, R., Peden, B. and Hall, R. E. (1994) 'Cool pose: A symbolic mechanism for masculine role enactment and copying by Black males' in Majors, R. G. and Gordan, J. U. (eds) *The American Black Male: His Present Status and His Future*, Chicago, IL: Nelson-Hall pp. 245–59.

Mincy, R. B. (ed.) (1994) *Nurturing Young Black Males: Challenges to Agencies, Programs, and Social Policy*, Washington, DC: The Urban Institute.

Parry, O. (1997) '"Schooling is Fooling": Why Do Jamaican Boys Underachieve in School?' *Gender and Education*, **9** pp. 223–31.

Polite, V. (1993) 'Educating African-American males in suburbia: Quality education . . . Caring environment?', *Journal of African American Male Studies*, **1**, pp. 92–105.

Polite, V. and Davis, J. E. (eds) (1994) 'Pedagogical and contextual issues affecting African American males in school and society', Special Issues of *The Journal of Negro Education*, **63**, p. 4.

Rong, X. L. (1996) 'Effects of race and gender on teachers' perception of the social behavior of elementary students', *Urban Education*, **31**, pp. 261–90.

Rys, G. S. and Bear, G. G. (1997) 'Relational aggression and peer relations: gender and developmental issues', *Merill-Palmer Quarterly*, **43**, pp. 87–106.

Sanders, E. T. and Reed, P. L. (1995) 'An investigation of the possible effects of an immersion as compared to a traditional program for African-American males', *Urban Education*, **30**, pp. 93–112.

Sewell, T. (1997) 'Teacher attitude: Who's afraid of the big black boy?' Paper presented at the Annual American Educational Research Association meeting held in Chicago, IL.

Slaughter-Defoe, D. T. and Richards, H. (1994) 'Literacy as empowerment: The case for African American males' in Gadsden, V. L. and Wagner, D. A. (eds) *Literacy among African American Youth: Issues in Learning, Teaching, and Schooling*, Cresskill, NJ: Hampton Press pp. 125–47.

Watson, C. and Smitherman, G. (1991) 'Educational equity and Detroit's male academies', *Equity and Excellence*, 25 pp. 90–105.

Wright, D. L. (1996) 'Concrete and abstract attitudes, mainstream orientation, and academic achievement of adolescent African-American males', Unpublished Dissertation, Howard University, Washington, DC.

13 Black boys and schooling: an intervention framework for understanding the dilemmas of masculinity, identity and underachievement

Tony Sewell and Richard Majors

INTRODUCTION

Not all black boys are the same. This may seem a simple or common-sense assertion but in terms of teacher perception and the popular discourses that underpin 'black masculinity' there is evidence of an acceptance of cultural and ethnic essentialism (Dhondy 1974; Ofsted 1999). This chapter is written with data drawn from an ethnographic study of an inner-city boys' school. It seeks to challenge the homogenisation of black (i.e. African-Caribbean) boys into one big lump of rebellious, phallocentric underachievers. We want to point to the differences between those who conform to the requirements of schooling and those who do not. Within this, we want to show the fluid, multifarious, shifting and hybrid constructions of black masculinities that operated in this school. We will argue that a more heterogeneous perspective of black boys has been missing from the literature which has failed to look at class, context and the complex intersections of masculinity and ethnicity. Emancipation from the canon of 'black masculinity' gives us a more sophisticated understanding of 'underachievement' and the survival strategies of these children. Those teachers who were most successful with African-Caribbean boys were aware that too many boys were tagged with the label of 'Black Machismo'. Their success was not in the ignoring of masculinity and ethnicity but in realising the complex identities of the boys in a context where racism worked on a number of levels.

The key part of this empirical evidence is drawn from 'Township School', an inner-city boys' comprehensive school. The school faced an on-going battle to avoid closure. It had a roll of 500 but this had been falling over the last five years. The school was unpopular because of its exam results and reputation of being a school with a poor discipline record. The school is located in a rich suburb, uncomfortably nestling between a number of public schools. The appointment of the school's first African-Caribbean headteacher marked a new start for the school with the expectation that this new leader would change the fortunes of the school.

At the time of research there were 61 students of Asian origin, 63 of African origin, 140 of African-Caribbean origin, 31 mixed-race students, 127 white boys and 23 others. African-Caribbean boys were six times more likely to be excluded from school compared to other groups. In spite of this disproportionate amount of punishment, African-Caribbean boys adopted various strategies to survive the problems of racism and the inadequacies of teaching and management in the school. In order to understand the range of responses we reworked Merton's (1957) typology of the four ways in which subjects negotiated their schooling. These were: the 'Conformists' who accept both the means and goals of schooling, the 'Innovators' who accept the goals but reject the means of schooling, the 'Retreatists' who reject both and the 'Rebels' who reject both but replace them with their own agenda. Merton's perspective could easily be seen as four stereotypes; the Merton model presupposes that student behaviour can be regimented into these fixed categories. We argue to the contrary, that students are de-centred subjects changing their social identity depending on the context and their role(s) within it.

There is a need to look at positions around different discourses and cultural forms and regard Merton's categories not as fixed entities but as rooted in positions that come from an acceptance or resistance to the various discourses and cultural forms of the school and the boys' subculture. A reworked model would look as follows:

Positioned: (Discourse and cultural forms of the school and the way they are perceived as goals and means)

Position themselves: Communities and sub-culture; producing discourses of acceptance or resistance)

Categories: (From a multiplicity of axes for the production of possibly conflicting subject positions and potential practices and interactions)

It is impossible to talk of 'goals' and 'means' without first unpacking the cultural influences or relationships available to different students. The 'categories' then become the result of different discourses and cultural forms and the way individuals are positioned and position themselves in relation to them.

THE CONFORMISTS: THE ULTIMATE SACRIFICE OR DOING YOUR OWN THING?

It must be noted that by far the largest single category (41 per cent) was Conformist. This meant that most African-Caribbean boys were not rebelling against school and most accepted its means and goals. There has been a concentration in the literature on so-called 'Black underachievement' and black conflict with school but little on those boys who say they like school and do relatively well. Therefore we have the danger of perceiving African-Caribbean boys as a single entity who are all disillusioned with schooling.

What did unite the range of 'Conformist' students was the notion of a conflict between the 'fictive Black culture' of the peer group and the goals, values and expectations of school. It was this characteristic which helped us develop the

Conformist typology. It is not necessarily boys who did very well academically but from observation and their own perceptions we get a picture of boys who feel that they cannot embrace the values of school and those of their own black peer group. They tended to have a mixture of friends from different ethnic backgrounds, unlike the exclusively black peer group of the Rebels. Some of these Conformists tended to go to the extreme in their break from the collective, so much so that it borders on a racialised discourse. Kelvin, who is a year 9 student, gives this 'individualistic' perspective as the reason why he has avoided exclusion:

TS: Do you belong to a gang or posse?
Kelvin: No, because my mum says I shouldn't hang around students who get into trouble. I must take my opportunity while I can.
TS: What students in this school do you avoid?
Kelvin: They are fourth years, you can easily spot the way they walk around in groups, they are mostly black with one or two whites. They're wearing baseball hats and bopping (black stylised walk).
TS: Don't you ever 'bop'?
Kelvin: Sometimes for a laugh, but it's really a kind of walk for bad people. I might walk like this at the weekend with my mates but not in school in front of the teachers. It sets a bad example.

Kelvin has not only linked group or community dynamics with bad behaviour, but is also using a racialised discourse. It is this perceived anti-school sub-culture of African-Caribbean fourth years that Kelvin links with 'bad people'. He cannot reconcile an 'innocent' cultural expression, which he shares even if it is only on weekends, with the values and norms of being a 'good' student. There is a cost to doing well in Township and that sacrifice is made by Kelvin and his mother.

Fordham (1988) describes the collective identity that Kelvin resists as 'fictive-kinship'. In her study of black American children she looks at how a sense of racialised 'brotherhood' and 'sisterhood' affects their attitude to schooling. This desire to flee from the black collective and cut an individual path is not only shown in attitudes to work but in music and cultural tastes. Kelvin echoes this in his comments on black music:

TS: What music do you like?
Kelvin: I like UB40 and Meatloaf.
TS: What do you think of rap and ragga music?
Kelvin: It's not my favourite because some of the rappers are offensive to women and cuss. It makes you want to dance to the beat, but the words about women are bad. It's not fair.
TS: What do the rest of the kids in your year think about your musical tastes?
Kelvin: They think I'm weird, but I say to them 'I don't have to listen to the same music or dress up like you'. I am my own person. My mum told me to be my own person and not copy other people. I just follow that.

In Fordham's study, the students who conformed to the schooling process also felt they could not share the same music as the students who were anti-school. Although Kelvin does express some of these attitudes, he's too complex an individual to simply be categorised as 'acting White' in order to progress. The information from his parents could easily be interpreted as a 'survival' or 'tactical' strategy in a racist context as distinct from an act of self-denial or what Fordham calls 'racelessness'. The problem with Kelvin's rationale is that he sees little that is good in the black collective identity. It is perceived as oppositional to schooling and therefore bad. One of the most important attributes of fictive-kinship is the blanket of security it gives in a hostile context. Weis (1985) notes this ambivalence when she argues that being a Conformist is more than just an act of individual will:

> The ethic of co-operation is deeply rooted among the urban poor, and individuals do not break these ties easily. While individualism may be a desired goal, it may be impossible to live out in a context of scarce resources. It must be stressed that the desire for dominant culture embodies its own contradictions: while dominant culture may be desired on one level, it is white, not black. Given that student cultural form at Urban College acts largely to reproduce the urban underclass, success in school represents a severe break with the underclass community. Since the collective offers the only security students have, the individual must carefully weigh his or her chances for success against the loss of security that the community provides.
>
> (Weis 1985: 125)

There was in Township a capacity amongst many of the Conformist students to work at a compromise between the tensions that Weis describes. The tragedy in Township is that too many of these students did not have the capacity or the 'luck' to fine-tune the balance between keeping their distance and at the same time staying 'in' with their friends.

This tension was not just an example of student weaknesses, often there were times when Conformist students would attempt to claim the 'individual' ground but this was taken away by negative teacher expectation. Stephen, an African-Caribbean year 10 student was determined not to be linked with the 'Posse' (African-Caribbean gang) but his teachers were not prepared to separate him from the group when it came to punishments. Stephen shows some similarity to Gillborn's (1990) student, Paul Dixon:

> Like the members of the clique discussed earlier, Paul Dixon recognised and rejected the negative image which some staff held of him. Rather than reacting through a glorification of that image within a culture of resistance, however, Paul channelled his energies into succeeding against the odds by avoiding trouble when he could and minimising the conflicts which he experienced with his teachers.
>
> (Gillborn 1990: 63)

Like Paul Dixon, Stephen was too often perceived as being in the same category as the anti-school students, despite his efforts to claim individual ground. This individuality was also challenged by his peer group and, most strongly, by the year 10 'Posse':

TS: What do the 'Posse' think of you?

Stephen: I think they think I'm part of them, even though I'm doing my own things now. When I go to my class and they bunk off, they will say to me I'm a goody goody. But I turn to them and say that when I get my flash car and you're begging for money, then you wished you had behaved like me.

TS: What do they say when you tell them this?

Stephen: They call me a pussy.

Being called a 'pussy' Stephen suffers the ultimate attack for being a Conformist, which is a charge against his masculinity. Being pro-school cannot be reconciled with the machismo of sub-culture. Mac an Ghaill (1994) comments on how some anti-school African-Caribbean boys have linked academic achievement with being gay or effeminate.

The category of Conformist student becomes in Township a fluid context with these students positioning themselves and being positioned by others. Their own stance in school may come from a series of influences: parental, class and even religion. However, no Conformist student was really allowed 'to be themselves'. In fact this 'individualistic' stance was seen to be most objectionable not only by the fictive-kinship of the peer group but ironically from many teachers. Although these boys claimed to share the dominant ethos of the school, which saw black peer grouping as a negative, too many were still perceived as part of a wider African-Caribbean challenge. They could never really escape the castle of their skins and gender. However, the important point is that many of them wanted to. The kind of escape path that many of them desired was not a denial of their race and gender but the restrictive 'Positioning' that came from the teachers and the peer group.

INNOVATORS: LEARNING TO BALANCE ON THE TIGHTROPE OR A STEP TOO FAR FOR 'MANKIND'

The second largest grouping (35 per cent) of African-Caribbean boys surveyed came under the category of innovation. This category accepted the goals of schooling but rejected the means. The origins of their pro-school values are mostly parental. However, they reject the means of schooling. At the heart of 'Innovation' is a conflict: you are positive about the wider values of education but you cannot cope with the schooling process. We arrived at this category by looking first at the research done on black girls. Fuller (1980) has shown how the black girls in her study managed subtly to resolve this dichotomy. She describes their attitude as 'pro-education and not pro-school'. They managed to distance themselves from Conformists (keeping themselves close to their peer groups) and yet achieve academic success.

The category of innovation as applied to the boys in Township is really about their 'desire' or 'struggle' rather than a successful accomplishment of this typology. In other words we need to examine why black girls have been more successful at 'innovation' compared to African-Caribbean boys.

Frank Sinclair is a year 10 student and a key member of the clique in his year called the 'Posse'. He was expelled from two schools before coming to Township. He has already had five short-term exclusions since he has been at his new school:

TS: What did your mum say when she found out about your latest exclusion?
Frank: She just sent me to my Dad's house. And my Dad would talk long, long, long.
TS: What did he say?
Frank: He says it would be harder for me to get a job than a white man. He's always
          talking about this; it's like when he starts he can never finish. Most of the time
          I go up on Saturdays, get my pocket money – I only want to speak to him.
          He would just keep on about education. Then as I'm about to go he would
          get a book out and I would have to sit down and do some weird maths. And
          if I can't do a sum he would start getting mad.
TS: Do you think it is worth coming to school?
Frank: Yes, I have some friends who are about 21 and they're just loafing around.
          I just want to go to college do a B-Tec National and go and work in a bank.

Frank is representative of many boys at Township School who were positive about education but rejected the schooling process. These boys were unable/disabled to fine-tune these two opposing instincts in order to avoid open conflict with teachers.

One popular reason why 'Innovation' is said to be never successfully accomplished is that black boys face greater pressure and teacher racism compared to girls. This might be the case but the work of Mirza (1992) still shows black girls having to work against the racist discourses of their teachers and experiencing more exclusions compared to their white counterparts. Another popular reason is the power and pressure of a peer group that demands an antischool hypermasculinity. Mac an Ghaill (1994) points to this pressure:

> The Black Macho Lads were particularly vindictive to African-Caribbean academic students who overtly distanced themselves from their anti-school strategies. In response, the Black Macho Lads labelled them 'batty men' (a homophobic comment). As Mercer and Julien (1988 p. 112) point out, a further contradiction in subordinated Black Masculinities occurs, 'when Black men subjectively internalise and incorporate aspects of the dominant definitions of masculinity in order to contest the conditions of dependency and powerlessness which racism and racial oppression enforce.' Ironically the Black Macho Lads, in distancing themselves from the racist school structures, adopted survival strategies of hyper-masculine heterosexuality that threatened other African-Caribbean students, adding further barriers to their gaining academic success.
>
> (Mac an Ghaill 1994: 87–8)

These two popular reasons for the difficulty of 'Innovation' both can be reduced to notions of underachievement and hypermasculinity. However, there is a danger of overplaying the achievement of black girls and making an exaggerated comparison. Second, is that Mac an Ghaill's analysis needs to be balanced by the fact that there were boys who did successfully negotiate the pressures of peer group and the demands of school. For them there was no psychic pressure between the so-called 'two worlds'. To use a cliché, they 'worked hard and played hard'.

In Township a combination of teacher racism and peer group pressure led to 'Innovation' being a tightrope that many of these boys failed to cross, but not all. What we need to take from the Innovators is not simply an analysis of them as victims but to listen to the reasons why they feel the 'means' of schooling cannot work for them. In many cases it was to do with the class management of individual teachers and the irrelevancy of the curriculum where they or their interests were never featured.

RETREATISM: AN INVISIBLE RESISTANCE OR GLAD TO BE UNNOTICED?

There were a minority of African-Caribbean students in our sample who can be classified as 'retreatist' (6 per cent). These are students who reject both the goals and means of schooling but for whom these are not replaced by the subculture. In fact schooling is replaced with no significant alternative; their task is simply to reject work. The characteristics behind this typology stem from a psychological perspective where a student is marginalised within the margin. In Township we have already established that the black male presence itself could be perceived by some teachers as threatening. For 'Retreatism' to be successful it needs an additional characteristic to 'accommodate' this negative teacher expectation. Therefore the African-Caribbean boys who best avoided exclusion were those who were perceived as non-threatening. In physical terms they were either very slight or very overweight and usually having Special Educational Needs.

Joseph is a third year student. He spends most of his day walking around the corridors. He claims never to have been 'picked up' by his class teachers who regard him as a 'slow learner'.

TS: Why do you spend so much time outside lessons?
Joseph: It's just boring and the teachers that I have are weak and they can't control the class.
TS: Do you ever hang around with the Posse?
Joseph: You must be joking. I hate them. They go around trying to bully students and get their dinner money. They just want to start trouble.
TS: Have you ever been excluded?
Joseph: No.
TS: Why?
Joseph: Because I'm not that rude when I'm around teachers.

TS: How long can you get away with not turning up to lessons?

Joseph: Weeks. Teachers sometimes see me on the corridor but they don't say anything. They don't think I'm a bad boy because I'm not aggressive.

Joseph is not only opposed to teachers; he also hates the sub-culture of the Posse. It is because he is not visibly rejecting the schooling process that he avoids open conflict with teachers. Retreatists are never seen in groups of more than two and they resist schooling through subversion. They might walk the corridors pretending that they are on an errand for a teacher. In Township it was significant that this form of resistance was open to only a minority of black boys. However, it is more evidence of the qualitative difference of the 'black masculine' experience in the school. Joseph was overweight for his age and the teachers perceived him as 'soft and cuddly' – to quote his form teachers. The physically aggressive signals that teachers picked up from the Posse were not present in a student like Joseph. He was therefore more likely to be ignored because he was perceived as non-threatening.

In the case of the Retreatists, their experience was not one of a phallocentric charged rebellion. They resisted school through subversion. They add another complex layer to any notion of a uniform 'black masculine' experience in Township school. Even their relationship to the dominant values of the black 'peer group' is different to that of many other boys: they refuse to give the Posse any legendary status. They claim an invisible ground marginalised by the schooling process and despised by the dominant peer group.

REBELS: PHALLOCENTRIC REVENGE OR EXPLODING BLACK CANONS?

At the heart of some black feminist critique (hooks 1992) is a debate about the motivation and consequences of 'black male' rebellion to racist oppression. It is suggested that because of the sexualised way in which black males are excluded from mainstream society, the only way they can find an alternative power is in an exaggerated phallocentricity which exploits women. What is interesting about this debate is that there are some black nationalist scholars (Staples 1982) who read this as an 'understandable' response and others like bell hooks who feel that this is an internalised oppression:

> If Black men no longer embraced phallocentric masculinity, they would be empowered to explore their fear and hatred of other men, learning new ways to relate. How many Black men will have to die before Black folks are willing to look at the link between the contemporary plight of Black men and their continued allegiance to patriarchy and phallocentrism?

(hooks 1992: 112)

It is our argument that both Staples and hooks have not allowed for the complex nature of black male rebellion, particularly when it manifests itself in the context of school. Rebellion in Township was really a rather damp squib affair. There were a number of boys who did translate their experience into a phallocentric discourse but there were other forms of rebellion which were more sophisticated and were not a form of internalised oppression. Those boys who did fit into bell hooks' category I called 'Hedonist'. They replaced the goals and means of schooling with their own agenda. They were frequently excluded and did find comfort in an anti-school black machismo. One afternoon, I showed a video of a programme by the comedian Lenny Henry to a group of year 9 and 10 African-Caribbean students, in which Henry plays the feckless Delbert who makes his living doing scams. This was their response:

TS:	Why does Delbert have to keep using 'scams'?
Michael:	It's the only way he, as a black youth, can survive.
Donald:	Check it, no one is going to give him a job, he has to do a bit of illegal business or else he's going to go hungry.
Michael:	Most black kids do scams.
TS:	Why?
Dennis:	It's how we are – we have to go crooked because the system is like that.
TS:	What do you mean?
Dennis:	The police and employers, let's face it, they don't like black people.
Allan:	I don't think it's just black kids that pull scams. Loads of white boys always do it. They just do it differently.
TS:	What do you mean?
Allan:	Yes, the black kids do it up front and they don't care.
TS:	Do you think that the white boys are more clever with their sneaky scams?
Allan:	No way, the white boys are just pussies, they haven't got the balls like a black man, most of them go on as if they are batty men [homosexual].
TS:	Do you all agree with that?

There is universal agreement.

These responses do confirm an attitude that has internalised oppression and that sees 'black masculinity' in a narrow patriarchal and phallocentric framework. What is particularly interesting is the contemptuous attitude that these boys have for white boys. This again must be contextualised with many black students having close relationships with white students. However, as part of the construction of hedonistic rebellion white students are perceived as effeminate and featuring low in terms of the values of the dominant peer group.

The problem with Township is that no one had the insight or 'courage' to take on the issue of how black masculinity is constructed and its influence on the wider society. The nearest that the students came to any sort of discussion about these issues was when the new black headteacher took a group of boys for their Personal and Social Education class; however, he failed to grasp the opportunity. He felt too threatened by the boys' phallocentric sub-culture:

TS: What do you think about the African-Caribbean boys' attitude to women?

Mr Jones: During a Social Education class, we were talking about children's reading books and we were trying to identify stereotypes. I told them I had 10 year-old twins, one boy, one girl, and my wife and I decided we would not create this gender divide in the twins. Then one of the boys in the class said to me: 'You've only got two kids sir?'

I said 'Yes, that's right.' He then asked: 'What about the others back in Jamaica?'

I said: 'I've only got two children.' He said: 'Well sir, you're not really a true Yard Man!'

The term 'Yard man' is a reference to Jamaicans who are from 'back home' or affectionately the 'back yard'. He is linked with a street 'hard man' life style and he is notorious for fathering many children with different mothers and taking no responsibilities for his actions. Mr Jones had an ideal opportunity to deconstruct the Yard Man and examine the cultural process that goes into his construction. Instead, he saw this as just more evidence of lost youth, who have become irresponsible and who worship destructive role models.

Rebellion in Township was not just phallocentric; there were those who articulated their rebellion on a political level. Calvin is a year 10 pupil. His dad died, leaving his mum to raise five boys. He has good contacts and a strong network of friends outside of school who are a lot older. This helps to bolster his reputation in the Posse as a man who does business with 'big people'. He has most conflict with a white teacher, Ms Kenyon. In one class Calvin was sharing a joke with a group of boys at the back of the class. Ms Kenyon's response was to seek confrontation in a battle of the wills:

Ms Kenyon: Calvin, will you shut up. I don't know why you come to my lessons because you're not interested in doing any work.

Calvin: I would do if you didn't give us rubbish work. Look around, half the class haven't got a clue what you're on about.

Ms Kenyon: And you have, have you?

Calvin: The lesson is boring and so are you.

Calvin does not see a link between schooling and getting a good job. He has already set up his own small business as a 'mobile barber', cutting hair at people's homes. He said he could make up to £300 a week. He carries a mobile phone in school so that clients can make appointments:

TS: How important is it for you to own your own business?

Calvin: It is important for black people to make money because white people don't take us seriously because we're poor.

TS: Is education important to you?

Calvin: Not really, I know what I need to know from the street. I'll give it three years and I bet no one will bother with school. There ain't no jobs for no one and they don't want to give jobs to black people.

The national figures on levels of unemployment for black youths compared to whites confirmed Calvin's claims that job prospects were bleak for school leavers. Calvin has rejected the world of schooling and replaced it with his alternative source of income and his most valued contact with the adult world in his community. He spoke about 'real' education which gave black people economic independence and pride in their race.

Calvin has contempt for what Dhondy (1974) calls the functions of school:

> The reaction of Black youth to discipline, grading and skilling processes is substantially different and potentially more dangerous to schools. And it is precisely because the education of Black youth starts and continues within the communities of which they are still a part.
>
> (1974: 46)

Although Calvin exercises individualism in terms of his contempt for many of his peers and his desire to be his own boss, he looks positively towards his local black community for inspiration, guidance and success. He has not distanced himself from the power and knowledge; it is school knowledge that he despises most. He firmly believes that knowledge can be used for collective action and the eventual betterment of the condition of black people. It is proof that students in this category do not close off the possibility of pursuing an emancipatory relationship between knowledge and dissent. He has realised that there are other sources of knowledge which meet his material and psychological needs and they can be found within his community.

The emphasis on framing all the rebels as phallocentric is incorrect. Indeed, much theory and analysis of phallocentrism seems always to be pointing to black boys. What about the sexist and misogynistic attitudes which have been the inspiration for white working-class rebellion? Yet teachers seem only to find these problems with black boys. The category of rebel has a wide spectrum within it, much of which is political and pedagogic. It is simply an analysis and rejection of an education system that works against many black boys. This more sophisticated response has often been silenced by the 'obsessive' preoccupation with the dynamics of the black phallus.

EGO-RECOVERY

What then are some of the solutions for schools, teachers and black boys in a context of racism and poor self-esteem? How can we reduce the number of exclusions of African-Caribbean boys? What can administrators, teachers and the children themselves do to counter the complex oppressive and repressive schooling process that these boys face every day? First, there needs to be change at the level of the school and how it is organised; second at the level of teacher attitude and how those expectations can be changed and third at the level of the student, where African-Caribbean boys have the opportunity to deconstruct black masculinity and take control of their own behaviour. All these levels feed into what can be called 'ego-recovery' a social and psychological position where African-Caribbean boys can achieve, driven by a reconstructed masculinity.

Hardiman and Jackson (1996) have produced a model of racial identity development that can help teachers to evaluate their own strengths and shortcomings on the issue of social justice and race. What makes this such a powerful tool is that it requires the 'individual' to make the self-reflecting journey on issues that are generally, at best, hidden by slogans or, at worst, totally ignored. The same model can be used by students, black and white, for confronting the crises and anxieties in their own development. (Figure 13.1)

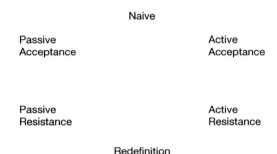

Radical identity development

Naive

| Passive | Active |
| Acceptance | Acceptance |

| Passive | Active |
| Resistance | Resistance |

Redefinition

Figure 13.1 Model of racial identity development

INTERNALISATION

At a conference in Texas in 1996 Hardiman and Jackson were asked to explain each of these categories with examples to support their case. They came up with the following:

Naive: a state of no social consciousness, usually from birth to age 3, when children accept what they see. Only with the development of social consciousness comes the potential for race awareness.

Passive Acceptance for many African-Caribbean boys is when a student internalises all the negative images of himself. Passive in this context means unconscious. They are boys who unconsciously believe the negative perceptions that are held by teachers and the wider society. This was illustrated by two dominant beliefs in Township school. First, there were some boys who shared the racist perception that it was the black children who gave the school a bad name. Second, there were boys who bought into the black male hypersexual image as a normative value.

Active Acceptance links to those students who carry the 'burden of acting white'. These were the rebel students who felt that to conform to schooling was a form of betraying a radical black consciousness. They linked black culture/masculinity only with anti-school and anti-education. In other words they played host to their own oppression.

Passive Resistance links to the innovators in Township who were unable to operate a limited form of resistance which was sufficient to satisfy their peers and also avoid confrontations with teachers. It is a strategy that black girls have been able to operate more successfully than black boys.

Active Resistance These are either failed passive resistors or those able to see the workings of racism in teachers and the institution. This is a cleansing process where the students begin to fight against all those aspects of consciousness that are working against them. They begin to see the racialised way in which school operates and actively fight against this.

Redefinition This will demand African-Caribbean boys to re-think black masculinity. They will have to deconstruct black masculinity. The question that needs to be asked is, what does it mean to be a black male?

Internalisation This is what bell hooks calls 'black ego recovery'. This comes only after you have decolonised your mind. For young black men it will mean understanding how racism is often linked with other oppressions. It may even mean making coalitions with other groups, be they racial or gender.

There were three aspects of the 'black ego recovery' to be found in Township. First, the abandonment of black nationalism, not black pride but a theoretical framework that has its roots in the European Enlightenment. Second, the need not to engage in a mind/body split, which should have the same subversive implications it had for feminist theory. Third was the need for black youth subculture to shift from an 'uncritical' reportage in learning and play to a more creative framework that explores new avenues and opens fresh spaces.

When talking to African-Caribbean boys about these issues I would illustrate this by alluding to a popular icon that they know or can relate to. One can use the racial development profile to explain the development of the life of major black figures like Malcolm X. A good exercise would be to show an edited version of Spike Lee's film and get the students to plot his racial development using the profile. One of the key problems with this type of exercise is clarity. I would use a different type of jargon for students compared to teachers (Figure 13.2).

Trusting (toddlers)

Passive	Active
Acceptance	Acceptance
(Parents, Sports stars)	(Black kids who are
	ashamed of themselves)

Passive	Active
Resistance	Resistance
(Awareness that the	(Awareness that the
world/school has a	world/school has a
problem about your	problem about your
race)	race)

Do little or nothing	Stand up against the system,
	demanding that school and
	teachers change

A new rhythm

(Doing well at school without taking anything off anyone.
What does it mean to be a black male?)

A change from within

(Look at Malcolm X, don't be limited by the narrow lens of
being a race victim, don't split your mind from your body, don't be
afraid to be an individual and follow your own instincts)

Figure 13.2 Extending the model of racial identity development

EXPLORING RACIAL DEVELOPMENT PROFILES THROUGH POPULAR CULTURE

The gangster lifestyle as represented in rap music has come under incredible assault, not only from the white establishment but from black feminists and concerned black parents. The only times I witnessed the boys in Township in a mood of self-reflection about this gangster lifestyle was when one of their heroes fell. When top rappers suffered from the contradictions and self-inflicted wounds inherent in their lifestyle, it became the topic for discussion during registration. These discussions soon broke down into the boys accepting that a rapper who was shot or jailed must be honoured for his street credibility.

However, there was one exception. This was the gangster rapper Tupac Shakur, the only artist in the history of popular music to have his album ('Me against the world' (1995)) rise to number one, while still in prison. What gave the strongest impression to the boys in Township School was not his jail sentence but the fact that he had decided to give up his gangster lifestyle.

Tupac Shakur was black America's most famous tough rapper. The gangster lifestyle in rap was always about the expression of rage, frustration and hopelessness. It was a strategic option adopted by many young black men in the materialistic 1980s as the most effective way to go through life and get 'paid'. All that these rappers did was give voice to a mood that was already playing itself out in some aspects of black urban culture. In the process, however the gangster lifestyle became romanticised and celebrated. It was no longer the life to avoid or dread but became one that a black youth could aspire to. Bad was indeed good and 'good' was for the weak.

When interviewed about this gangster style, rappers confidently said that they were only reflecting reality. It was an easy way out because they were not just holding up a mirror to nature, it was more like taking the mirror and smashing it over the heads of rival gangs and women. Gangster rap was no longer a simple reporting of reality, but the creation of a fantasy gangster world which fed into the real world and then made it more extreme.

Tupac Shakur survived a shoot-out and when he was in jail for violence and accused of rape, he decided to give up this old life, where gangsters rarely get old. A year later he was shot dead. In his own words (1995):

> When you do rap albums, you got to train yourself. You got to constantly be in character. You used to see rappers talking all that hard shit, and then you see them in suits and shit at the American Music Awards. I didn't want to be that type of nigga. I wanted to keep it real, and that's what I thought I was doing. But now that shit is dead. That Thug Life shit . . . I did it, I put in my work. I laid it down. But now that shit is dead . . . I'm going to start an organization called Us First, I'm going to start to save these young niggaz, because nobody else wants to save them. Nobody ever came to save me. They just watch what happened to you. That's why Thug Life to me is dead. If it's real, then let somebody else represent it, because I'm tired of it. I represented it too much. I was Thug Life. I was the only nigga out there putting my life on the line.
>
> (Tupac Shakur 1995: 55)

The story of Tupac Shakur is the story of how the black ego can be recovered. His shift from a gangster style to new perception of black masculinity has important theoretical implications. First, he wanted to be able to be free from the restrictions of black nationalism that did not allow him to cultivate contacts with white friends (1995):

> I was letting people dictate who should be my friends. I felt like because I was this big Black Panther type of nigga, I couldn't be friends with Madonna. And so I dissed her, even though she showed me nothing but love. I felt bad, because when I went to jail, I called her and she was the only person that was willing to help me.
>
> (ibid.)

This part of Tupac's black ego recovery was that his realisation that the whole concept of Black Nationalism really is restrictive. He realised that the world is too large and varied to limit oneself to any race or idea. This point was also stressed by tennis star Arthur Ashe (1993) in his autobiography. In the last chapter he writes a personal piece to his young daughter, advising her on the best path to success:

> You must also learn to feel comfortable in any company, as long as those people are good people. Travelling the world as a tennis player, I discovered that deep friendships with an infinite variety of people are not only possible but can definitely enrich one's life beyond measure. Do not hem yourself in, or allow others to do so. I am still dismayed when I go to some college campuses and find out that in the cafeteria, for example, black students, by choice, sit separately at a table with only other black students. Whether from force of habit, thoughtlessness, or timidity, this practice is usually a waste of time – time that should be used by these students to get to know people of other cultures and backgrounds. This mixing is an essential part of education, not something extraneous to it. I hope you will summon the courage to forge friendships with as many different people as you can. Some African-Americans may tease or even scorn you, and some other people may rebuff you, but I want you to persevere anyway.
>
> (Ashe 1993: 321)

Black ego recovery must tackle the complex notion of the way black fictive-culture translates itself into an experience where to be good in school means one is 'acting white'. It needs to give black youths a desire and a knowledge to feel comfortable about their identity (however shifting) and yet not feel restricted by a narrow nationalism. Glenn Loury (1993), a black American academic, talks of this challenge to the 'black psyche':

> I now understand how this desire to be regarded as genuinely black, to be seen as a 'regular brother,' has dramatically altered my life. It narrowed the range of my earliest intellectual pursuits, distorted my relationships with other people, censored my political thought and expression, informed the way I dressed and spoke, and shaped my cultural interests. Some of this was inevitable and not all of it was bad, but in my experience the need to be affirmed by one's racial peers can take on a pathological dimension. Growing into intellectual maturity has been, for me, largely a process of becoming free of the need to have my choices validated by 'the brothers.' After many years I have come to understand that until I became willing to risk the derision of the crowd I had no chance to discover the most important truths about myself or about life. I have learned that one does not have to live surreptitiously as a Negro among whites in order to be engaged in a denial of one's genuine self for the sake of gaining social acceptance. This is a price that blacks often demand of each other as well.
>
> (Loury 1993: 6–7)

Loury shows that black ego-recovery is not about a black 'Amen' corner where children are deprogrammed from a white perspective to black one through so called positive images. It is a wider and harder project that demands a willingness to risk derision as one breaks from the restrictive confines of 'race' and 'nation'. Loury (1993) goes on to explain the restrictions of a personal identity wholly dependent on racial contingency:

> Thus, and ironically, to the extent that we individual blacks see ourselves primarily through a racial lens, we sacrifice possibilities for the kind of personal development that would ultimately further our collective, racial interests. We cannot be truly free men and women while labouring under a definition of self derived from the perceptual view of our oppressor, confined to the contingent facts of our oppression. In *A Portrait of the Artist as a Young Man* James Joyce says of Irish nationalism: 'When the soul of man is born in this country there are nets flung at it to hold it back from flight. You talk to me of nationality, language, religion. I shall try to fly by these nets . . . Do you know what Ireland is? . . . Ireland is the old sow that eats her farrow'. It seems to me that, too often, a search for some mythic authentic blackness works similarly to hold back young black souls from flight into the open skies of American [British] society. Of course there is the constraint of racism also holding us back. But the trick, as Joyce knew, is to turn such 'nets' into wings, and thus to fly by them. One cannot do that if one refuses to see that ultimately it is neither external constraints nor expanded opportunity but rather an indwelling spirit that makes this flight possible.
>
> (Loury 1993: 10)

These theoretical possibilities must be taken up by black and white teachers and worked within a curriculum that is open to black and white boys. The notions of 'masculinity', 'race' and 'nation' influence teachers and pupils from all backgrounds.

Tupac Shakur also points to the Western division of mind and body, which was a trait of his former Thug Life. He is aware that these diversions exist in the psyche of white people and adopted in the lifestyle of many black youths is an attitude that suggests that physicality is everything for the black man:

> I'm not trying to make people think I'm faking it, but my whole life is going to be about saving somebody. I got to represent life. If you saying you going to be real, that's how you be real – be physically fit, be mentally fit. And I want niggas to be educated. You know, I was steering people away from school. You gotta be in school, because through school you can get a job. And if you got a job, then that's how they can't do us like this.
>
> (Shakur 1995: 55)

Black ego recovery must be about the healing body a mind which has been wounded/divided by slavery, colonialism and cultural racism. It has been left to what Gramsci calls the organic intellectuals such as Bob Marley and the radical tradition in rap music to keep black youth sub-culture as intellectually dynamic as anything coming out of a university. This point is supported with feminist thinking having always recognized the legitimacy of a pedagogy that dares to subvert the mind/body split and allow us to be whole in the classroom, and as a consequence wholehearted.

(hooks 1994b)

In this model we have attempted to take the best of theory and practice of the African-centred academies and apply it, not to separate schools but to mainstream institutions. For me black ego-recovery has to take place within the world in which we work and play. It is more than giving African-Caribbean boys a new set of textbooks that contain black characters and pictures. It presupposes a commitment by staff to a form of emancipatory teaching, as distinct from a white patriarchy dressed up in black nationalism.

CONCLUSION

In this chapter we have tried to unpack some of the oversimplifications that exist in the current debate about boys' achievement. African-Caribbean boys are seen in research (e.g. Mac an Ghaill 1994) and popular discourse as the tip of the iceberg in a general doomsday scenario of male disillusionment with school. This analysis links gender identity to an anti-school attitude. Boys, the argument runs, try to show their maleness by being as unfemale as possible and, in doing so, contrast themselves with girls, who are generally more committed to school work. This has been made worse by peer group pressure which boys are highly sensitive to, and this allows generalisations to be made about boys as a group. African-Caribbean boys have been seen in this context as a unified lump, who underachieve academically and are driven by a phallocentric revenge impulse to repair their oppressed maleness. There is a need to seriously question this overall pessimism of boys' alleged failure and in particular examine the complex, ambivalent and contradictory male identities that are constructed in school.

There are a number of costs and benefits to the boys in occupying each ideal position and this impacts on other relations (i.e. male and female teachers, parents, other black boys and white boys). If we look at the parents of conformist students we see them divided on the issue of whether Kelvin should bop (black stylised walk) in front of the teachers. We put the example to many black parent groups and it divides them. Some say he should curb his cultural style in order to 'get on' and not draw attention to himself, while others are adamant that for teachers to see his cultural expression as a threat is really racist and the teachers should change their attitudes. This example shows that even when African-Caribbean boys occupied the ideal of conformist, it was not unproblematic.

What we can say which goes against the tide of pessimism is that there was no evidence that boys were less positive towards school work than girls. Many of the

African-Caribbean boys positioned themselves in the pro-school categories of Conformist and Innovation, while 24 per cent saw themselves as rejecting the goals and means of schools. Even those boys who could be categorised as Rebels were not a simplified and unified group. Rebellion was complex and was not solely based on a phallocentric revenge but in many cases the boys had adopted a political position to explain their rejection of school.

In trying to solve the problems of teaching black boys, teachers need to avoid two falsehoods. The first is to deny that African-Caribbean boys face a disproportionate amount of punishment in school which is based on a wider myth of a greater African-Caribbean challenge. Second, that African-Caribbean boys are a homegenous lump of rebellious phallocentric underachievers.

The use of the 'ego-recovery' model is really a powerful tool both for teachers and pupils. In the case of African-Caribbean boys it can be the source in which these boys really begin to engage with the damaging features of racism. It also allows them to see if their survival strategy is really counter-productive. Ego-recovery is not race awareness training. It acknowledges that 'autobiography' and 'self-reflection' are the cornerstone of any learning process. Race and racism, just like gender and class, will work in different ways on different boys. The best interventions into children's lives are the ones that acknowledge this complexity.

REFERENCES

Ashe, A. (1993) *Days of Grace*, London: William Heinemann.
Back, L. (1992) PhD thesis: *Youth, Racism and Ethnicity in South London*, University of London.
Back, L. (1994) 'The White Negro revisited' in Cornwall, A. and Lindisfarne, N. (eds) *Dislocating Masculinity*, Comparative Ethnographies. London: Routledge.
Dhondy, F. (1974) 'The Black explosion in schools' *Race Today*, **6** 2, February, 44–50.
Fordham, S. (1988) 'Racelessness as a factor in Black students' school success: Pragmatic strategy or pyrrhic victory?', *Harvard Educational Review*, Vol. 58 No. 1.
Foucault, M. (1982) *Discipline and Punish*, London: Peregrine Books.
Fuller, M. (1980) 'Black girls in a London comprehensive school', reprinted in M. Hammersley and P. Woods (eds) (1984) *Life in School: The Sociology of Pupil Culture*, Milton Keynes: Open University Press.
Gillborn, D. (1990) *Race, Ethnicity and Education*, London: Unwin Hyman.
Gillborn, D. and Gipps, C. (1996) *Recent Research on the Achievements of Ethnic Minority Pupils (Ofsted)*, London: HMSO.
Gilroy, P. (1993) *Small Acts: Thoughts on the Politics of Black Cultures*, London: Serpent's Tail.
Hardiman, R. and Jackson, B. (1996) Lecture notes at the National Conference on Race and Ethnicity in American Higher Education, San Antonio, Texas, May 30–June 4.
Hebidge, D. (1982) *Subculture: The Meaning of Style*, London: Routledge.
Hewitt, R. (1996) *Routes of Racism: The Social Basis of Racist Action*, Stoke-on-Trent: Trentham Books.
Holland, S. (1996) Interview on Choice FM radio: London.
hooks, b. (1992) *Black Looks: Race and Representation*, London: Turnaround.
Loury, G. (1993) 'Free at last? A personal perspective on race and identity in America' in

Early, G. (ed.) *Lure and Loathing: Essays on Race, Identity and the Ambivalence of Assimilation*, New York: Penguin.

Mac an Ghaill, M. (1994) *The Making of Men, Masculinities, Sexualities and Schooling*, Buckingham: Open University Press.

Merton, R. (1957) *Social Theory and Social Structure*, Chicago: Chicago Free Press.

Mirza, H.S. (1992) *Young, Female and Black*, London: Routledge.

Ofsted (1999) *Raising the Attainment of Minority Ethnic Pupils*, London: HMI.

Powell, K. (1995) *Tupac Shakur*, New York: Time Warner.

Sewell, T. (1997) *Black Masculinity and Schooling: How Black Boys Survive Modern Schooling*, Stoke-on-Trent: Trentham Books.

Shakur, T. interview with Kevin Powell, *Vibe Magazine*, 9 April 1995 pp. 20–25.

Staples, R. (1982) *Black Masculinity: The Black Man's Role in American Society*, San Francisco: Black Scholar Press.

Weis, L. (1985) *Between Two Worlds: Black Students in an Urban Community College*, London: Routledge and Kegan Paul.

Part V
Mentoring and education

14 Mentoring Black males: responding to the crisis in education and social alienation[1]

Richard Majors, Vincent Wilkinson and William Gulam

INTRODUCTION

Young African Caribbean males are over-represented within the British criminal justice system, within the ranks of the unemployed, amongst those who are academically underachieving and those subject to exclusion from school (Sewell 1997). Additionally, African Caribbean males suffer disproportionately from poverty, violence, substance and alcohol abuse and higher mortality rates (Majors and Gordon 1994; Majors and Billson 1992). The social construction of Black males as dangerous and destructive exaggerates their current position and alienates them from the mainstream of British society.

Consequently, the prevalent negative image serves to sanction and facilitate the structural inequalities that particularly affect young African Caribbean males and contributes to the legitimisation of punitive exclusions of Black school pupils (Majors, Gillborn and Sewell 1988). Currently, African Caribbean boys are between four and six times more likely to be permanently excluded from school than their white counterparts (Gillborn and Gipps 1996). Black boys become isolated and alienated from the education process, reinforcing the syndrome that legitimises the structural inequalities they face in their adult years.

One of the ways in which professionals have sought to counteract this culture of alienation and discrimination is through mentoring. This chapter aims to review developments around the various mentoring initiatives among young African Caribbean males in Britain today, focusing on the localised but significant example of Manchester. It will explore some of the gaps in present programme delivery and suggest ways forward.

BACKGROUND

Historically, a significant thrust of government policy towards problems involving young people in the inner cities has been to direct funds and resources towards containment and control. Through racist stigmatisation, the focus for many of the enforcement programmes of the criminal justice system and social welfare has been the Black male (Majors and Wiener 1995; Solomos 1988). In many respects, the British response follows the American approach, where one out of every three Black males between the ages of 20 and 29 is now involved in the criminal justice system (Mauer 1990). In Britain too, despite the fact that 'ethnic minorities' constitute 4.2 per cent of the population, in 1990 they made up 15.5 per cent of the prison population (Foster 1990).

Clearly then, what is arguably needed as an alternative to the current blighting of the life chances of many young Black males is a set of new policies and interventionist paradigms that acknowledge the current waste in human resources and the need to improve the social status of Black males. Rather than using crisis management strategies and punitive programmes to solve the problem, the new paradigms must be proactive and collaborative, with the emphasis on nurturing and developing the potentialities of Black males (Majors and Wiener 1995). Importantly, they require race- and gender-specific strategies to obviate what is a stark and dysfunctional situation.

Most recently, the government has lent its support to mentoring as a remediative and interventionist strategy (Social Exclusion Unit 1998), bringing it into line with developments over the decade, which has seen a growing interest in mentoring and a proliferation of programmes over the country. There is now slow but growing evidence that mentoring programmes, particularly those targeting high-risk youth, can make the difference between wasted and productive lives (Majors and Wiener 1995). Increasingly, they are seen as a way to arrest the underdevelopment of Black males and the underutilisation of their abilities.

THE ORIGINS OF MENTORING

> Mentoring is an ancient concept. The Greek poet Homer first used the word 'Mentor' in his poem, the *Odyssey*. When Odysseus knew he would be away from home for many years to fight in the Trojan War, he entrusted a man named Mentor to be the guardian and tutor of his son Telemachus. Mentor's job was not merely to raise Telemachus, but to develop him for the responsibilities he was to assume in his lifetime. Thus mentor came to mean any 'trusted counsellor or guide'. In fact, mentoring is probably one of the most ancient forms of human development.
>
> (Jeffrey 1994: 1)

In traditional African societies too, the practice was very common, with young people being entrusted to elders, heads of craft associations, societies or extended family members for personal development, job training and general guidance. A mentor is therefore someone who provides guidance and support to a younger or less experienced person over a period of time. Mentors are likely to be sources of inspiration and act as coaches, professional friends, sponsors, facilitators and role models to their mentees (Jeffrey 1994). They listen, motivate and provide constructive intervention at critical and key transitional points (Clutterbuck 1994). The mentor provides non-judgemental support and an interaction that is beneficial to the less experienced partner (Sheriffe 1997).

Research has found that mentoring can have a major impact on the lives of young people. In 1993, Tierney, Grossman and Resch conducted the first impact study of the Big Brother/Big Sister mentoring organisation in the USA. It found that young people who met with their mentor regularly for a year were:

- 46 per cent less likely than their peers to start using illegal drugs;
- 27 per cent less likely to begin using alcohol;
- 52 per cent less likely than peers to skip school and 37 per cent less likely to miss a class; and
- more likely to have confidence in their abilities in school and more likely to get along with parents.

Recently, an audit of mentoring schemes in Britain was commissioned by the Commission for Racial Equality (CRE) to audit mentoring schemes in Britain. A major aim of this study was to determine whether mentoring could be used as a tool to address racial equality, disadvantage and underachievement among ethnic minorities. The study found that mentoring was one of the most effective means of helping disadvantaged young people. However, it found that the majority of the mentoring schemes did not specifically address issues of race equality. This situation is currently being addressed by the development of race- and gender-specific mentoring schemes, even though too much attention appears to be focused on London initiatives. In Manchester, for example, some of the most innovative developments are taking place and making a positive impact on the lives of young African Caribbean people.

MENTORING IN MANCHESTER

In Manchester, there is now an emerging infrastructure of mentoring schemes that is unique for its dynamic interaction and collaboration amongst the professionals. This collaboration is largely informal, partly arising from the fact that the educational area within the city where many of the schemes are located is physically a series of connecting blocks bound by interest and political affinities. Irrespective of the age or subject specialism of a given professional, there is a city-wide horizontal layering produced by 'interest/affinity' groups (Stirton and Spencer, personal communication, 1997).

These groups meet at various conferences and converge frequently around specified issues, producing 'a kind of perpetual internal market in ideas and attitudes' (Marr 1998). One significant clustering or identifiable focus is race and ethnicity, resulting in various mentoring strategies specific to age and the various phases of education.

MENTORING IN FURTHER EDUCATION

One of the most significant mentoring schemes for 'ethnic minorities' in Manchester is offered by City College Manchester (CCM). Following the pioneering work of Howard Jeffrey, CCM became in 1994 the second further education college in the UK to establish a mentor service for ethnic minority students. The CCM approach advocates a community-based mentoring model, working with young Black men at risk. It aims to ensure that disadvantaged 'ethnic minorities', both students and the unemployed, are provided with guidance, advice, support and personal, educational and professional training. It also matches Black males with role models from their own community. This is seen as essential since Black mentors have an insider knowledge of the culture, values and attitudes of the mentee, as well as an intimate and shared understanding of racial dynamics and racism. This encourages a more rapid establishment of empathy, which is deemed crucial in the evolving relationship between mentor and mentee. The argument for such a race-specific solution partly reflects the argument developed by Stanfield and Dennis (1993) and Mirza (1995) that white led initiatives on Black issues more often than not produced 'outsiders' or 'pathologized' outcomes.

The CCM initiative has been particularly successful in the mentoring of young African Caribbean females. In March 1995, for example, 66 per cent of the students using the service were female (Sheriffe 1997). The persistence of underachievement and the high numbers of school expulsions and dropouts among African Caribbean males has, however, led the CCM to focus on male recruitment and to develop new approaches to empower Black males. Two of the most important initiatives so far are the 'Pilot Project: Mentoring for African Caribbean Men' and a 'Summer Workshop Roadshow'.

A preamble to these new initiatives was a wide-ranging consultation process involving questionnaires and one-to-one in-depth interviews with students of CCM and members of the local African Caribbean community. The respondents ranged from 'those with no formal qualifications to those who have a good educational track record; from those who have never been employed, to those who may have had periods of voluntary or paid employment' (Sheriffe 1997: 2). Interviews with African Caribbean male students of CCM were conducted across all five CCM sites spread across the city. This geographical and vocational mix ensured a diverse representation of African Caribbean males.

In all, a total of 158 males between the ages of 13 and 35 were contacted and either interviewed or asked to complete a questionnaire. Of these 104 questionnaires were returned (64 CCM students and 40 from the local African Caribbean community). Out of this total, 45 were randomly selected and interviewed on a one-to-one basis. Nine were randomly grouped and interviewed as a focus group.

The research findings indicated that African Caribbean males benefited from the mentoring scheme at CCM when they knew about it and made use of the service. However, outside the college, only a small number of African Caribbean males knew about it, and therefore only a few used it. The research also made three other critical points:

- 85 per cent of African Caribbean males did not know what a mentor was, and 65 per cent of African Caribbean male students did not know that a mentor service was available to them;
- 50 per cent of the group reported that financial problems were the primary barriers that prevented them from attending further or higher education;
- 60 per cent of African Caribbean males said they would attend further or higher education if they received more encouragement and support from those who in their view were 'significant' others.

As a result of these findings, the CCM tested a new initiative, the 'Summer Workshop Roadshow', for African Caribbean males in the summer of 1996. The aim was to provide them with an opportunity to discuss barriers that prevented them from attending further or higher education, and information on the CCM mentor service. The Summer Workshop found that:

- 30 per cent of the African Caribbean males who attended the workshop subsequently enrolled in further or higher education courses;
- all those who attended the workshop were in favour of being mentored.

These workshop outcomes broadly substantiated the initial research findings and led to a series of recommendations, one of which was to provide mentor services in schools. This was taken up and developed into one of the interconnecting blocks of the interest/affinity groups.

MENTORING IN SCHOOLS

The use of school-based mentors and role models has generally had a significant impact on the lives of young Black males throughout the UK. Some of the more successful mentor schemes are BUILD in Nottingham; the Black Mentor Scheme in Southwark, London; the Second City – Second Chance and KWESI in Birmingham. In Manchester, schemes also operate in a range of primary and secondary schools.

One of the crucial targets of these schemes is to reduce exclusions. This practice is heading towards a national scandal, with young people being excluded from school at an increasingly young age – in some cases as young as 4. The *Truancy and School Exclusion Report* 1998 states that many of the excluded children – two out of three – fail to return to mainstream education. It is estimated that in 1996 and 1997 the cost of the additional drain on education, police time, the courts, social and youth services involvement and remediation was in excess of £81 million (Parsons 1998).

Placing Black males in the classroom as mentors and role models to Black boys has resulted in a decrease in exclusions (*Truancy and Exclusions Report* 1998). It has also increased achievement among African Caribbean boys (Hulme 1997; Victor 1997).

Arguably, however, these mentoring interventions cannot in themselves exact significant changes to the life chances of the mentees. Institutions need to change. They need to evolve policies that reflect the cultural diversity of the school and address discriminatory practices. As recently as 1985, the Swann Report gave credence to the issue of racism in education and described how African Caribbean males were particularly affected. More recently, Sewell (1997) has described how racism leads to exclusion, poor achievement and disaffection among African Caribbean males. Sewell's contention is supported by the DfEE, with its inspection arm, OFSTED, concluding that 'African Caribbean young people, especially boys have not shared equally in the increasing rates of achievement; in some areas their performance has worsened, even when differences in qualifications, social class and gender are taken into account' (Gillborn and Gipps 1996: 2). The factors that have produced this situation include negative stereotyping and low teacher expectancy. The media have frequently portrayed Black males as drug pushers, pimps and misfits (Majors and Gordon 1994). Middleton (1983) found evidence to support this generalisation in a northern comprehensive school. He found that African Caribbean males were considered as a source of trouble to be controlled in non-academic classes.

In another study, Wilkinson (1994) found that, from a sample of 300 parents of African Caribbean heritage children in Manchester, as many as 57 per cent felt that teachers paid less attention to Black children; 56 per cent felt that teachers had a lower expectation of Black children, and 51 per cent felt that teachers were not keen to listen to them.

These negative stereotypes and their consequences are not limited to Britain. Foster's research (1996), based on a sample of 3,130 subjects, came to similar conclusions in the USA, in relation to African American males. Mentors and Black role models in the classroom have helped Black boys to cope more effectively with racism and negative stereotyping in schools (Holland 1987). They have also helped to engender in Black children a greater sense of identity, security and mutual respect. They can also stimulate male 'bonding' and solidarity between Black boys and Black men.

MENTORING IN HIGHER EDUCATION

Complementing the mentoring efforts in schools and in further education is a new initiative in the university sector. This comes in the wake of a growing acceptance of the value of mentoring to both mentor and mentee, backed by evidence from studies supporting the value of mentoring for 'disadvantaged groups' and improved graduate retention, lowering dropout and reducing unemployment at the exit points of study.

The Manchester higher education sector comprises five institutions that currently have the largest concentration of students in the UK. Four of the institutions formed a consortium to launch 'Interface', a mentoring initiative that targeted final-year Black undergraduates who were also UK citizens. Initial research had confirmed that Black undergraduates faced a problematic future. Irrespective of their degree or grades, they faced poorer job prospects than their white peers. They made more job applications, faced more rejections, and, if fortunate enough to secure employment, generally started at a lower level than their similarly qualified white peers (Kirschenman and Neckerman 1991).

Following discussions within further education, between mentoring practitioners and employers in both the private and public sectors, and negotiations with government, the Government Office of the North West agreed to fund a pilot mentor scheme for fifty Black students to operate across the Manchester and Salford Universities.

The Interface scheme has proved popular and successful, with appreciative feedback from participating employers as well as students. This success has been partly based on the strategy of establishing a cadre of Black mentors and matching them with students via particular interest or subject specialisms. The aim was, in addition to providing role models, to engender a supportive Black network at the university and in employment to empower the mentees and increase job opportunities. It was also intended to create a 'comfort zone' for Black males, to compensate for their exclusion from mainstream networks.

Further funding was secured from the Government Office in 1998. It was intended to consolidate the progress and develop a centre of excellence in mentoring for the North-West. The centre will house various relevant resources and offer training in Black mentoring. To underpin the significance of the latter, a post-graduate certificate in mentoring has already been established in Salford University, and negotiations are under way to form a steering committee of educators from all sectors and interests. This steering group notion is an affirmation of the thesis of the horizontal interconnecting blocks of 'interest/affinity' groups and their value to developing initiatives.

The developments in Black mentoring in Manchester are exemplary. Significantly, they have developed as part of an organically evolved strategy at each level of the education system. Clearly, the existence of the 'interest/affinity' groups has helped to structure and co-ordinate the responses to the failings of the system as they coalesce and collaborate on the various initiatives. Given the added impetus of government funding, there is now the real possibility of developing a holistic Black mentoring model. Nevertheless, it must also be acknowledged that there are potential pitfalls, not least those that come with governmental intervention on race-related issues. The affinity/interest groups are also community-driven and need to remain so to maintain the momentum for change.

SOCIAL POLICY RESPONSE AND RECOMMENDATIONS

Substantial research undertaken in the USA by Majors and Wiener (1995) to determine what factors were crucial to the successful development of African American male youth, found that nurturing and developmental programmes such as mentoring were cheaper, cost-effective and socially more beneficial than punitive strategies centred on control, maintenance and monitoring. These findings are borne out by the success of the Manchester initiatives, which have the support of the community.

CONCLUSION

The current situation of Black male disaffection, underachievement and unemployment in Britain is morally untenable and politically destabilising in the long run. As the riots of the 1980s testify, occasionally it explodes into civil unrest with dire consequences. It is too costly to contain and a waste of vital human resources. Currently race- and gender-specific mentoring schemes which intervene directly in the education process, and which have the potential to impact in other areas such as employment, appear to provide a workable and effective alternative. This alternative needs to be given wider recognition and supported with adequate resources if the momentum for change such as in Manchester is to be maintained.

ACKNOWLEDGEMENT

We would like to thank Valerie Kahn and Duncan Scott of the University of Manchester Social Policy Department for their editorial assistance on an earlier draft.

NOTE

1   This Article originally appeared in Owusu, K (2000). *Black British Culture and Society*, London: Routledge pp. 385–392 entitled, 'Mentoring Black Males in Manchester, Responding to the crisis in education and social alienation'. It reappears here re-titled, 'Mentoring Black Males, Responding to the crisis in education and social alienation' with the kind permission of the publishers.

REFERENCES

Birmingham Court Social Enquiry Report Monitoring Exercise (1987) Birmingham: West Midlands Probation Service.
Clutterbuck, D. (1994) 'Business mentoring in evolution', *Mentoring and Tutoring* **2**, 1.
Foster, H. (1996) '"Educators" and "Non-educators": Perceptions of Black Males: A Survey', *Journal of African American Men* pp. 37–70.
Foster, K. (1990) *General Household Survey*, London: Office of Population Censuses and Surveys: HMSO.
Gillborn, D. and Gipps, C. (1996) *Recent Research on the Achievement of Ethnic Minority Pupils*, London: HMSO.
Gulam, W. (1997) 'Paradigm lost', *Multicultural Teaching*, **15**, 3.

Gulam, W. and Zulfiqar, M. (1998) 'Dr Plum's Elixir and the Alchemists' Stone', *Mentoring and Tutoring*, **5**, 3.

Holland S. (1987) Positive primary education for young black males: inner-city boys' male role models, *Education Digest*, **53** pp. 6–7.

Hulme, J. (1997) *The Teacher*, January/February, news update.

Jeffrey, H. (1994) *Developing a Mentoring Strategy*, London: CPW Associates.

Kirschenman, J. and Neckerman, K. (1991) '"We'd love to hire them, but ... " The meaning of race for employers', in Jencks, C. and Peterson, P. *The Urban Underclass*, Washington, DC: The Brookings Institute.

Majors, R. (1986) 'Coolpose: The proud signature of Black survival, changing men', *Issues in Gender, Sex and Politics*, **17** pp. 5–6.

Majors, R. and Billson, J. (1992) *Coolpose: The Dilemmas of Black Manhood in America*, Boston: Lexington.

Majors, R. and Gordon, J. (1994) *The American Black Male: His Present Status and Future*, Chicago: Nelson-Hall.

Majors, R. and Wiener, S. (1995) *Programs that Serve African American Male Youth*, Washington, DC: The Urban Institute.

Majors, R., Gillborn, D. and Sewell, T. (1988) 'Exclusion of Black children: A racialised perspective', *Multicultural Teaching Spring*, 35–7.

Marr, A. (1998) *The Observer*, 7 June p. 31.

Mauer, M. (1990) *Young Black Men and the Criminal Justice System: A Growing National Problem?*, Washington, DC: The Sentencing Project.

Middleton, B. (1983) *Factors Affecting the Performance of West Indian Boys in a Secondary School*, MA thesis, University of York.

Mirza, M. in M. Griffiths and B. Troyna (eds) (1995) *Antiracism, Culture and Social Justice in Education*, Chester: Trentham Books.

Parsons, C. (1998) 'Excluded children', *International Journal of Inclusive Education*, **2**.

Sewell, T. (1997) *Black Masculinities and Schooling: How Black Boys Survive Modern Schooling*, Chester: Trentham Books.

Sheriffe, G. (1997) *Pilot Project: Mentoring for African Caribbean Men: Manchester*, Manchester City College.

Social Exclusions Unit (1998) *Truancy and School Exclusions Report*, London: HMSO.

Solomos, J. (1988) *Black Youth, Racism and the State*, Cambridge: Cambridge University Press.

Stanfield, J. and Dennis, R. (eds) (1993) *Race and Ethnicity in Research Methods*, London: Sage.

Swann, M. (1985) *Education for All: Final Report of the Committee of Inquiry into the Education of Children from Ethnic Minority Groups*, Cmnd 9453, London: HMSO.

Tierney, J., Grossman, J. and Resch, N. (1993) *Making A Difference: An Impact Study of Big Brothers/Big Sisters*, Philadelphia: Public/Private Ventures.

Truancy and School Exclusion Report (1998) London: Social Exclusion Unit.

Victor, P. (1997) *The Independent*, 11 July.

Wilkinson, V. (1994) *Parental Attitudes Towards the Multiracial Education Policies and Practices of a Local Education Authority*, M Phil thesis, University of Manchester.

15 School-based mentoring for minority youth: program components and evaluation strategies

Teresa Garate-Serafini, Fabricio E. Balcazar, Christopher B. Keys and Julie Weitlauf

INTRODUCTION

The evaluation of mentoring programs designed to meet the needs of at-risk populations is of particular interest to the authors. We recognize the challenges: as Blechman (1992) stated, 'attempts to evaluate existing mentoring programs seem premature because the term *mentoring* is now applied to diverse programs united only by an interest in helping inner city, minority youth'. We propose that mentoring programmes should evaluate their impact on two levels: the overall impact of the program and the impact on individual participants. All mentoring programs should have clear guidelines that govern their operation and goals (National Mentoring Partnership 1998). Without linking these goals to the individual success of the youth being mentored, the evaluation process is weakened. The youth's outcomes should be the measure of the program's effectiveness.

The model presented in Figure 15.1 assumes that a successful youth mentoring program requires assessment within four domains: goal attainment, competency skills, social support, and participant's motivation. In addition to assessing the goals of the overall program, the evaluation of the youths' successes in several areas is a central component for any comprehensive evaluation of mentoring programs. The proposed four domains indicate a holistic approach to the development of mentoring programs that address major life areas. These domains evaluate an individual youth's ability to develop and achieve goals, learn competency skills, develop a positive social support network, and develop an efficacy in their power to affect change in their lives.

The United States National Mentoring Partnership defines responsible mentoring programs as those that meet the needs of both parties involved, the mentee and the mentor (National Mentoring Partnership 1998). A mentor is defined as a role model who may serve as a teacher, adviser, sponsor and peer (Balcazar and Keys 1994; Slicker and Palmer 1993). A successful mentor is one that encourages, guides and praises, while impacting the mentee's sense of competence and self-concept (Kaufman, Hamel, Milan, Woolverton and Miller 1986). A productive mentor is not defined by who they are, but by what they do in the mentoring relationship.

Self Regulating Competencies

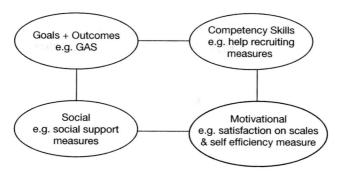

Figure 15.1 Evaluation domains
This figure outlines the four domains that are assessed by the proposed model.
These domains are identified as the key factors affecting the mentored youth. They
serve as a guideline for developing evaluation strategies that will assess all domains in
question.

Definitions have also been formulated to describe an individual seeking to be
mentored. A successful mentee is one who recognizes and values the support of the
mentor and is able to reap the benefits of the relationship by achieving success
in their area of interest (National Mentoring Partnership 1998). The qualities of the
mentor and mentee can be assessed by evaluating the outcomes of mentoring
relationships based on goals set by either the mentor or the youth being mentored.

As schools, social service agencies and local, state, and national organizations
continue to develop programs to meet the needs of at risk populations, effective
mentoring is becoming an innovative and useful tool all over the world. Although
mentoring has long been used as a positive tool in the business world and in higher
education, there is insufficient information regarding the effectiveness or lack thereof
of its use with youths in the United States (Freedman and Baker 1995; Slicker and
Palmer 1993). The increase of immigration from developing nations to more
prosperous nations (i.e. the United States and the United Kingdom) has increased
those societies' concerns with how to meet the demands of serving minority youths
in educational systems which were not developed to serve them. This concern has
given rise to a new type of mentoring within school and community settings which
focuses on young people living in disadvantaged environments (Freedman and
Baker 1995).

Mentoring programs for youth can take a variety of forms, both structured and
non-structured. It is important to note that the great majority of school and
community-based mentoring programs in the United States are facilitated by an
agency or organization involved in the program; thus the young person involved is
matched with a predetermined individual to serve as their mentor. A number of
unstructured 'mentoring' programs have actually been set up more as peer-support
groups than individual mentoring relationships (Roberts and Cotton 1994).

Most of the literature available on mentoring programs for youth focuses on how to develop programs, examine characteristics of mentoring adults, describe existing programs, and describe identifying characteristics of youth who would benefit from mentoring programs (Diem 1992; DuBois and Neville 1997). A small percentage of the literature discusses the effectiveness of mentoring programs based on outcomes experienced by the participating youth. For instance, Furano, Roaf, Styles and Branch (1993) have developed some investigations that examine the characteristics of mentoring relationships as factors affecting the success or failure of said relationships. DuBois and Neville (1997) examined the relationship characteristics and perceived benefits in two types of mentoring programs. The results indicated that mentees perceived a positive relationship with their mentors based on the degree of closeness they felt. The more mentor–mentee contact, the greater the feeling of closeness in the relationship (DuBois and Neville, 1997). These researches also found the need for training and support of volunteer mentors to ensure that the outcome of the established relationship is effective in supporting youths with their perceived needs. Overwhelmingly, mentored youths report that effective relationships were ones in which there were continuity and consistency in the contacts that occur (Freedman 1988). While this information is useful, it does not render tangible information regarding long-term outcomes for the mentees as a result of the mentoring relationship.

In the proposed model, mentoring is presented to youths as a means of achieving personal, educational, and/or vocational goals. Through training the youths realize that the mentoring relationship can be a means for pursuing relevant life goals. Without this outcome as a central purpose of the relationship, mentoring loses its effectiveness as a mechanism for affecting both the lives and futures of disadvantaged youth. The proposed model does not provide mentors to the participating youth; rather, youths receive instruction on how to recruit and initiate mentoring relationships. It is assumed that by developing individuals' competencies in the area of recruiting help, disadvantaged youth will be more capable of becoming proactive partners in a true mentoring relationship (Balcazar, Majors, Blanchard, Paine, Suarez-Balcazar, Fawcett, Murphy and Meyer 1991). This approach also decreases the probability that youths will become dependent on the adult mentor that they may be assigned to in traditional mentoring programs. This can be the limitation of traditional mentoring programs since in those programs the mentors are preselected and matched with the mentee (Freedman and Baker 1995).

Minority youth, often overwhelmingly at-risk for both academic failure and dropout, are typically characterized as having difficulty developing positive relationships with adults, teachers and even peers who take on a role of authority (Diem 1992). This is one of the factors affecting the selection of possible mentors across mentoring programs in the US. Great efforts are made to recruit adult mentors that match youth on aspects such as race, gender and interests. By doing this, programs are making the assumption that at-risk factors are influenced by the environment in which minority youth live. It is assumed that mentors who are not part of the youth's immediate environment could serve as positive role models and provide alternative perspectives on life issues, such as education and careers. Because of the importance that has been placed on mentoring programs to alleviate some of the greatest needs of minority communities in relation to the future of their youth, it is essential to develop evaluation strategies that will render relevant information with regards to the effectiveness of these programs and their components. Agencies and organizations sponsoring mentoring programs are continually attempting to develop effective strategies for assessing their mentoring programs based on outcomes. Since mentoring has become an intervention tool for meeting the needs of minority at-risk youth, professionals in the field are interested in discovering what works for what youths. Unfortunately, in the US there is little information available regarding the success of most mentoring programs, with the exception of school-based programs.

School-based mentoring programs usually take on the form of peer tutoring or buddy programs. These built-in programs, are often credited with improving academic achievement and peer relationships (Cohen 1986; Greenwood, Carta and Hall 1988; Neill 1979; Wells 1990). These programs are goal oriented, which makes their evaluation more feasible. Bhareman and Kopp (1988) found that school-based programs with appropriate staff support also have the potential for improving race relations and developing positive attitudes toward school. These programs also provide positive outcomes for the student mentors who volunteer (Bhareman and Kopp 1988).

A number of studies conducted in the US have shown that youth with mentors were more likely to complete an increased amount of years in school (Torrance 1983). Kaufman (1986) found that of 604 presidential scholars recipients, a large portion 66 per cent reported that they had experienced significant benefits from mentoring relationships in which the mentor was a secondary school teacher. Further review of the literature indicates that there are notable benefits among gifted students who are involved in mentoring relationships (Kaufman 1986; Torrance 1983). Unfortunately, comparable information regarding the effects of mentoring on at-risk high school students who have the potential to dropout is not available (Fine 1986; Roberts and Cotton 1994; Slicker and Palmer 1993).

For example, at the Seattle Center Arts and Sciences Academy (1998), a group of innovative artists and teachers use peer-aged mentors to help youth with disabilities develop their talents and interest in the arts. They use Hellison's responsibility model (1995) to train youth with disability and peer mentors to work together. They evaluate the experience of their peer mentors supporting younger students with disabilities using both satisfaction surveys and mentor generated reports. Anecdotal information also speaks to student mentor satisfaction. In the four years of operation, between 60 per cent and 70 per cent of the peer mentors and students have asked to return the following year. If the peer mentors receive support, training, and become personally invested in the relationship, they are more likely to be effective and feel positively rewarded through the relationship (Srebnik and Elias 1993).

MENTOR RECRUITING MODEL

Few mentoring programs provide specific training for empowering youths to set goals, develop effective action plans to pursue their goals, and search out and start their own mentoring relationships in an effective way. Facilitated mentoring programs can be successful in providing designated mentors for participating youths. These programs are more successful when they contain the following key elements. The National Mentoring Partnership (1998) suggests that having a well-defined mission statement; providing participants with clear operating guidelines; facilitating regular contact between the mentees and their mentors; having the family support; accessing additional community supports; recruiting qualified paid or volunteer staff; having access to financial and in-kind resources; being inclusive of racial, economic and gender representation; having an established long-range plan with community input and collaboration; and providing for program evaluation and assessment based on outcomes are important components of successful mentoring programs.

On the other hand, several investigations of mentoring programs have rendered results that indicate only minimal benefits (Freedman 1991). Complicating the process of successfully evaluating these programs is the fact that disadvantaged individuals are often involved in several interventions sponsored by schools and/ or local communities. In addition there are many disparities among mentoring programs, their components and their guidelines (Roberts and Cotton 1994). While the components may vary from program to program, some common goals identified include improving academic performance and enhancing personal self-concept (Freedman 1988). As mentoring programs grow within school communities, effective evaluation will become increasingly necessary to develop consistent and useful programs.

Mentoring relationships can be an avenue for disadvantaged youth to accomplish personal life goals. A review of the literature indicates that traditionally, mentoring relationships for minority youths in the US have served as vehicles of prevention against the development of social problems including dropping out and gang involvement (DuBois and Neville 1997). Research shows that youths at risk of dropping out of high school demonstrate a lack of positive engagement with their school environment (Barnes, Balcazar and Keys 1997; Srebnik and Elias 1993). Gang involvement and other social problems such as drug use, drinking and delinquency also seem to be related to various environmental factors, such as peer pressure, fear for personal safety, lack of strong family support, low-income and lack of positive role models in youths' natural surroundings (Srebnik and Elias 1993).

The proposed model

The proposed model for developing and evaluating mentoring relationships is based on an empowerment approach designed to allow minority youth to become increasingly independent. Empowerment, which is at the root of this model, is defined as a process by which individuals obtain a greater degree of control over the situations, events and resources that are of interest or needed by them (Fawcett, White, Balcazar, Suarez-Balcazar, Mathews, Paine-Andrews, Seekins and Smith 1994). The model has three main components: 1) goal setting; 2) action planning; and 3) help recruiting skills development. Based on past research conducted by the authors, these three components were determined to be essential to the success of a school-based intervention mentoring program.

An analysis of contextual factors that lead youths with disabilities to engage in early school leaving (Barnes, Balcazar and Keys 1997) led the authors to recognize the great need to develop school programs, including mentoring programs, that would motivate youths and help them in the process of developing personal and vocational goals and action plans. In addition to the emphasis on goal setting, youths who partake of this mentoring model are encouraged and taught skills aimed at developing self-reliance and increased independence. The focus on independence ensures that youths will become active participants within the mentoring relationships and thus become increasingly invested in the process of improving outcomes for themselves in school and in relevant aspects of their personal life (finding a job, getting a driver's license, etc.) Other researchers have used similar intervention components which have included goal setting, action planning and self-monitoring in relation to developing programs that support the needs of minority youth (Gallup and Gallup 1986; Mithaug, Martin and Agran 1987).

Balcazar, Fawcett, and Seekins (1991) developed a program designed for teaching young adults with disabilities how to set goals, develop action plans, and recruit mentors for the purposes of achieving goals. Upon completing training all participants had improved their competencies in social skills for help recruiting and were able to use mentors to pursue and attain personal and vocational goals. Similar results were found applying this model (Balcazar, Keys and Garate-Serafini 1995; Balcazar, Keys, Gianneschi and DeYoung 1992) with adjudicated youths with severe emotional and behavioral problems transitioning from a residential high school facility and with adults with severe disabilities receiving vocational rehabilitation services in a classroom setting. In both of these studies participants were able to develop mentoring relationships that in turn helped them in the process of attaining their personal goals. Finally, researchers working specifically with a group of African American youths (Balcazar, *et al.* 1991) found that a training intervention which included instruction in goal setting, action plan development and the application of specific set of behaviors for meeting with and developing a relationship with a mentor was successful at increasing the participants' attainment of post high school goals.

Assessment tools

Based on our experiences with minority youth and the development of interventions that effectively meet the needs of these youth, we strongly support designing mentoring programs which include evaluation strategies that render information regarding their impact. The model described above uses a number of assessment tools for the purpose of assessing program effectiveness with regard to youth outcomes. The measures that will be described in this section were chosen as indicators of the degree of success achieved with each participating youth. The measures assess goal attainment, skills competence, social support, self-efficacy, and satisfaction. Goal attainment is measured with the use of goal attainment scaling (GAS) in order to assess outcomes achieved by the participating youth. Skills competence is evaluated to determine the degree of improvement in the performance of specified skills for recruiting help from mentors. Social support looks at the youths' network of support for achieving relevant life goals. The self-efficacy measures are used to gather information about the youths' beliefs with regards to their performance in several domains (school, home and work). Finally, satisfaction surveys are used to determine degree of satisfaction with our mentoring program model.

Goal attainment

Goal attainment scaling has traditionally been used as an evaluation tool for assessing the effectiveness of human service programs (Davis 1973). A number of researchers enlisted to objectively evaluate such programs have developed variations of the concept and have used them effectively to provide useful information based on program outcomes (Davis 1973). Kiresuk and Sherman (1968) first developed the concept as an objective tool for assessing mental health program effectiveness based on identifiable outcomes. Because of its flexibility for adaptation to special situations, it is a useful tool for the evaluation of structured or unstructured mentoring programs. It can be used to measure outcomes for both the mentees and the mentors. It is also applicable to a variety of populations varying in gender, race, age and other personal variables. Regardless of its flexibility, goal attainment Scaling (see a copy of the GAS in appendix 1) has been used widely with required internal consistency coefficients and inter-rater agreement reliability coefficients (Emmerson and Neely 1988; Garwick and Lampman 1972). Because this scale is based on an individualized measurement system, program participants and their mentors are actively involved in specifying goals and outcomes to be measured (Balcazar, Keys and Garate-Serafini 1995).

In an intervention based on the proposed model, the GAS was used to assess outcome data based on individual's independent living, educational, and vocational goals set by project participants learning how to recruit mentors to attain their personal and rehabilitation goals (Balcazar *et al.* 1996). For the goal setting process, participating youth were asked to set goals using action words (e.g. 'obtain, acquire, become') in their statements. Additionally, the process is facilitated by the program staff and recorded on individual GAS forms (Balcazar *et al.* 1991) (see Appendix 1). Examples of commonly stated goals are 'to get a summer job,' 'to open up a savings account,' 'to pass math class this semester,' 'to stay in school.' The process of goal attainment scaling gives participating youth an opportunity to increase self-awareness and to develop a sense of themselves as individuals with the power to affect their lives and their futures in a positive way. The information contained on the GAS form is collected by a staff member who can clarify the various options of the goal. By rating each goal on its level of importance and difficulty, youth are encouraged to think about their goals in a realistic way. They also have the opportunity to track their progress throughout the process and to select options to follow that will possibly result in the achievement of a greater number of goals.

Goal outcomes are rated based on eight possibilities. These possibilities are outlined and described in Appendix 2. Once the initial goals are written by the participating youths with the necessary support from project staff, they are not evaluated again until a pre-determined amount of time, possibly three to six months, depending on the group of youth participating in the program. This interval should give the participants sufficient time to work on meeting the objectives designated for each of the goals they have developed. Participants' GAS scores are determined by a formula using the level of importance (1=little important, 2=moderately important, 3=very important), level of difficulty (1=not difficult or easy, 2=moderately difficult, 3=difficult), level of functioning (used with individual with disabilities, but could be modified to address levels of personal competency – 1=low, 2=high), and the outcome for each goal (from 1 to 8 in a scale).

Formula
Goal attainment = GAS * [1.5(importance) + 1.5(difficulty) + 2.5 (level of functioning)]

These weights were determined by a panel of experts who rated the relative importance of each of the three factors that could modify the goal attainment score. This formula is used to compare goals and goal attainment between individuals with different levels of functioning and identified degrees of importance, difficulty and work required to attain them.

Each project staff member who is involved in the application of the GAS receives training on how to use the scale. The following are steps for collecting goal attainment data:

Step 1: determine the importance of the goal

In this step the participant is asked to listen to and think about the goals that he/she set at the onset of the intervention; the goals were ranked by the participants using the following guidelines: 3=very important, 2=moderately important, and 1=a little important. Project staff supports the youth in understanding and clarifying the differences between these three ratings and assigning a rating to each goal.

Step 2: determining the outcome for each goal

In this step the participant has the opportunity to assess the progress they have made toward achieving each goal by discussing their actions with the program staff; scorer will start by reviewing the information they have thus far from their interactions with the youth and asking for clarification and updates along the way. The youth are asked to give details about their actions attempted and completed. Sample probes include, 'How much progress have you made toward achieving this goal?' 'What steps have you taken to reach this goal?' 'When did you take these steps?' 'Are you going to continue with this goal?' Using the information provided by the participants, the project staff determines the status of each goal following a scale of 1 to 8; where 1=goal deterioration and 8=higher than expected outcome. (Please see Appendix 2 for sample outcomes within each rating.)

Step 3: assigning a level of difficulty for each goal

Difficulty scores are assigned by a panel of experts who rate a complete list of goals from a group of participants. These scores are assigned independently and only on the basis of the perceived degree of complexity of the proposed goal. The levels are as follows: 1=not difficulty/easy, 2=moderately difficulty, 3=difficult. The levels are determined using the participants' input as to what is challenging and non-challenging for them.

[Sample GAS]

Goal: <u>To get a summer job</u>   Outcome Score: <u>7</u>
Importance: <u>3</u>   Level of Difficulty: <u>3</u>   Level of Functioning: <u>low</u>
# of actions: <u>3</u>

Youth set a goal of obtaining a summer job.
(1) He proceeded to speak with both
     a teacher and mentor regarding his goal.
(2) Student was able to get Bridges Foundation involved in the process and received
     a referral to Wrigley Field. His mentor provided support with transportation for
     initial interview.
(3) Youth was hired and maintained employment for the whole summer.

Additional Information:
Youth received positive feedback from employer. Youth used this experience and obtained part-time job after school for the semester following the summer months.

Formula:
Goal Attainment = 7* [1.5(3)+1.5(3)+2.5(1)]=80.5

Table 15.1 Evaluating a mentoring program

Step 4: level of functioning

For use with individuals with disabilities, level of functioning is assigned based on the diagnosis of the person. This information is obtained from records already available, such as special education files or medical forms. This can be modified for use with non-disabled individuals by using perceived levels of competency for pursuing desired outcomes in life. Individuals familiar with the students, such as teachers and parents, should be involved in the process of assigning these ratings.

Step 5: repeat the process with each goal written

Here the steps are repeated for any additional goals that were set during the mentor training program. Goals that were dropped are also noted in this process. Participants are asked about new goals that may have been set since the completion of the training intervention.

Table 15.1 demonstrates an example of a completed GAS form. As can be seen the GAS formula takes into account the youth's individual level of functioning, the level of difficulty of the goal and the importance that it was given. This form can be used to monitor the youth's progress in the goal-driven mentoring relationship and to develop new goals.

Using goal attainment scaling as a tool we have been able to collect data regarding the success of past program participants. The data from one particular project, which focused on developing the skills of minority youth who had dropped out of school for developing mentoring relationships, indicated that 82 per cent of the youths attained their goal of enrolling in some type of educational program, including GED programs, alternative schools, and integrated high schools. With regard to the employment goals set by the students, 88 per cent of them were able to secure employment. Interestingly, 72 per cent of the students achieved their goals of securing employment without the direct assistance of project staff. These youth were able to apply the training skills taught to develop mentoring relationships to make connections and attain employment on their own (Balcazar, Keys, Barnes, Isaza-Rivera and Ortiz 1996). These findings indicate that the empowering approach of this mentoring model encouraged and supported students at increasing their independence and becoming more self-reliant.

Skills competence

Using role plays assessments in a study conducted with six adjudicated male youths, researchers found that a training intervention for developing mentoring relationships and recruiting help from mentors was successful at improving the help-recruiting skill levels of the participants (Balcazar *et al.* 1995). In this study the average baseline level for all the targeted behaviors was 29.6 per cent and at follow-up it was 74.1 per cent. These findings demonstrate the impact of training on the development of the skills proposed by this mentoring model.

As stated previously, in the proposed model, youths are not provided with or matched with mentors. Instead they are taught a series of social skills designed to enhance their degree of control over relevant aspects of their lives with help from others.

The proposed model uses role-play assessments at both pre- and post-test to measure improvement in a specified skill area. Participating youths are asked to act out a situation (see Appendix 3 for a sample situation) which calls them to request help from someone they do not know, such as a counsellor, potential employer or tutor. Trained project staff serve as the second party in the role play and are instructed to respond either positively or negatively to elicit certain pre-determined behaviors. At baseline we expect role-play assessments to indicate the degree of proficiency in the performance of the needed skills. Post-role play data, collected following the training, should demonstrate improvement in the performance of the target skills. This measure gives a clear view of the effect of the intervention on participants' social competencies. It also evaluates the success and/or failure of the mentoring program by determining concrete growth among the participating youth.

The model encourages participants to develop a proficiency for conducting themselves in a professional, almost a businesslike manner when they are both on the phone and in person for the purpose of gathering information or requesting support or services. The set of skills are classified into four categories:

1   opening the meeting;
2   making a request;
3   action planning/handling rejections; and
4   closing the meeting.

These skills are flexible enough to be used in various settings. In addition to helping youths learn about the importance of mentoring and how to seek mentors, the skills can also be applied in educational settings, employment opportunities, and social services. Figure 15.2 outlines the skill sections and behaviors that are targeted. Proficiency in the skills is measured to monitor progress and accomplishments within the overall goal of the mentoring program. Using this tool as a mechanism for evaluating a mentoring program needs to be done in a systematic and structured way.

The role-play situations (Appendix 3) were developed with the input of project staff working directly with the youths to ensure that they were relevant and applicable to the experiences of the participants. For individuals interested in using this form of assessment, it is important to get the input from professionals who have an understanding of the factors affecting the lives of the disadvantaged youth they are working with. We use four situations at pre-test time and four at post-test time. They are intentionally developed so that half of the situations at each time elicit positive responses and half elicit negative ones. In this way, participants are able to demonstrate skills needed for both developing an action plan and handling rejections in the process of recruiting help from potential helpers and mentors.

Social support

Measuring social support provides valuable information regarding the environment and influences affecting the lives of all individuals. Historically, minority populations around the world have been victims of discrimination and limited opportunities. Furthermore, minorities who also have low socio-economic status are more likely to have restricted social support networks which do not typically include individuals with access to education and/or employment opportunities (Balcazar *et al.* 1991).

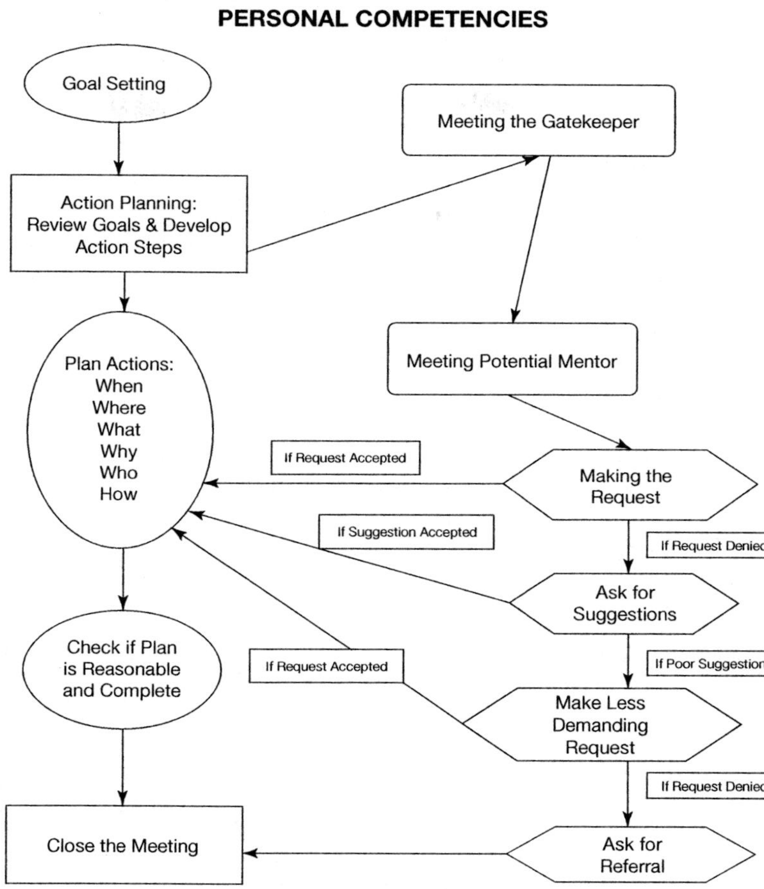

PERSONAL COMPETENCIES

Figure 15.2 Skill Competencies

In this model, we used a modified version of the Arizona Social Support Interview Schedule (ASSIS) (Barrera 1981) to collect information about relevant people in someone's life as well as the type of support they need and receive (see Appendix 4 for a sample). Specific for this model, the instrument identifies three categories of social support and social engagement. Participating youth perceived themselves as receiving inadequate social support from individuals other than immediate family members. Interestingly they indicated that the majority of their social support came from paid professionals (i.e. teachers, social service agency personnel). Encouraging minority youths with disabilities to learn how to set up mentoring relationships on their own will increase their independence from the social service agencies and organizations that are paid to provide services.

One important element of effective mentoring programs is social support. Pre- and post-measures of social support as described above can help evaluate this program component. The assumption is that by encouraging youth to seek out mentors and develop long-lasting relationships, their social network of support will expand. If a mentoring program is successful, the youth will be able to identify individuals able to support them in their efforts to pursue personal goals. Two scenarios are possible when taking a pre-test social support measure: one, you could find that individuals will name an extensive amount of people in their lives who are not necessarily capable of providing the type of support needed to achieve life goals; the second could find that individuals are at a loss for people to put into the various categories of social support which are defined for each mentoring program. Suggested categories include caring and emotional support, advice and guidance, material aid, support with discrimination issues, support for academic success, and crisis support. Elements of social support highlighted here centered around caring and emotional support, support with needs and identification of people who were a source of stress.

If the at-risk youth find that their social support networks are becoming not only larger, but also more effective by including people who are in a position to provide effective support toward reaching personal success, the measure can be used as an indicator for evaluating program success.

Self-efficacy

It is believed that an individual's self-efficacy is affected by three factors: natural endowment, socio-cultural experiences, and circumstances that alter one's life (Bandura 1986). In the proposed mentoring model, self-efficacy was examined as a way of determining how effective the intervention was at impacting the participating youths' view of themselves as determiners of their futures. In schools, teachers and adults are continuously telling youngsters how well they are doing, or how badly they are doing. While self-esteem is an interesting domain to examine, it is not as clear a determiner for success as self-efficacy. Beliefs of self-efficacy act as key factors in an individual's competence (Bandura 1997). Several studies reveal that perceived self-efficacy is an essential contributor to the performance of any task, regardless of the underlying skills present (Bandura 1977).

A primary focus of the evaluation of our program was the development of self-efficacy for the specific skills offered in our training as well as the generalization of self-efficacy beliefs to more global perceptions of individual competence. Specifically we measured self-efficacy in multiple domains. First, we administered all participants a general self-efficacy questionnaire, tapping into global self-referent beliefs. Second, we measured self-efficacy specific to the tasks directly addressed in the program (specific goal setting and goal attainment skills, communication and assertiveness training skills, and help recruiting skills). Finally, we assessed efficacy perceptions on skills that were related but not specifically addressed in training, such as perceptions about one's ability to obtain a job, success in school and behave appropriately at work and/or school.

Self-efficacy perceptions, both discrete and general, are excellent indices of the effectiveness of any training program and its impact on the participants involved. We encourage others to assess efficacy in monitoring the outcomes of future mentoring programs. Assessing self-efficacy for the specific tasks related to the intervention will help both to predict individual successes within the training program, and to measure the effectiveness of the training program. Assessing the impact of training on more general self-efficacy beliefs is appropriate if the mentoring program is especially powerful, or it is desirable that it have widespread impact. Assessing self-efficacy generalization to related domains and general self-efficacy in terms of global self-perception are useful ways to assess the size and spread of an intervention's impact.

For use with the proposed model, three specific efficacy measures were adapted from the Generalized Self-Efficacy Scale (GSE) (Schwarzer, Bäbler, Kwiatek and Shröder 1997) which was originally developed to assess individuals' beliefs of self-efficacy. The adapted version of the GSE used a simplified four-point scale and language appropriate to youth with learning or cognitive disabilities. (Please see Appendix 5 for a sample.) Two additional measures were developed to measure skills specifically related to the training component of the mentoring program. These two measures, the Academic Self-Efficacy measure (ASE; Appendix 6) and the Situation Specific Self-Efficacy measure (SSSE; Appendix 7), were focused on assessing youth's perceived self-efficacy with skills related both to academic success and school engagement, as well as the interpersonal skills needed to recruit help from mentors, set goals and develop action plans (Weitlauf, Hayes and Garate-Serafini 1997).

Satisfaction surveys

Satisfaction surveys are commonly used to assess an individual's opinions about a program or service. It is worthwhile to acquire knowledge about a program from the perspective of the people involved. As a caution, there may be information gathered from this type of survey that implies effectiveness within programs, and at the same time, data indicating that the outcomes achieved by participants were not significant (Blum and Jones 1993; Slicker and Palmer 1993).

In the proposed model, satisfaction surveys were developed for several individuals: the youth being mentored, the mentors, and parents or guardians of the youth, and if available, the school personnel involved in the process. For the mentored youth, the purpose was to determine their satisfaction with the skills they learned and their relevance in helping them recruit mentors, as well as satisfaction with their own social skills competence and goals attained (see Appendix 8 for sample questions and scale used). For the mentor, the survey attempted to determine their perspective on the skills the youth applied to set up the mentoring relationship. For the parents or guardian of the youth, the survey was designed to gain an understanding of what improvements, if any, they saw in their children with regard to their readiness skills for transitioning out of high school. Parents were asked about the materials used for the intervention, the support received from project staff and the mentoring experience that their children underwent. School personnel involved in some capacity, either as mentors that were sought out by the youth, or as cooperating teachers for the intervention training components were asked to give their opinions on three areas: the intervention effectiveness, the support for the student to achieve outcomes, and future uses of the proposed model. We try to keep this survey simple and short. In addition to using a Likert-type grading scale, there is also an opportunity for individuals to make their own comments about their experiences with the program.

CONCLUSION

A mentoring program which trains youth to plot their futures over time is empowering. The main purpose of the proposed mentoring model was to ensure that disadvantaged youth were given an opportunity to develop, pursue and attain goals that would enhance their quality of life. The means for achieving this purpose is to increase self-awareness in participating youth with regard to their strengths and their capacity to recruit help from others effectively. Teaching a set of social skill compentencies enables students to recognize individuals as potential mentors and to know how to approach them and initiate relationships that can be mutually beneficial both for the youth and the mentor. The goal attainment component of this model ensures that participating youth are active participants in both the mentoring process and the attainment of their personal goals. 'Mentoring' without goal attainment becomes meaningless. Traditional mentoring programs provide mentors, support, and even guidelines and suggested activities, but without goals as a central focus, the relationship becomes useless. The positive interactions and role models become just that, models and nice experiences that often do not allow the youth to take advantage of a unique relationship that could have a lasting effect on their lives.

The overall benefits of this model lie not only in the program components but also in the evaluation strategies that have been developed to evaluate its effectiveness. Too often, programs are expounded for being successful and beneficial without data to support these declarations. While there may be some truth to the positive aspects of said programs, they are not easily replicable because of the lack of a systematic evaluation. Table 15.1 recaps the list of measurement tools recommended for use in the process of evaluating mentoring programs.

It is important to recognize, however, that this model does have limitations. The success of this model depends in large part to the effort and time that is spent by the program staff who are assigned to work directly with the youth. Many organizations and/or schools do not always have the resources to provide as much support as is needed to make this program truly effective. We have found that there are lasting effects of the relationships developed between the youth participating in our programs and the staff that work directly with them. A second limitation centers around the instances when youth have not been able to learn the skills in the training component to the degree of being able to apply them in varying situations. In these situations, youth have required additional supports to develop mentoring relationships and access resources. A third limitation has been related to seeking out mentors. Not all the participating youth have been able to identify positive mentors and have required referrals for possible candidates. Some have chosen to use the

Table 15.2 Methods for evaluating mentoring programs

Instrument	Purpose	Format
Goal Attainment Scaling (GAS)	Assess participant outcomes in relation of goals set	one-on-one interview
Role-Play Assessment	Assess skills development	audio-taped role plays
Social Support Questionnaire (SS)	Assess social support network and type of support	questionnaire
General Self-efficacy (GSE)	Assess general beliefs about control over life situations	questionnaire
Academic Self-efficacy (ASE)	Assess beliefs related to academic success	questionnaire
Situation Specific Self-Efficacy (SSSE)	Assess beliefs specifically related to program components	questionnaire
Satisfaction Surveys	Assess satisfaction with program components	questionnaire

skills taught and supports given to access resources instead of developing mentoring relationships. Lastly, there is always the possibility of abuse of the mentoring relationship. This is one area which our model has not addressed. Youth who find supportive mentors may be inclined to resort to one person for a great number of things. This may jeopardize relationships in which one person is providing a large amount of support to the youth. Future research is needed to evaluate program effectiveness with different populations. Developing a program that uses the model's components with junior high school or middle school students would provide valuable information about program effectiveness with a younger population. Simplified versions of the model that are less time-consuming but equally effective need to be implemented and evaluated. Engaging individuals already serving youth, i.e. teachers, in the program implementation process would build the capacity of local organizations. Involving these individuals would increase the use of natural trainers to provide direct service to at-risk youth. The last area of need is examining the cost of implementing and evaluating a program based on the proposed model components. This cost–benefit analysis would provide schools and community organizations interested in the implementation of this program with valuable information as to its feasibility.

The researchers that developed this model have been working on developing relationships with schools in inner-city neighborhoods whose youth would benefit from this program. In addition to this effort, attempts are underway to support agencies and schools in the development of creative ways to implement some or all of the program components proposed in the model.

APPENDIX 1

Goal Attainment Scale Outcome Examples

Outcome Scale 1–8		Sample goal: 'obtain a job'	Sample goal: 'graduate from high school'
Deterioration	(1)	Youth has become unable to work.	Youth was expelled from school.
Goal dropped, no intent to continue	(2)	Youth no longer wants a job and has stopped looking for one.	Youth stopped going to school and does not want to return.
Clear intent to pursue goal, may be on hold	(3)	Youth states he/she still wants to get a job but has not looked at all.	Youth enrolled but didn't start school. He/she still plans to attend.
Active pursuit of goal; little or no response or progress	(4)	Youth has filled out some applications but has not heard anything.	Youth has been attending but is absent frequently and/or failing many courses.
Active pursuit, some response, some progress	(5)	Youth has gone to some interviews and is waiting to hear.	Youth still attending high school regularly at time of assessment and is progressing.
Accomplished less than desired goal; action might continue	(6)	Youth got a job but for less pay or worse hours than desired. Youth may look for something better.	Youth passed all but two courses needed for graduation; will retake those two courses.
Goal attained as expected, no further action	(7)	Youth obtained a job and is satisfied.	Youth graduated from high school.
Accomplished more than expected success	(8)	Youth got a job with benefits or better pay than expected.	Youth graduated on the honor roll.

APPENDIX 2

Goal Attainment Scale

NAME _____ INTERVIEWER _____ DATE _____ ID# ___

GOAL# _____ IMPORTANCE _____ LEVEL OF DIFFICULTY _____

Outcome
Deterioration (1)
Goal dropped, no intent to continue (2)
Clear intent to pursue goal, may be on hold (3)
Active pursuit of goal; no response, no or little progress (4)
Active pursuit; some response, some progress (5)
Accomplished less than desirable goal; action might continue (6)
Goal attained as expected, no further action (7)
Accomplished more than expected success (8)

LEVEL OF   # OF ACTIONS
FUNCTIONING _____   TAKEN _____

GOAL: _____

PROBES:
How important was this goal to you when you set it? (Compared to other goals you set)
State what YOU know about progress on this goal.
What steps have you taken to reach this goal?
When did you take these steps?
How important is this goal to you now?
(IF NOT MET) Are you going to continue this as a goal you want to work on and reach?
(IF NOT MET) How close are you to reaching this goal compared to when you set it?

APPENDIX 3

Post-role Plays – 'Empowering Choices'

> Instructions.
> Read through this handout carefully before you start. Mark the spots where the audiotape is turned on and off. Familiarize yourself with the process.

With the tape-recorder off say:

Do you remember a few months ago we acted out some situations and recorded them? We are going to do the same thing again. The situations are a little different this time around. Once again the four situations can occur regarding your school and employment. I will read the specific situations to you, and we are going to act them out. Please relax and be natural. This conversation is going to be audiotaped so that we can see how much better you got at doing this. I will first read each situation to you and then start the role play. We will not start until you are sure you know what the situation is about. If you need me to reread and review the situation, just let me know.

> Turn the tape-recorder on
> State the following:
>
> interviewer name, participant name, situation #, school, project, and project ID # (NOT THE SCHOOL ID)

Tape on say . . . . Situation #1
You are trying to get financial aid for technical school. You have an appointment with a financial assistant at the WestSide Technical School. His/her name is Mrs/Mr Jones. You go to the desk in the front of the office where the receptionist sits. Act as though I am the receptionist. What do you say?

> **Tape off**
> Give the participant time to think;
> say: Do you understand?
>   Would you like me to repeat anything?
>   Please repeat the situation back to me.
> If you are assured that the participant understands the activity, begin, START THE TAPE and LET THEM START TALKING!!!

- If the participant asks for Mr/Mrs Jones, you respond by saying: '**Mrs/Mr Jones is in. I'll call him/her for you.**'

Tape off
Give the following explanation to the participant:
After the receptionist calls, Mrs/Mr Jones comes out and takes you back into an office and you sit down. Act as though I am Mrs/Mr Jones now. What do you say? (Repeat the situation if necessary)

- Participate in the role play following the lead of the participant. Do not volunteer any information but do respond to questions and comments appropriately.
- Finally, if the participant makes a request for financial aid information, you respond by saying: '**You may be eligible for financial aid. However we won't know for sure until you complete the required FAF forms. You will need to pick those up from your high school counsellor.**'
- If asked for more information on how to do this, say, '**All high school counsellors have FAF forms for their students and can give you one.**'
- If the participant asks what to do following this step, say, '**Once you have completed the proper FAF forms and been accepted by us, we will have another meeting to discuss the kind of financial aid you are eligible to receive.**'
- If the participant continues to action plan, respond to his questions in a positive way. If the participant stops, **Do not continue or probe**.

Tape off, ask if the they are ready to continue with the next situation. Answer any questions they had about the process for doing the first one.

Tape on say . . . . Situation #2
There is a video store in the area you live. Last week, you saw an ad on the bulletin board at school for jobs at that store. You decide to walk in on your way home from school. You walk in and ask for the store manager. You are going to ask him/her about the job. Act as though I am the manager. What do you say?

Tape off
Give the participant time to think;
say: Do you understand?
　　　Would you like me to repeat anything?

> Please repeat the situation back to me.
> If you are assured that the participant understands the activity, begin, **Start the tape** and **Let them start talking!!!**

- Participate in the role play following the lead of the participant. Do not volunteer any information but do respond to questions and comments appropriately.
- If the participant asks about the job and/or how to apply, you respond by saying: **'I'm sorry, but the position has just been filled.'**
- If asked for an alternate suggestion, say: **'We may be hiring for the summer. You can come back in a month and see if there are any openings then.'**
- If asked for a referral, say: **'I heard that the music store on the other side of town is presently hiring. Why don't you try there?'**
- If asked for name, say: **'I can't remember any of the managers' names there, but you can tell them that we told you about it.'**

> **Tape off**, ask if they are ready to continue with the next situation. Answer any questions they had about the process for doing the last one.

Tape on say . . . . Situation #3
You have an appointment set up to meet with the counsellor at your school. His name is Mr/Mrs Martinez. You need to speak to the counsellor about your options for going to school after graduation. You want to find out exactly what you need to do to apply. When you get to the office you find another student working as an assistant. He/she will tell you where to find Mr/Mrs Martinez.

> **Tape off**
> Give the participant time to think;
> say: Do you understand?
>   Would you like me to repeat anything?
>   Please repeat the situation back to me.
> If you are assured that the participant understands the activity, begin, **Start the tape and let them start talking!!!**

- Participate in the role play following the lead of the participant. Do not volunteer any information but do respond to questions and comments appropriately.

- If the participant asks for Mr/Mrs Martinez, you say: '**Mr/Mrs Martinez is in room 305, you go right in.**'

Tape off
Give the following explanation to the participant:
Now you will talk to the counsellor, so now act as if I was Mrs/Mr Martinez. What would you say?
(Repeat the situation if necessary.)

- Participate in the role play following the lead of the participant. Do not volunteer any information but do respond to questions and comments appropriately.
- If the participant asks about applying to school, you respond by saying: '**Where are you interested in applying and for when? You need to have an idea because application deadlines are different for fall, summer and spring semesters.**'
- If the participant gives an example of a program, respond in a negative way by saying: '**I'm sorry, but I don't have any information on that school.**'
- If asked for a suggestion say: '**The other counsellor has worked with that school in the past. Why don't you talk to her?**'
- If asked for a specific referral say: '**Her name is Ms Gordon and she is in room 105. I think she may be able to help you out.**'

Tape off, ask if the they are ready to continue with the next situation. Answer any questions they had about the process for doing the last one.

Tape on say . . . . Situation #4
A teacher just made an announcement about job openings for Sears over the summer. You want to get more information about how to apply for the position. You get the phone number from your teacher call the place to speak with the department manager who is Mr/Mrs Hayes. The receptionist will first answer the phone. What would you say?

Tape off
Give the participant time to think;
say: Do you understand?
    Would you like me to repeat anything?
    Please repeat the situation back to me.
If you are assured that the participant understands the activity, begin, **Start the tape and let them start talking!!!**

- Participate in the role play following the lead of the participant. Do not volunteer any information but do respond to questions and comments appropriately.
- You start by answering the phone as the receptionist, say: '**Good afternoon, how may I help you?**'
- If the participant asks for Mr/Mrs Hayes, you respond by saying: '**Sure, one moment please.**'

Tape off
Give the following explanation to the participant:
The receptionist now gives the phone to the department manager Mrs/Mr Hayes, so now I'm the manager. What would you say?
(Repeat the situation if necessary.)

- Participate in the role play following the lead of the participant. Do not volunteer any information but do respond to questions and comments appropriately.
- If the participant asks about how to apply for the job or expresses the desire to apply for the job, you say: '**Yes, we are looking for additional help right now, you can come in to pick up an application.**'

Allow the participant to continue the dialogue and ask for the specifics. Possible questions:

a)   Where do I go?
b)   Who do I ask for?
c)   Whom do I turn the application in to?
d)   How long will it take to get an interview?

If they ask these questions respond in the following way:

a)   'You may pick up an application at any of our stores. There is one at the six corners intersection. You have to go to the human resources department. Do you know where that is?'
b)   'When you come in ask for the extra help manager. At the six corner store, her name is Tina. If you go somewhere else anyone in that department can help you.'
c)   'When the application is completed you should return it Tina.'
d)   'If everything on the application looks good, you will be contacted within the next week. We want someone to start as soon as possible.'

Tape off, Answer any questions they had about the process of doing the last one.

(Developed 5/99)

APPENDIX 4

(Pre/Post   School ID#)

Social support questionnaire

Part 1: Caring and emotional support

There are many people in your life who give you caring and emotional support (help). These are people you can count on to care about you no matter what is going on in your life at the moment. These people accept you completely, including your good and bad qualities. These people are ready to help you when you are upset. They truly care about your feelings and what is best for you.

(Take some time now, and think about who these people are for you in your life. If you want write them down on this piece of paper. Let me know when you are done.)

Now look at the the list of people on the next page. Let's go through each person together. If the person does not exist in your life (is not in your social network), put an X in the first column. For each person think about how helpful they have been in the past or would be in giving you caring and emotional support (all the things we talked about in paragraph 1 of this handout).

For example, if you think your dad would be very helpful in giving you this kind of support by either listening to you or giving you advice, then circle the number 5. If you don't think he would very helpful for whatever reason, then circle the number 1.

Do you understand the directions? Can you tell me in your own words what you are supposed to do?

Advocacy and Empowerment for Minorities Program, IDHD, UIC, 6/98

SSNI – Table

Person	Do not have	Not at all helpful	Not very helpful	Somewhat helpful	Helpful	Very helpful
Father		1	2	3	4	5
Mother		1	2	3	4	5
Step-father		1	2	3	4	5
Step-mother		1	2	3	4	5
Bro/Sis		1	2	3	4	5
Cousins		1	2	3	4	5
Aunt/uncle		1	2	3	4	5
Grandparent		1	2	3	4	5
Teacher		1	2	3	4	5
School counsellor		1	2	3	4	5
School principal		1	2	3	4	5
Best adult friend		1	2	3	4	5
Church		1	2	3	4	5
Best friend		1	2	3	4	5
Boy/girl friend, partner		1	2	3	4	5
Other friends		1	2	3	4	5
Boss		1	2	3	4	5
Classmate/co-worker		1	2	3	4	5
Other		1	2	3	4	5

How happy are you with the amount of caring and emotional support you get from the people in the list above?

Very Unhappy			It's alright			Very Happy
1	2	3	4	5	6	7

How often do you go to other people to get caring and emotional support?

Never			Sometimes			Always
1	2	3	4	5	6	7

Part 2: Help and guidance

Some people can be counted on to give you help and guidance. These people would be there to help you with figuring things out at school or work. If you have ideas on how to reach your goals about work and school but are not sure how to develop the best plan to reach these goals, you might go to one of these people. If you needed advice about how to apply for college or get financial aid they might be the right individual to go to.

(Take some time now, and think about who these people are for you in your life. If you want write them down on this piece of paper. Let me know when you are done.)

Now look at the the list of people on the next page. Let's go through each person together. If the person does not exist in your life (is not in your social network), put an X in the first column. For each person think about how helpful they have been in the past or would be in giving you guidance and advice (all the things we talked about in paragraph 1 of this handout).

For example if your gym teacher is someone who is always telling you how to improve yourself or reminding you to do your homework and study hard, then you may want to circle the number 5, for very helpful. On the other hand, if your uncle has never been able to answer your questions about the training program he went to even though you've asked him to do so, then you might circle the number 1, for not helpful.

Do you understand the directions? Can you tell me in your own words what you are supposed to do?

Advocacy and Empowerment for Minorities Program, IDHD, UIC, 6/98

SSNI – Table

Person	Do not have	Not at all helpful	Not very helpful	Somewhat helpful	Helpful	Very helpful
Father		1	2	3	4	5
Mother		1	2	3	4	5
Step-father		1	2	3	4	5
Step-mother		1	2	3	4	5
Bro/Sis		1	2	3	4	5
Cousins		1	2	3	4	5
Aunt/uncle		1	2	3	4	5
Grandparent		1	2	3	4	5
Teacher		1	2	3	4	5
School counsellor		1	2	3	4	5
School principal		1	2	3	4	5
Best adult friend		1	2	3	4	5
Church		1	2	3	4	5
Best friend		1	2	3	4	5
Boy/girl friend, partner		1	2	3	4	5
Other friends		1	2	3	4	5
Boss		1	2	3	4	5
Classmate/ co-worker		1	2	3	4	5
Other		1	2	3	4	5

How happy are you with the amount of help and guidance you get from the people in the list above?

Very Unhappy			It's alright			Very Happy
1	2	3	4	5	6	7

How often do you go to other people to get help and guidance?

Never			Sometimes			Always
1	2	3	4	5	6	7

Part 3: Needs issues

There are people in your life who are there for you when you need support in school or at work. These people may also support you by providing transportation, help with getting around, or getting financial assistance (money) for things you need (equipment, living expenses, etc.). This type of help would also be the type of help needed to learn a new skill, or pass a test, or understand the instructions at a job. If you need physical help, like getting to an important appointment for work, you might ask someone on this list.

(Take some time now, and think about who these people are for you in your life. If you want write them down on this piece of paper. Let me know when you are done.)

Now look at the the list of people on the next page. Let's go through each person together. If the person does not exist in your life (is not in your social network), put an X in the first column. For each person think about how helpful they have been in the past or would be in giving you support with your needs (all the things we talked about in paragraph 1 of this handout).

For example, if the high school counsellor is always telling you about special programs to apply for which will give you support in obtaining special equipment, then you would probably circle a 5 for very helpful. If your friends are rarely ever there for you to give you help with transportation then you probably would circle a 2 for not very helpful.

Do you understand the directions? Can you tell me in your own words what you are supposed to do?

Advocacy and Empowerment for Minorities Program, IDHD, UIC, 6/98

SSNI – Table

Person	Do not have	Not at all helpful	Not very helpful	Somewhat helpful	Helpful	Very helpful
Father		1	2	3	4	5
Mother		1	2	3	4	5
Step-father		1	2	3	4	5
Step-mother		1	2	3	4	5
Bro/Sis		1	2	3	4	5
Cousins		1	2	3	4	5
Aunt/uncle		1	2	3	4	5
Grandparent		1	2	3	4	5
Teacher		1	2	3	4	5
School counsellor		1	2	3	4	5
School principal		1	2	3	4	5
Best adult friend		1	2	3	4	5
Church		1	2	3	4	5
Best friend		1	2	3	4	5
Boy/girl friend, partner		1	2	3	4	5
Other friends		1	2	3	4	5
Boss		1	2	3	4	5
Classmate/ co-worker		1	2	3	4	5
Other		1	2	3	4	5

How happy are you with the amount of support you get from the people in the list above?

Very Unhappy			It's alright			Very Happy
1	2	3	4	5	6	7

How often do you go to other people to get support for your special needs?

Never			Sometimes			Always
1	2	3	4	5	6	7

Part 4: People who upset you

Whether they mean to or not, some people in our lives upset us in many ways. Sometimes these are people whom we do like but still bother us. A teacher may be such a person. You may like your teacher and she may be very helpful, but sometimes you get angry with them for scolding you or giving you too much homework. This can also happen with other people in our lives, like parents, brothers and sisters.

(Take some time now, and think about who these people are for you in your life. If you want write them down on this piece of paper. Let me know when you are done.)

Now look at the the list of people on the next page. Let's go through each person together. If the person does not exist in your life (is not in your social network), put an X in the first column. For each person think about how how often you get upset with these people.

For example, if your mother and you are always arguing, you might circle 5 for often upset. If you and your science teacher have a great relationship and they never upset you, then you might want to circle 1 for never upset.

Do you understand the directions? Can you tell me in your own words what you are supposed to do?

Advocacy and Empowerment for Minorities Program, IDHD, UIC, 6/98

SSNI – Table

Person	Do not have	Never upset	Not often upset	Somewhat upset	Upset	Often upset
Father		1	2	3	4	5
Mother		1	2	3	4	5
Step-father		1	2	3	4	5
Step-mother		1	2	3	4	5
Bro/Sis		1	2	3	4	5
Cousins		1	2	3	4	5
Aunt/uncle		1	2	3	4	5
Grandparent		1	2	3	4	5
Teacher		1	2	3	4	5
School counsellor		1	2	3	4	5
School principal		1	2	3	4	5
Best adult friend		1	2	3	4	5
Church		1	2	3	4	5
Best friend		1	2	3	4	5
Boy/girl friend, partner		1	2	3	4	5
Other friends		1	2	3	4	5
Boss		1	2	3	4	5
Classmate/ co-worker		1	2	3	4	5
Other		1	2	3	4	5

How do you feel about the amount of upsetting or negative feelings you go through in your relationships with these people?

Very Negative Definitely a Problem			It's alright			Very Positive No real Problem
1	2	3	4	5	6	7

APPENDIX 5

(Pre/Post   School ID#)

Generalized Self-efficacy

Read each sentence. Think about how this applies to you. Circle the number that shows how true this is for you. Remember there is no right or wrong answer. This is just how you feel.

1. If I try really hard, I can always solve my tough problems.

No way	Not really	Maybe	Yes
1	2	3	4

2. When someone doesn't want me to do well, I can still find ways to do well.

No way	Not really	Maybe	Yes
1	2	3	4

3. It is easy for me to reach my goals.

No way	Not really	Maybe	Yes
1	2	3	4

4. I know that I can handle anything that comes my way.

No way	Not really	Maybe	Yes
1	2	3	4

5. Because I am creative, I know I can deal with things that come up as a surprise.

No way	Not really	Maybe	Yes
1	2	3	4

246 *Teresa Garate-Serafini* et al.

6. I can solve most problems if I try as much as I can.

No way	Not really	Maybe	Yes
1	2	3	4

_____

_____

7. I have learned ways to deal with problems. That is why I can stay calm when there are tough times in my life.

No way	Not really	Maybe	Yes
1	2	3	4

_____

_____

8. When I have a problem, I can find more than one solution.

No way	Not really	Maybe	Yes
1	2	3	4

_____

_____

9. If I am in a bind, I can think of something to do.

No way	Not really	Maybe	Yes
1	2	3	4

_____

_____

10. No matter what comes my way, I am usually able to handle it.

No way	Not really	Maybe	Yes
1	2	3	4

_____

_____

(Revised 3/13/98)

APPENDIX 6

(Pre/Post   School ID#)

Academic Self-efficacy

Please read the following sentences. Think about the sentence and decide if you think you could be able to do the action. Remember, most people can not do *all* of these things! There are no right or wrong answers! Tell us about you. Once you have decided which number matches you the best, circle it.

1. I am a good student.

No way	Not really	Maybe	Yes
1	2	3	4

2. The goals written in my IEP are tough, but I can still reach them.

No way	Not really	Maybe	Yes
1	2	3	4

3. I am able to go to school almost every day.

No way	Not really	Maybe	Yes
1	2	3	4

4. I can make good grades.

No way	Not really	Maybe	Yes
1	2	3	4

5. I can do what is required of me to graduate from high school on time.

No way	Not really	Maybe	Yes
1	2	3	4

6.   Because of my talents I have been able to do things which others can't do.

No way	Not really	Maybe	Yes
1	2	3	4

_____

_____

7.   Sometimes my grades embarrass me.

No way	Not really	Maybe	Yes
1	2	3	4

_____

_____

8.   I am able to follow school rules on most days.

No way	Not really	Maybe	Yes
1	2	3	4

_____

_____

9.   I have good study skills.

No way	Not really	Maybe	Yes
1	2	3	4

_____

_____

10.   I feel good about answering questions in class.

No way	Not really	Maybe	Yes
1	2	3	4

_____

_____

11.   I care about what my teachers think of me.

No way	Not really	Maybe	Yes
1	2	3	4

_____

_____

12.   Most of the time, 'A' students do not get more attention than I do.

No way	Not really	Maybe	Yes
1	2	3	4

13.   I find most subjects in school easy.

No way	Not really	Maybe	Yes
1	2	3	4

14.   People think badly of me because I am not 'smart' or doing well in school.

No way	Not really	Maybe	Yes
1	2	3	4

15.   Because I am creative, I have solved some difficult problems in the past.

No way	Not really	Maybe	Yes
1	2	3	4

16.   Sometimes I am jealous of students who are smarter than me.

No way	Not really	Maybe	Yes
1	2	3	4

17.   I am proud of my schoolwork.

No way	Not really	Maybe	Yes
1	2	3	4

18.   I am not afraid to tell a teacher when I think that she/he has the wrong answer.

No way	Not really	Maybe	Yes
1	2	3	4

19.   I would call myself a smart person.

No way	Not really	Maybe	Yes
1	2	3	4

20.   I can think on my feet (quickly).

No way	Not really	Maybe	Yes
1	2	3	4

(Revised 3/13/98)

APPENDIX 7

(Pre/Post   School ID#)

Situation Specific Self-efficacy Questionnaire

Please read the following sentences. Pretend that you are in this situation. Think about the sentence and decide if you think you could be able to do the action. Remember, most people cannot do *all* of these things! There are no right or wrong answers! Tell us about you. Once you have decided which number matches you the best, circle it.

1.   If I see an ad for a job I really like, I can make an appointment with the manager in a week.

No way	Not really	Maybe	Yes
1	2	3	4

2. I can make a meeting for a job interview even if I can't get a hold of the person in charge.

No way	Not really	Maybe	Yes
1	2	3	4

_____

_____

3. I find a job I want. I can get to the interview even if it is far from my house.

No way	Not really	Maybe	Yes
1	2	3	4

_____

_____

4. I can get to a job interview on time and dressed nicely, even if it is at 7:00 in the morning.

No way	Not really	Maybe	Yes
1	2	3	4

_____

_____

5. If I had a job, I could get to work on time even if I didn't have my own transportation.

No way	Not really	Maybe	Yes
1	2	3	4

_____

_____

6. If I was confused about how to do something at a job, I could get help from my boss or co-workers.

No way	Not really	Maybe	Yes
1	2	3	4

_____

_____

7. I can ask for help at school even if I feel embarrassed.

No way	Not really	Maybe	Yes
1	2	3	4

_____

_____

8. I can ask for help from my teachers even when I am in trouble.

No way   Not really   Maybe   Yes
1   2   3   4

_____

_____

9. I can find help from an adult at school to fill out my applications for school (college, technical school, etc.).

No way   Not really   Maybe   Yes
1   2   3   4

_____

_____

10. I can ask this adult for help even if I don't know them very well.

No way   Not really   Maybe   Yes
1   2   3   4

_____

_____

11. When I feel like I have to make some hard decisions (about drugs, gangs, school, etc.) I can find an adult in my school to help me think about my choices.

No way   Not really   Maybe   Yes
1   2   3   4

_____

_____

12. I want to go to school (college, technical school) but don't have the money. I can find some help from public assistance, loans, grants, etc.

No way   Not really   Maybe   Yes
1   2   3   4

_____

_____

13. I am not sure of what I should work on or study after graduation. I can talk to an adult in my school to help me learn more about my options.

No way   Not really   Maybe   Yes
1   2   3   4

_____

_____

14.   I can save enough money to open a savings account in two months' time.

No way	Not really	Maybe	Yes
1	2	3	4

15.   I am trying to save money to buy a car. I can stop buying things I don't need so I don't waste money.

No way	Not really	Maybe	Yes
1	2	3	4

(Revised 3/13/98)

APPENDIX 8

(Student ID#)

Satisfaction Survey

This is your chance to let the project staff know what you think about the program. Think about each question carefully and choose a number that describes how you feel. Be honest. This information will help us improve the program.

1.   How well did you understand the information taught?

Not very well			Very well
1	2	3	4

2.   How useful were the skills that you learned?

Not very useful			Very useful
1	2	3	4

3.   How useful was the book?

Not very useful   Very useful
      1   2   3   4

_____

_____

4.   How well did the teacher(s) explain the information?

Not very well   Very well
      1   2   3   4

_____

_____

5.   How helpful were the teachers with problems outside of the
     classroom?

Not very helpful   Very helpful
      1   2   3   4

_____

_____

6.   How helpful is the training for helping you get a job?

Not very helpful   Very helpful
      1   2   3   4

_____

_____

7.   How difficult were the homework assignments?

Not very difficult   Very difficult
      1   2   3   4

_____

_____

8.   How useful were the role-playing activities?

Not very useful   Very useful
      1   2   3   4

_____

_____

9. How useful was it seeing yourself on the videotape?

    Not very useful   Very useful
        1   2   3   4

---

10. How useful was it setting goals and short-term objectives?

    Not very useful   Very useful
        1   2   3   4

---

a) What did you like the best about the program?
b) What did you like the least about the program?
c) What would you change about the program and why?
d) If a friend asked you about the program, would you tell them to participate? Why?

REFERENCES

Balcazar, F.E., Fawcett, S.B. and Seekins, T. (1991) 'Teaching people with disabilities to recruit help to attain personal goals', *Rehabilitation Psychology*, **36**, 1 pp. 31–42.

Balcazar, F.E. and Keys, C.B. (1994) 'Teaching self-help to vocational rehabilitation clients', *Directions in Rehabilitation Counselling*, **5** pp. 3–11.

Balcazar, F.E., Keys, C.B., Barnes, H., Isaza-Rivera, V. and Ortiz, G. (1996) *The Back to School and Work Project: Annual Report to the US Department of Education*, Chicago, IL: University of Illinois.

Balcazar, F.E., Keys, C.B. and Garate-Serafini, J.T. (1995) 'Learning to recruit assistance to attain transition goals: A program for adjudicated youth with disabilities', *Remedial and Special Education*, **16** 4 pp. 237–46.

Balcazar, F.E., Keys, C.B., Gianneschi, A. and DeYoung, R. (1992) *Teaching goal setting and help-recruiting skills in the vocational rehabilitation counseling process*, Unpublished manuscript, Chicago, IL: IDHD, University of Illinois at Chicago.

Balcazar, F.E., Majors, R., Blanchard, K.A., Paine, A., Suarez-Balcazar, Y., Fawcett, S.B., Murphy, R. and Meyer, J. (1991) 'Teaching minority high school students to recruit helpers to attain personal and educational goals', *Journal of Behavioral Education*, **1** pp. 445–54.

Balcazar, F.E., Seekins, T., Fawcett, S.B. and Hopkins, B.L. (1990) 'Empowering people with physical disabilities through advocacy skills training', *American Journal of Community Psychology*, **18**, 2 pp. 281–96.

Bandura, A. (1977) 'Self-efficacy: Toward a unifying theory of behavior change', *Psychological Review*, **84** pp. 191–215.

Bandura, A. (1986) *Social Foundations of Thought and Action: A Social Cognitive Theory*, Englewood Cliffs, NJ: Prentice Hall.

256 *Teresa Garate-Serafini* et al.

Bandura, A. (1997) *Self-efficacy: The Exercise of Control*, New York: W.H. Freeman and Company.

Barnes, H., Balcazar, F.E. and Keys, C.B. (1997) 'A Contextual Analysis of the Reasons for Dropping Out from Special Education among Latino Youth with Disabilities', Unpublished manuscript, Chicago, IL: IDHD, University of Illinois.

Barrera, M. (1981) 'Social support in the adjustment of pregnant adolescents: Assessment issues' in Gottlieb, B.H. (ed.) *Social Networks and Social Support*, Beverly Hills, CA: Sage Publications.

Bhareman, R.D. and Kopp, K.A. (1988) 'The school's choice: Guidelines for drop-out prevention at the middle and junior high school' (*Drop-out Prevention Series*), Columbus, OH: National Center for Research in Vocational Education.

Blechman, E.A. (1992) 'Mentors for high-risk minority youth: From effective communication to bicultural competence', *Journal of Clinical Child Psychology*, **21**, 2 pp. 160–68.

Blum, D.J. and Jones, L.A. (1993) 'Academic growth group and mentoring program for potential dropouts', *The School Counsellor*, **40**, 2 pp. 207–17.

Cohen, J. (1986) 'Theoretical considerations in peer tutoring', *Psychology in the Schools*, **23** pp. 175–86.

Davis, H. (1973) 'Four ways to goal attainment: An overview', *Evaluation*, **1**, 2 pp. 43–48.

Diem, R.A. (1992) 'Dealing with the tip of the iceberg: School responses to at risk behaviors', *The High School Journal* pp. 119–25.

DuBois, D.L. and Neville, H.A. (1997) 'Youth mentoring: Investigation of relationship characteristics and perceived benefits', *Journal of Community Psychology*, **25**, 3 pp. 227–34.

Emmerson, G.J. and Neely, M.A. (1988) 'Two adaptable, valid and reliable data-collection measures: Goal attainment scaling and the semantic differential', *Counselling Psychology*, **16**, 2 pp. 261–71.

Fawcett, S.B., White, G.W., Balcazar, F.E., Suarez-Balcazar, Y., Mathews, R.M., Paine-Andrews, A., Seekins, T. and Smith, J.F. (1994) 'A contextual–behavioral model of empowerment: case studies involving people with physical disabilities', *American Journal of Community Psychology*, **22**, 4 pp. 471–96.

Fine, M. (1986) 'Why urban adolescents drop into and out of public high school' *Teachers College Record*, **87**, 3 pp. 393–409.

Freedman, M. (1988) *Partners in Growth: Elder Mentors and At-risk Youth*, Philadelphia, PA: Private/Public Ventures.

Freedman, M. (1991) *The Kindness of Strangers: Reflections on the Mentoring Movement*, Philadelphia, PA: Private/Public Ventures.

Freedman, M. and Baker, R. (1995) *Workplace Mentoring for Youth: Context, Issues, Strategies*, Washington, DC: National Institute for Work and Learning, Academy for Educational Development.

Furano, K., Roaf, P.A., Styles, M.B. and Branch, A.Y. (1993) *Big Brothers/Big Sisters: A Study of Program Practices*, Philadelphia, PA: Private/Public Ventures.

Gallup, G. and Gallup, A.M. (1986) *The Great American Success Story: Factors that Affect Achievement*, Homewood, IL: Dow Jones-Irwin.

Garwick, G. and Lampman, S. (1972) 'Typical problems bringing patients to a community mental health center', *Community Mental Health Journal*, **8**, 4 pp. 271–80.

Greenwood, C., Carta, J. and Hall, V. (1988) 'The use of peer tutoring strategies in classroom management and educational instruction', *School Psychology Review*, **17** pp. 258–75.

Hellison, D. (1995) *Teaching Responsibility Through Physical Activity*, Champaign, IL: Human Kinetics.

Kaufman, F., Hamel, J., Milan, C., Woolverton, N. and Miller, J. (1986) 'The nature, role and influence of mentors in the lives of gifted adults', *Journal of Counselling and Development,* **64** pp. 576–78.

Kiresuk, T.J. and Sherman, R.E. (1968) 'Goal attainment scaling: A general method for evaluating comprehensive community mental health programs', *Community Mental Health Journal,* **4** pp. 443–53.

Mithaug, D.E., Martin, J.E. and Agran, M. (1987) 'Adaptability instruction: The goal of transitional programming', *Exceptional Children,* **53,** pp. 500–05.

National Mentoring Partnership (1998) *Mentoring: Elements of Effective Practice* [online]. www.mentoring.org

Neill, S. (ed.) (1979) *Keeping Students in School: Problems and Solutions, AASA Critical Issues Report,* Sacramento, CA: American Association of School Administrators.

Poe, J. (1998) 'No quitting on dropouts', *The Chicago Tribune,* pp. A1, A4.

Roberts, A. and Cotton, L. (1994) 'Note on assessing mentor programs', *Psychological Reports,* **75** pp. 1369–70.

Schwarzer, R., Bäbler, J., Kwiatek, P. and Shröder, K. (1997) 'The assessment of optimist self beliefs: Comparisons of the German, Spanish and Chinese versions of the general self-efficacy scale', *Applied Psychology: An International Review,* **46,** 1 pp. 69–88.

Slicker, E.K. and Palmer, D.J. (1993) 'Mentoring at-risk high school students: evaluation of a school-based program', *The School Counsellor,* **40,** 2 pp. 327–34.

Srebnik, D.S. and Elias, M.J. (1993) 'An ecological, interpersonal skills approach to dropout prevention', *American Orthopsychiatric Association,* **63,** 4 pp. 526–35.

Torrance, E. (1983) 'Role of mentors in creative achievement', *The Creative Child and Adult Quarterly,* **8,** 8–15 p. 18.

Weitlauf, J., Merner, J., Filley, L. and Wright, P. (1998) 'Training youth mentors in the arts', Unpublished manuscript, Chicago, IL: University of Illinois.

Weitlauf, J., Hayes, E. and Garate-Serafini, T. (1997) 'The academic and situation-specific self-efficacy scales', Unpublished manuscript, Chicago, IL: University of Illinois.

Wells, S. (1990) *At-risk Youth: Identification, Programs and Recommendations,* Englewood, CO: Teacher Idea Press.

List of contributors

Cheryl S. Ajirotutu, Ph.D. (University of California, Berkeley) has been a faculty member in the Department of Anthropology at the University of Wisconsin-Milwaukee for the past seven years. She has several years of research experience in both national and international settings. Her research has focused on the influence of culture in school and work settings. In addition to research in public school settings, she has studied informal learning situations, the culture of work traditions, particularly in the use of indigenous technology, and issues concerning language and society. She has also taught at the University of Ibadan in Nigeria and at the Davis and Berkeley campuses of the University of California.

Keith Alford, Ph.D., ACSW, LISW, is an Assistant Professor in the School of Social Work, Syracuse University where he is chair of the Family Mental Health Concentration and project director for the Rosamond Gifford Community Exchange Forums. He teaches in the practice sequence at both the undergraduate and graduate levels. He received his doctoral degree in Clinical Social Work with a concentration in Family Therapy from The Ohio State University. A former child protective services worker and therapeutic foster care supervisor, Dr Alford focuses his research on cultural specificity in human services. Dr Alford holds membership in the Council on Social Work Education and the National Association of Social Workers. In Syracuse, New York, he is a member of the Family Find Advisory Council for the Dunbar Association, Vera House Domestic Violence Coalition, and a facilitator for the Racial Dialogue Circles sponsored by the Inter Religious Council.

Fabricio E. Balcazar, Ph.D. is Associate Professor of Disability and Human Development and Psychology at the University of Illinois at Chicago. Dr Balcazar's primary interest is in developing methods for enhancing and facilitating consumer empowerment and personal effectiveness of individuals with disabilities and their families. Dr Balcazar has conducted research over the past 15 years on the development of systematic approaches for effective involvement of people with disabilities in consumer advocacy organisations and their communities through both employment and positive community engagements. He has served as the Principal Investigator on numerous federally funded projects from the U.S. Department of Education since 1990 and has developed a mentoring curriculum for supporting minority youth with disabilities in their efforts towards recruiting mentors and pursuing personal, educational and vocational goals. Dr Balcazar has had extensive practical experience in developing and evaluating training materials in areas including advocacy skills, goal setting, action planning, and help-recruiting. With over 50 publications and more than 150 presentations, Dr Balcazar is a leader in the field of a consumer empowerment for individuals with disabilities and continues to contribute to the field of disability and minority.

Maud Blair is a Lecturer in Education at the Open University. She is Chair of the Open University course ED356, 'Race' Education and Society, and of the M.A. course E826, Gender Issues in Education: Equality and Difference. Her publications include, *Racism and Education: Structures and Strategies*, which she co-edited with D. Gill and B. Mayor; *Identity and Diversity, Gender and the Experience of Education*, and *Debates and Issues in Feminism and Pedagogy*, both co-edited with Janet Holland.

Karl Brooks works as a senior Educational Psychologist in the London Borough of Enfield. As well as conducting research on exclusion and related issues, he has given talks and facilitates numerous workshops on the subject. He is a member of the Association of Black Psychologists (UK).

James Earl Davis is currently a visiting scholar at the University of Michigan in the Institute of Research on Women and Gender (1998–99) and on leave from the University of Delaware where he is an Associate Professor in the School of Education. At Delaware, he is also a faculty affiliate in the Centre for Community Development and Family Policy in the College of Urban Affairs and Public Policy. He received a B.A. in sociology from Morehouse College and a Ph.D. in Evaluation Research and Social Policy from Cornell University. Professor Davis completed a postdoctoral fellowship in the Division of Education Policy at the Educational Testing Service in Princeton, New Jersey. A former National Academy of Education-Spencer Foundation Postdoctoral fellow, Dr Davis' research and teaching are in the areas of sociology of education, program evaluation, educational assessment and public policy. His current research focuses on Masculinities in Schools and the Social and Educational Experiences of Black boys/men.

Teresa Garate-Serafini, M.Ed. is a Project Director at the Department of Disability and Human Development of the University of Illinois at Chicago. Ms Garate-Serafini currently directs two federally funded model demonstration projects and one state funded project all targeting African American and Latino youth with disabilities within the Chicago Public School System. Ms Garate-Serafini is a bilingual special education teacher by profession and has seven years of experience working in urban schools and surrounding suburbs. She has co-authored a curriculum on mentoring for youth with disabilities that has been implemented with adjudicated youth, high school dropouts and youth transitioning from school to work, and is highlighted in the present chapter. She has been working in the area of transition for the past nine years and her interests continue to lie in the area of improving services for youth with disabilities by following a 'self-determination' approach. Her experience as an advocate for minority families working to improve the education outcomes of students with disabilities has earned her a place as an Illinois TASH Board Member. In her role as Advocate, Educator and Researcher, Ms Garate-Serafini has been involved in over 30 presentations and workshops related to Transition, Inclusion, and Parent/Consumer Empowerment. She is also pursuing her Ph.D. in the College of Education at the University of Illinois at Chicago.

Stephen Gavazzi, Ph.D. is Associate Professor in the Department of Human Development and Family Science, The Ohio State University. His research interests include the impact of family process variables on adolescent adjustment and well-being, the development of biopsychosocial models to predict domestic violence, psychoeducational programming for families containing a child/adolescent with a mood disorder, and culturally specific/ community-based rites of passage initiatives. Dr Gavazzi is the creator of the Growing Up FAST: Families with Adolescents Surviving and Thriving Program. This program serves families of delinquent youth as both a diversion program and a parole programming option.

David Gillborn is Head of Policy Studies at the Institute of Education, University of London. He is best known for his research on equality and ethnic diversity in education. David's previous publications include the books *Racism and Antiracism in Real Schools* (1995) and *Rationing Education*, with Deborah Youdell (2000): both published by Open University Press. He is author of the influential review *Recent Research on the Achievements of Ethnic Minority Pupils*, with Caroline Gipps (Ofsted, 1996). David is the founding editor of the international journal, *Race Ethnicity and Education*.

Mekada Graham is a social work educator, lecturer, author and practitioner. She has published several scholarly articles and essays in academic journals in Britain and the USA. Mekada is a member of the editorial board of the *Journal of Black Studies*, Temple University, USA. She is currently completing her Ph.D. research at the University of Hertfordshire. Mekada has designed and implemented community rites of passage programmes. She is a regular contributor to the *Afrikan Business and Culture Magazine*.

Denny Grant works as a Principal Educational Psychologist for Enfield. He has given talks at a national level on the problem of exclusion and his articles with Karl Brooks have been informed by seminars with parent and community groups. He is a past chair and secretary of the Association of Black Psychologists (UK).

William Gulam is a Senior Lecturer in the Education Development Unit at Salford University, Manchester. Until 1993 he was an Inspector of Education.

He has also taught in schools, FE colleges and at the John Moores University in Liverpool.

Richard Harris is Associate Dean of the School of Education and Chester College of Higher Education. He has produced a number of publications together with Professor Parsons on a variety of aspects of school exclusions. He is a lawyer and his particular focus has been upon the rights of excluded children and those with parental responsibility for them.

Aminifu Richard Harvey is currently tenured Associate Professor at the School of Social Work at the University of Maryland, Baltimore. Dr Harvey earned his doctorate of social work degree from Howard University in 1983 having received a National Institute for Mental Health Fellowship for doctorate study. From June 1986 until July 1997 he served as the Executive Director of MAAT Centre for Human and Organizational Enhancement Inc., which he founded in order to provide culturally competent services to African American families and youth. Dr Harvey has been a practising clinician for 24 years and is one of the pioneers in developing and implementing an Afrocentric approach to psychotherapy and social service delivery systems. He is a certified hypnothera-pist and has served as a consulting editor to the journal *Social Work*.

Dr Harvey has conducted numerous workshops and training events within this area with a special interest on African American families and youth. A former Woodrow Wilson Foundation Fellow, he is the author of a number of books.

Christopher B. Keys, Ph.D. is a Professor of Psychology and Disability and Human Development and Chair of the Department of Psychology at the University of Illinois at Chicago. Dr Keys is a President of the Society for Community Research and Action and past Chair of the Council for Program Directors in Community Research and Action. Author of more than 100 articles.

Richard Majors is a former Harvard Medical School Clinical Fellow and is a former Senior Fellow at the David Walker Research Institute at Michigan State University and a Senior Fellow at the University of Manchester, in the Department of Applied Social Science (formerly the Dept. of Social Policy and Social Work). He is the founder and Deputy Editor of the *Journal of African American Men* and has written extensively on education, race, class and gender. His book *Cool Pose: The Dilemmas of Black Manhood in America* (cowritten with J. Billson) was on the Publishers Bestsellers List. He has been selected by the International Biographical Centre as one of the 2000 outstanding people of the twentieth century. Currently Richard Majors is the Deputy Director of the Leigh Education Action Zone. He has been on Working Groups for the Qualifications and Curriculum Authority, Department for Education and Employment and the Commission for Racial Equality. The *New York Times* describes his work as 'being at the forefront of a movement of black social scientists who are seeking ways to understand inner city youths better and to marshal the strengths of the black middle class to help these troubled young people survive'.

Patrick McKenry, Ph.D. is a Professor of Human Development and Family Science, and Adjunct Professor of African American and African Studies at The Ohio State University. He received his Ph.D. in Child and Family Studies from the University of Tennessee. He has held academic positions at the University of Georgia, University of British Columbia, and University of North Carolina-Chapel Hill. His research has focused on cultural and gender variations in family stress and coping. He has written three books and more than 80 journal articles.

Jason W. Osborne is an Assistant Professor of Educational Psychology at the University of Oklahoma. His current research interests focus on understanding the processes that lead to inquities in educational outcomes, particularly racial and gender inequities. Ongoing work particularly focuses on exploring Stereotype Threat, and how the findings from this line of research can be implemented to improve outcomes for disadvantaged groups.

Carl Parsons is Professor of Education at Canterbury Christ Church University College. He has been funded to carry out research on school exclusions by the Joseph Rowntree Foundation, the Commission for Racial Equality and the Department of Education, twice. He has monitored permanent exclusion in schools in England over the last four years and his book, *Education, Exclusion and Citizenship* has sought to explain the phenomenon, which is unique amongst the education systems of Western Europe.

Diane S. Pollard, Ph.D. (University of Milwaukee) is currently Professor of Educational Psychology and Director of the Urban Education Doctoral Program at the University of Wisconsin-Milwaukee. She has conducted research on factors underlying successful coping and achievement among African American students in urban school settings, the implications of the intersection of race and gender for the perceptions, motivations, achievements and coping of African American youth and adults, and the interrelationships between social and cultural contexts and individual behaviour in urban educational institutions.

Diane Reay is a Research fellow at King's College, London where she is engaged in research on Social Justice and Education. Her book, *Class Work: Mothers' Involvement in their Children's Primary Schooling* (Taylor and Francis 1998) explores the influences of social class and 'race' on the maintenance of educational difference and the reproduction of social inequality. Prior to her academic career at King's she worked for twenty years as a primary school teacher in inner London.

Heidi Safia Mirza is a Reader in Sociology at South Bank University, London, where she is also Director of the Postgraduate Programme in Social Sciences. Her academic career includes teaching Afro-American Studies at Brown

University, USA, and research on race and gender issues in the Caribbean and Britain. She is the author of *Young, Female and Black* (Routledge 1992). Her current research is on black women in higher education and educational strategies of the black community in Britain and Africa. She has recently been appointed to the Government's Schools Standards Task Force. Her latest book is an edited collection entitled *Black British Feminism* (Routledge 1997).

Dr Tony Sewell is a Lecturer at the University of Leeds; he is also a columnist for the *Voice* newspaper and has published many books. His latest work, *Keep On Moving: Caribbean History from 1948,* was written to celebrate the fiftieth anniversary of the coming to Britain of large numbers of Caribbean immigrants.

Julie Weitlauf, M.A. received her Bachelor's degrees in Anthropology and Psychology from the University of Washington in 1996 and a Master's degree in Clinical Psychology from the University of Illinois at Chicago (UIC) in 1998. She is currently a doctoral student in Clinical Psychology at UIC. Here her clinical specialisation in neuropsychology and research programme in personality and individual differences converge on a key question: how does self-efficacy generalise? As is highlighted in the present chapter, a key mechanism for such generalisation is the development of strong self-regulatory and coping skills. Mentoring youths, as discussed throughout the chapter, can help to foster such skills and contribute to the development of robust efficacy in social and academic domains in youth.

Vincent Wilkinson grew up in Leeds, West Yorkshire. He graduated from Salford University in 1976 with honours in Biomedical Electronics and worked in the further education sector as a lecturer for 14 years. He carried out research on issues involving school policy and practice leading to the award of an M. Phil. degree in 1994. He completed his PhD in 1999, looking into permanent exclusions of African Caribbean pupils in a northern LEA. He worked part time for the Open University as an education adviser followed by a temporary contract with the Leeds Education Department as a service team leader with responsibilities for mentoring prior to taking up his present post as a Senior Research Fellow with Sheffield University.

Index

3S's 15, 65
Abdenoor, A. 6
Aboud, F. E. 132
academic ability 5, 29
academic achievement 3, 20, 31–2, 45–58,
    86, 141–56, 171, 187, 210
academic disidentification 45–58
accommodation without assimilation 54
Acland, H. 117
adolescents needs 35–7
Advisory Group on Ethnic Minority
    Achievement 1, 106
African American Immersion Schools
    experiment 79–89
African American Rites of Passage
    (AA-RITES) 141–54
Africentric immersion 145–8
Afrikan Studies 35, 40, 64
Afrocentrism 61–78, 160–5, 172
Agran, M. 219
Ajirotutu, C. S. 79–89
Akbar, N. 68, 170
Alderson, P. 6
Alexander, C. 144
Alexander, K. L. 45
Alford, K. 141–56
alienation 205–13
Allen, B. A. 80
Ansell, A. E. 18
Arewa, C. S. 68
Argyle, M. 136
Arnold, S. 6
Aronson, J. 51, 52, 56
Asante, M. 66, 67, 68
Ashe, A. 198
Assante, K. A. 162, 163
Assem, K. 163
assimilation model 63–4, 132
Association of Educational Psychologists
    120

Audit Commission 112

Bäbler, J. 226
Bain, N. 7
Baker, R. 215, 216
Balcazar, F. E. 214–56
Bandura, A. 225
Barker, M. 17–18
Barnard, N. 4
Barnes, H. 218, 219, 222
Barrera, M. 224
Barrett, M. 132
Bazron, B. J. 159
Bear, G. G. 178
Becker, J. T. 157
Beckett, J. O. 161
Bell, D. 68
Bell, Y. R. 80
Belton, D. 171
Bennett, W. J. 162, 163
Bentham 135
Bernstein, B. 111
Betts, H. 3–4
Bhareman, R. D. 217
Bidwell, W. W. 35
Billingsley, A. 162, 163
Billson, J. M. 52, 205; cool pose theory 45,
    48, 55–6, 131, 143, 149, 169; cultural
    awareness 2; masculinity 130, 174;
    social indicators 141
The Black Child Report 107
Blair, M. 4, 5, 28–44
Blair, T. 19, 106, 128
blame paradigm 132
Blanchard, K. A. 216
Blechman, E. A. 214
Blount, M. 171
Blum, D. J. 226
Blumenkrantz, D. 145
Blunkett, D. 21, 22

Boateng, F. 74
Botvin, G. J. 157
Bourdieu, P. 93
Bourne, J. 5, 61
Bowen, G. L. 152
Boykin, A. W. 80
Branch, A. Y. 216
Brandt, G. 16
Bridges, L. 61
British Psychological Society (BPS) 115
Brooks, K. 110–27
Brown, J. D. 46
Browne, R. 179
Bryan, B. 65
Burlet, S. 93
bussing 63, 111
Byrd, J. Jr 142

Callender, C. 111, 114
Calliste, J. 117, 118
Campbell, J. 46, 145
Campbell, T. 135, 136
Cao, H. 7
Carby, H. 61, 63
Carnegie Corporation 158
Carrington, B. 15
Carta, J. 217
Cashmore, E. 64
centrality 95
challenge model 53
Channer, Y. 28
Chestang, L. 148
child centredness 98–9
Childright 113
citizenship education 22, 23
Clawson, J. G. 206
Clutterbuck, D. 206
Coard, B. 61, 112
1994 Code of Practice 112, 118
Cohen, J. 217
Coleman, A. A. 163, 165
Coleman, J. B. 157
collectivity 69, 146, 157, 161, 185, 186, *see also* Ujima
Collinson, V. 7
colour-blindness 18–19, 30, 31
Comer, J. P. 80
Commission for Racial Equality (CRE) 2, 4, 15, 20, 61, 129, 144, 207
Commonwealth Immigrants Advisory Council 14
community 54, 55, 70, 87–8, 92–3, 94, 100, 150, 161
Cones, J. 6

Conformists 184–7, 201
Connell, R. W. 179
Connolly, P. 29, 33
cool pose theory 45, 48, 55–6, 131, 143, 149, 169, 172
cost 108, 129–30
Cotton, L. 215, 217, 218
counter-publics 94–5
Cretney, S. 135
Crick, N. R. 178
crime 205, 206
Crocker, J. 46, 49
Cross, T. L. 159
Cuban, L. 84
Cuff, E. C. 131
Cullingford, C. 29
cultural competence 159–60
cultural dissonance 28
cultural ecological theory 45, 47–8, 54–5
cultural pluralism 15
culture: differences 2–3; exclusions 107; respect 34–5
Cunningham, G. P. 171
Cunningham, M. 170
Curtis, T. E. 35
Cuttance, P. 31

Dadzie, S. 65
Daly, A. 161
Davidson, A. 7
Davies, H. 134
Davies, T. 136
Davis, H. 220
Davis, J. E. 169–82
Deakin, N. 63
Dei, G. 61, 62, 65, 66, 67, 68, 70, 71, 72, 74
Demo, D. H. 50
Denby, R. 150
Dennis, K. W. 159
Department for Education and Employment (DfEE) 2, 30, 61, 210; Circular 10/94 120; 1997 Education Act 115; *Excellence in Schools* 19–20; exclusions 106, 107, 128; Green Paper 1997 110; Stephen Lawrence Inquiry 22, 24; Youth Cohort Study 3
Department of Education and Science (DES) 14, 64, 113
Dew, M. A. 157
DeYoung, R. 219
Dhondy, F. 14, 183, 193
Diallo, Y. 73
Diem, R. A. 216

Diop, C. 66
disidentification 45–58
Dodson, J. 163
Dornbusch, S. M. 84
Dove, N. 70–1
Drew, D. 20
Driver, G. 28
Dryfoos, J. 157
DuBois, D. L. 216, 218
Dukes, R. 7
Dunn, J. 132
Durkin, K. 132
Dworkin, R. 135, 136

early intervention 118–19, 120
Eaton, J. 7
Education Acts 21, 112, 113, 115, 116, 136
educational psychologists 110–27
ego recovery 193–4, 195, 197–200, 201
Eke, E. 66
Elias, M. J. 217, 218
Elkin, F. 80
Elton Report 111
Emmerson, G. J. 220
emotional capital 93–4
employment 193, 205, 211
empowerment 152–3, 158, 218–19, 222–3, 227
Enfield Education Authority 120–3
Entwhistle, D. R. 45
equal opportunity 117–18
equiphobia 18
Excellence in Cities 23
Excellence in Schools 19–20
exclusion 1–3, 36, 103–38, 205; educational psychologists 110–27; mentoring 209
Eysenck, H. 29, 111

Fawcett, S. B. 216, 219
feedback 49–50
femininity 170, 172, 178–9
fictive-culture 198
fictive-kinship 185, 186
Fine, M. 79, 217
Finn, J. D. 47
Fitzherbert, K. 63
Fletcher, R. 179
Flew, A. 16
Foley, D. 100
Fordham, S. 28, 47, 48, 54, 96, 107, 174, 185–6
Fort, J. 151

Foster, H. 5
Foster, K. 206, 210
Foster, P. 29
Francis, D. W. 131
Franklin, C. 152
Fraser, B. 162, 163
Fraser, N. 94–5
Freedman, M. 215, 216, 218
Frierson, H. T. Jr 80
Fuller, M. 187
Furano, K. 216

Gaine, C. 16
Gallup, A. M. 219
Gallup, G. 219
Galton, M. 99
gangster lifestyle 196–7
Garate-Serafini, T. 214–56
Garibaldi, A. M. 169, 171
Garwick, G. 220
Gavazzi, S. 141–56
Ghouri, N. 4, 5
Gianneschi, A. 219
Gibbs, J. 141, 143, 169
Gibson, M. A. 51
Gilbert, P. 169
Gilbert, R. 169
Gill, D. 64
Gillborn, D. 1, 4, 13–27, 28, 33, 61, 96, 111, 205; academic achievement 210; blame paradigm 132; discipline 29; exclusions rise 114; masculinity 130; racialised perspective 105–9; racism 34; staff negativity 186
Gilroy, P. 16
Gipps, C. 20, 28, 114, 205, 210
goal attainment scaling 220–2, 227, 228, 229–30
Goldstein, H. 31
Gordon, J. 169, 210
Gould, C. 3
Graham, M. 61–78
Graham, S. 80
Grant, C. A. 52
Grant, D. 110–27
Greater London Council 16
Greemers, B. 133
Green, 28
Green, R. L. 152
Greenwood, C. 217
Gross, J. 117
Grossman, J. 207
Grotpeter, J. K. 178
Guishard, J. 117

Gulam, W. 205–13

Hale-Benson, J. E. 150
Hall, M. 73, 74
Hall, V. 217
Hamel, J. 214
Hamilton, C. 4
Hammond, N. J. 152
Hammond, R. 45
Handel, G. 80
Hansford, B. C. 50
Hardiman, R. 194
Hardy, K. 142–3
Hare, J. 153, 161
Hare, N. 153, 161
Hargreaves, A. 29, 33, 35, 39, 40, 42
Harper, P. M. 171
Harris, P. 132
Harris, R. 128–38
Hartley, D. 131
Hartnell, N. 119–20
Harvey, A. 141, 146, 157–68
Hassan, E. 5
Hattie, J. A. 50
Hayden, C. 39
Hayes, E. 226
Haynes, N. M. 80
Hellison, D. 217
Herrnstein, R. A. 29, 45, 53
Herskovitz, M. J. 67
Hey, V. 93
Hill Collins, P. 68, 92, 93, 97
Hill, P. 72, 145–6, 161
Hillier, S. 4
Hindelang, M. J. 47
Holdcraft, H. 134
Holland, S. 119, 151, 153, 170, 171, 172, 179, 210
Home Office 22, 23
hooks, b. 96, 190, 195
Hoover, M. E. R. 81
Hopkins, D. 133
Hornby, G. 118, 119
Howard, 208
Howard, J. 45
Hudley, C. A. 172
Hulme, J. 209

Imani 147, 162–3
immersion school 79–89, 172
independence 35–6, 219
Ingra, V. 158
Inner London Education Authority 16, 112

Innovators 184, 187–9, 201
integration model 64
intelligence 53
interconnectedness 68–9, 146, 153, 161
Interface 210–11
internalisation 194–5
intervention framework 183–202
Irvine, J. 2, 5, 171
Irwin, C. E. Jr 158
Isaacs, M. R. 159, 162
Isaza-Rivera, V. 222
Islamic schools 21

Jackson, B. 194
Jackson, V. 143
Jacob, E. 45
Jagers, R. J. 81
James, W. 46, 144
Jausovec, N. 53
Jeffrey, H. 206
Jenkins, R. 14, 64
Jennings, J. 161
Jensen, D. 29
Jensen, S. 111
Jesor, R. 158
John, G. 64
Johnson, D. 80
Johnson, J. A. 151
Johnson, W. 141
Jones, L. A. 226
Jones-Wilson, F. C. 81
Jordan, B. 92
Jordan, C. 45
Jordan, J. T. 50
Jordan, W. J. 171–2
Joseph, K. 17, 22, 24
Judd, J. 5
justice 134–6

Kambon, K. K. K. 165
Karenga, M. 69, 72, 161, 163
Kaufman, F. 214, 217
Kelly, G. 119
Kelsey, M. 147
Keys, C. B. 214–56
Killeavy, M. 7
Kimball, S. 80
Kinder, K. 6, 116
King, A. 69, 141
King, M. L. Jr 142
Kingsley, L. 157
Kinney, D. 7
Kiresuk, T. J. 220
Kirschenman, J. 211

Knapp, M. 129
Kopp, K. A. 217
Kujichagulia 72, 147, 162
Kunjufu, J. 151, 157, 165, 169, 170
Kuumba 73, 147, 162
Kwanzaa programmes 71
Kwiatek, P. 226

Ladson-Billings, G. 81
Lampman, S. 220
Langley, M. R. 170
Lantz, J. 145
Laszloffy, T. 142–3
Lawrence, Stephen 4, 22–3, 24, 62
Lay, R. 50
Leake, B. L. 171
Leake, D. O. 171
Leashore, B. R. 161
Lee, C. 81, 145, 146, 147–8, 150–1, 152,
    154
Lepkowska, D. 21
Lerner, R. M. 143
Lewis, F. 157
Lewis, J. 157
liaison meetings 118–19, 123
Lipman, P. 81
Little, K. 63
Long, L. C. 161
Loury, G. 198–9
Lunt, I. 117
Lynch, J. 14, 15

Ma'at 147, 161
MAAT Center program 161
Mac an Ghaill, M. 33, 34, 114, 130, 174,
    187, 188–9, 200
McAdoo, J. L. 143
McAlister, A. 157
McCall, N. 170
Macdonald, I. 16–17
McKenry, P. 141–56
Macpherson Report 3–4, 5, 22–3, 62
Madhubuti, H. 170
Major, B. 46, 49
Major, J. 18–19
Majors, R. 1–27, 52, 174, 216, 219; blame
    paradigm 132; cool pose theory 45, 48,
    55–6, 131, 143, 149, 169, 172;
    intervention framework 183–202;
    masculinity 130; mentoring 205–13;
    racialised perspective 105–9; social
    indicators 141; subjective preferences
    134; targets 115
manhood training 147, 149, 157–68

Marr, A. 207
Martin, J. E. 219
Martinez, R. 7
masculinity 130, 139–202
Massey, G. 143
Massey, I. 14, 15, 16
Masson, J. 135
Mathews, R. M. 216, 219
Mauer, M. 206
Mbiti, J. 67, 68, 69, 161
Mboya, M. M. 80
Measor, L. 29
Meeker, M. 83
mentoring 5, 37, 150, 170, 203–56
Merton, R. 184
Meyer, J. 216
Middleton, B. 210
Milan, C. 214
Millar, M. 46
Miller, 133
Miller, D. B. 141
Miller, J. 214
Millman, R. B. 157
Mincy, R. B. 169
Mirza, H. S. 33, 90–101, 188
Mirza, M. 208
Mithaug, D. E. 219
Mock, L. O. 81
Modood, T. 16
Moore, J. 46
morals 128–38
Morgan, G. 133
Morgan, H. 7
Morris, E. 1, 106
Morrison, J. 29
Morrow, V. 94
Mortimore, P. 29, 133, 136
Moyers, B. 145
Moynihan Report 145
Mullard, C. 14, 63, 64
Murphy, R. 216
Murray, C. 29, 45, 53, 145
Mutisya, P. 73
Myers, K. 18
Myers, L. 66, 68, 69

National Curriculum 5, 18, 19, 23, 35
National Mentoring Partnership 214, 215,
    218
National Middle School Association 84
Neckerman, K. 211
Neely, M. A. 220
Nehaul, K. 28
Neill, S. 217

Neville, H. A. 216, 218
Newcombe, E. 7
Newmann, F. M. 47
Nguzo Saba 72–3, 147, 162–3, 164
Nia 72–3, 147
Nobles, W. 66, 67, 68, 161
Noguera, P. 29, 30
Nowotny, H. 93–4
Nuttall, D. 31

Obonna, P. 72, 73
Office for Standards in Education
   (OFSTED) 3, 5, 31, 106, 114, 183, 210
Ogbu, J. U. 28, 45, 47–8, 51, 54–5
O'Leary, J. 3–4
Oliver, W. 161
orientation training 151
Ortiz, G. 222
Osborne, J. W. 45–58
Ouseley, H. 2, 3, 4

Paine, A. 216
Paine-Andrews, A. 219
Palmer, D. J. 214, 215, 217, 226
Palmer, F. 16
paradox of blackness 160
parents 38; African American Immersion
   Schools 86, 87–8; African-centredness
   70–1, 72, 74; attitude survey 210;
   empowerment 152–3; involvement
   117–18; partnerships 37–9; working
   with 30
Parker, K. D. 50
Parry, O. 178, 179
Parsons, C. 128–38, 209
Patterson, S. 63
peer groups 29, 36, 37, 54, 151, 175–8,
   185–7, 188–9, 190–3, 200
Pegram, M. 145
Penkower, L. 157
Perkins, U. E. 159, 161
Persaud, R. 132
personhood 69, 72
Peters, M. 143
Pettit, P. 135
phallocentricity 190, 191, 193, 201
Phelan, P. 7
Phillips, T. 133
Phoenix, A. 117
Pickering, J. 6
Pierce, C. 143
Pinkett, J. 161
Pitchford, M. 117
Plowden Report 111

Polite, V. 7, 170, 171
Pollard, A. 132
Pollard, D. S. 79–89
Portland Oregon Public School System
   152
positionality 169
positive learning approach 6, 7
postmodernism 67–8
power blocks 158
Preston, S. 7
profiling system 118, 119
psyche 198–9

Quinn, D. M. 51
Quinn, W. 145

Race Relations Act (1976) 15
racial development profiles 196–200
racial identity development 194, 196
Ramdin, R. 14
Rampton Report 15, 111
Rasheed, J. 141
Rattansi, A. 17, 29
Rauch, J. B. 141, 159, 160
Rawls, J. 134–6
Reay, D. 90–101
Rebels 184, 185, 190–3, 201
Reed, P. L. 172
Rehal, A. 118
Reid, H. 93
Rejtman, R. 4
Resch, N. 207
Retreatists 184, 189–90
reverse racism 34
Reynolds, D. 31, 133
Richards, D. M. 161
Richards, H. 171
Richman, J. M. 152
rights 135–6
rites of passage 71–4, 141–56, 159
Roaf, P. A. 216
Roberts, A. 215, 217, 218
Roberts, M. 4
Roderick, C. 117
role models 53–4, 160
role play 223–4, 228, 231–5
Rong, X. L. 171
Rose, E. 14, 63
Rosenberg, M. 49, 50
Rosenfeld, L. B. 152
Rys, G. S. 178

Saggar, S. 143
Sanders, E. T. 172

Santayana, G. 24
satisfaction surveys 226–7, 228, 252–4
Satz, P. 157
Scafe, S. 65
Schaerf, F. W. 157
Scheurich, J. 66, 68
Schiele, J. 67, 68
Schmader, T. 46
Schwarzer, R. 226
Scott-Jones, D. 29
screening 121
Searle, C. 61
Seattle Center Arts and Sciences Academy 217
Seekins, T. 219
Select Committee (1973) 64
self efficacy 225–6, 228, 244–52
self-esteem 5, 7, 28, 46–7, 49–50, 53, 225
self-presentation 177
Sewell, T. 1, 2, 4, 5, 66, 111, 130–1, 136, 205; blame paradigm 132; intervention framework 183–202; positionality 169; racialised perspective 105–9; racism 210; stereotypes 114; supplementary schools 99
Shade, B. 45
Shakur, T. 196–8, 199–200
Shapland, J. 129
Sharrock, W. W. 131
Sheppard, J. 117
Sheridan, K. 157
Sheriffe, G. 5, 6, 208
Sherman, R. E. 220
Short, J. 132
Shröder, K. 226
Simmons, R. 50
Singh, E. 64
Sivanandan, A. 16, 62
skills competence 223–4, 227
Sklar, M. 145
Slaughter–Defoe, D. T. 171
Sleeter, C. 42, 52
Slicker, E. K. 214, 215, 217, 226
Sluckin, A. 132
Smith, D. 31, 111
Smith, G. 81
Smith, J. F. 219
Smith, P. K. 132
Smith, V. 7
Smitherman, G. 170, 171
social capital 93–4
Social Exclusion Practitioner Group 1
Social Exclusion Unit 1–2, 20, 61, 92, 106, 128

social support 152, 224–5, 228, 236–43
socialisation 55–6, 170
Solomon, D. 158
Solomos, J. 143–4, 205
special education 112–13
Spencer 207
Spencer, M. 7, 84
Spencer, S. J. 51
Spindler, G. 80
Spindler, L. 80
spirituality 68, 72, 157, 161
Srebnik, D. S. 217, 218
Stanfield, J. 68, 208
Staples, R. 190
Steele, C. 45, 46–7, 49, 51, 52–3, 56
Stephenson, J. 7
stereotype threat theory 45, 46–7, 52–4
stereotypes 5, 15, 33, 36, 37–8, 114, 175, 210
Stevens, A. 71–2
stigma vulnerability 52–3
Stirton, 207
Stoll, L. 133
Stone, M. 112
Styles, M. B. 216
Suarez-Balcazar, Y. 216, 219
Sudbury, J. 94
supplementary schools 70–1, 90–101
Swann Report 15, 17, 18, 21, 24, 66, 111, 210
Swisher, J. D. 157

Taylor, M. J. 22
Taylor, R. 141, 143, 145
Taylor, S. E. 46
Teacher Training Agency 4
Tesser, A. 46
Thatcherism 17–19
Thornton, K. 1, 2
Tierney, J. 207
Times Educational Supplement 22, 105, 113, 115
Tizzard, B. 29
Tomlinson, S. 13, 14, 31, 97, 111, 112
Torrance, E. 217
Troyna, B. 15, 40, 64, 97

Ujamaa 72, 147, 162
Ujima 72, 147, 162
Umoja 72, 147, 162
utilitarianism 133–4, 135

Valencia, R. R. 45
Vance, M. 64

Victor, P. 209

Wakefield, A. 6
Wakstein, J. 50
Warfield-Coppock, N. 73, 145, 146, 159, 161
Warnock Report 112, 116, 118
Watson, C. 170, 171
Watt, D. 5, 6
Weddle, K. D. 143
Wehlage, G. 81
Weis, L. 79, 186
Weitlauf, J. 214–56
Wells, S. 217
West, C. 68
Whaley, A. L. 81
White, G. W. 219
White, J. 6, 151
Whitty, G. 19, 22

Wiener, S. 205, 206, 211–12
Wilcox, D. 73
Wilkin, C. 4
Wilkins, A. 6
Wilkinson, V. 205–13
Williams, B. 7
Wilson, J. 131
Woods, A. 110
Woods, P. 29
Woolverton, N. 214
Wrench, J. 5, 144
Wright, C. 29, 33, 61
Wright, D. L. 171

Youdell, D. 20
Young, I. M. 92
Young, M. 66, 68

Zulfiqar, M. 206